Frederic Ives Carpenter

Metaphor and simile in the minor Elizabethan drama

Frederic Ives Carpenter

Metaphor and simile in the minor Elizabethan drama

ISBN/EAN: 9783337304942

Printed in Europe, USA, Canada, Australia, Japan

Cover: Foto ©Thomas Meinert / pixelio.de

More available books at **www.hansebooks.com**

METAPHOR AND SIMILE

IN THE

MINOR ELIZABETHAN DRAMA

A DISSERTATION PRESENTED TO THE FACULTY OF ARTS, LITERATURE, AND SCIENCE, OF THE UNIVERSITY OF CHICAGO, IN CANDIDACY FOR THE DEGREE OF DOCTOR OF PHILOSOPHY

BY
FREDERIC IVES CARPENTER

CHICAGO
The University of Chicago Press
1895

ANALYTICAL TABLE OF CONTENTS.

	Pages.
INTRODUCTION: Aim and Scope of the Study — Literature of the Subject — Difficulty of the Subject — Method of Observation followed — Plan of Classification — The Theory of Trope — The Test of Trope — Significance of the Study of Dramatic Imagery	vii–xvi
GORBODUC AND THE BEGINNINGS OF THE ELIZABETHAN DRAMA: Pre-Elizabethan Dramatic Imagery — Influence of Foreign Models on Diction and Imagery — Characteristics in the use of Metaphor and Simile in *Gorboduc*	1–7
LYLY: List of Plays Analyzed	9
Characteristics and Influence of Lyly's peculiar Diction — Euphuism in Lyly's Plays — Conceits in Lyly — General Character of his Imagery	11–15
Analysis of the Range and Sources of Lyly's Imagery	15–20
PEELE: List of Plays Analyzed	21
Various Critics on Peele's Imagery — General Character of his Imagery	23–25
Analysis of the Range and Sources of Peele's Imagery	26–31
MARLOWE: List of Plays Analyzed	33
Quality and Value of Marlowe's Dramatic Imagery — Condensed Metaphors in Marlowe — Imagery Poetical rather than Dramatic — Mixed Metaphors — Hyperbole — Costly Phrases — Geographic Romance — Quibbling — The Earlier and the Later Plays distinguished	35–40
Analysis of the Range and Sources of Marlowe's Imagery	40–47
Summary: Chief Topics reflected in Marlowe's Imagery	47–48
KYD: Noteworthy Metaphors and Similes in *Jeronimo* and in *The Spanish Tragedy* — Tropes common to various Plays ascribed to Kyd	49–53
GREENE: List of Plays Analyzed	55
Quality of Greene's Imagery — His Favorite Forms	57–59
Analysis of the Range and Sources of Greene's Imagery	59–62

TOURNEUR: List of Plays Analyzed	63
The Dramatic Intensity of Tourneur's Diction — Hyperbole in Tourneur — His Imaginative Suggestiveness — Elliptical Figures — Striking Similitudes — Introspective Conceits	65–68
Analysis of the Range and Sources of Tourneur's Imagery	68–72
WEBSTER: List of Plays Analyzed	73
Striking Originality and Power of Webster's Dramatic Diction — Observance of Dramatic Decorum — The Short Simile his Favorite Form — Logical Quality of his Genius — Concentrated Comparisons — Persistence of the Ethical Motive — Sententiousness — Personifications — Trick of Self-Repetition	75–80
Analysis of the Range and Sources of Webster's Imagery	80–92
Summary: Morbid Quality of Webster's Comparisons	92–93
CHAPMAN: List of Plays Analyzed	95
Great Faults counterbalanced by Great Merits — General Manner of his Imagery — His Three Styles — Excesses of his Diction — Profuse Use of Tropes — Chapman and Marlowe — The Question of Bombast in Chapman — Quibbling and Conceits — The Introspective Conceit — His Epithets — Personification — Hall-marks of his Diction — Poetical and Vigorous Images	97–107
Analysis of the Range and Sources of Chapman's Imagery	107–123
Summary: Chapman's Treatment of Nature — Aspects of Life reflected in his Tropes	123–124
JONSON: List of Plays Analyzed	125
Two Noteworthy Features in Jonson's Imagery — Self-consciousness — Diction of his Tragedies — Of the Comedies — Narrow Theories of Art — Conceits — Pregnant Metaphors — Epithets — Nature in Jonson	127–136
Analysis of the Range and Sources of Jonson's Imagery	136–156
Summary: Aspects of Life emphasized in Jonson's Imagery	156
TABLE BY AUTHORS AND BY TOPICS OF TROPES INDEXED	159
GENERAL SUMMARY AND CONCLUSIONS	161–213
Chief Forms of Trope in the Elizabethan Drama: General Value and Quality of Elizabethan Dramatic Imagery — Methods of Composition among the Dramatists — The Evolution of Dramatic Imagery — Lyric Interludes — Characteristics of the later Elizabethan Drama — Metonymy and Synecdoche in the Drama — Simile as a Dramatic Figure — The Simile in Action — Metaphor, its various Forms as a	

Dramatic Figure — Exactness not an essential Merit in Trope — Two Types of Poetic Mind — Strong Figure and Metaphor; Weaker Figures and Simile — Function of Dramatic Metaphor — Two essential Classes of Tropes: The vivid Image *versus* The Sympathetic Metaphor — The Intensive Metaphor in the Drama — In Marlowe — Kyd — Chapman — Tourneur — Webster — Various Excesses in the Use of Tropes — Cumulative Effects — Sententious Figures — Catachresis and Mixed Metaphor — Conceits: Dramatic; Airy and Fantastic; Abstract and Metaphysical; and Hyperbolical — Hyperbole in the Drama — Personification in the Drama: Personal Metaphors; Formal Personification - - - - - - - - - 161–192

MATTER AND CONTENT OF ELIZABETHAN DRAMATIC IMAGERY: General Range and Sources of Tropes in the Drama — Treatment of Nature — The Pathetic Fallacy — Treatment of Human Life — Diction Fluent, not Conventional - - - - - - 192–202

THE TIMES AND THE PEOPLE AS REFLECTED IN THE ELIZABETHAN DRAMATIC IMAGERY: Multitudinous Aspects of Life revealed — Predominant Moralizing Tendency — Sombre Criticism of Life — Renaissance Traits reflected in the Drama — Costly and Gorgeous Images — Violent Metaphors — General Recapitulation - - - 202–213

BIBLIOGRAPHICAL INDEX - - - - - - - - 215–217

INTRODUCTION.

Aim and Scope of this Study

THE aim of this study is partly descriptive, partly theoretical. I have selected eight of the representative dramatists of the reign of Elizabeth and the early years of the reign of James I, not including Shakspere, have made an analysis of the characteristics of each author in his use of metaphor and simile, and in the range and sources of his imagery, and have endeavored to state the results of this study in each case in some detail. In conclusion I have attempted to formulate a few generalizations in regard to the Elizabethan drama as a whole, considered in relation to the characteristic diction and imagery employed in it. This is the descriptive part of the work. At the same time consideration of the theory and the classification of the figures of speech, especially of the higher and more imaginative figures, has been forced upon me by the extreme complexity and the elliptical abruptness and difficulty of many of the characteristic images to be found in the pages of the authors studied. I have however no new definitions or classifications of importance to offer; but the illustrations under the several heads of Simile, Implied Simile, Fable, Proverb, Allegory, Hyperbole, Conceit, and Personification, as herein presented, may possibly serve as material in the elucidation of the subject by others.

Literature of the Subject

Some sixteen years ago Dr. Friedrich Brinkmann began to publish an extensive work on the study of Metaphor,[1] of which however only one volume out of several proposed was ever published. This volume contains an extended statement of the theory of metaphor, suggestions and illustrations of various points of view in the study of metaphor, and finally a minute analysis of the principal metaphors which are drawn from domestic animals.

[1] Die Metaphern, Studien ueber den Geist der modernen Sprachen. (Bonn 1878.)

Among the subjects connected with the study of metaphor suggested by Dr. Brinkmann the one most important and fruitful for the student of literature as literature is doubtless the study of the characteristics and style of individual authors as revealed in their use of metaphor and simile.[1] It is to be regretted that a fuller exemplification of this side of his subject was not included in Dr. Brinkmann's work. Studies in this direction by others,[2] it is true, are not altogether lacking. Metaphor in poetry has been studied from various points of view from the days of Aristotle and the Greek critics to our own. And very recently a thorough study of Chaucer's imagery by Dr. Friedrich Klaeber, now of the University of Minnesota, has been published.[3] In its general outlines the present study follows the leading suggestions of Dr. Brinkmann in this direction, and its plan resembles in some particulars that of Dr. Klaeber's book.

The study of metaphor and simile in the Elizabethan drama is attractive, but it is also very difficult. In this essay it will be possible only to survey the way and to classify a part of the materials. I confess to a strong sense of the dangers of an analytical method in the study of things literary. The essence, the living spark always escapes us when we come to dissect. Quantity is taken into account; quality is neglected, and it is impossible to consider all the facts. Especially is this true in dramatic writing, where so much is left unexpressed, to be supplied by the actor or reader. "Images are either grand in themselves or for the thought and feeling that accompany them," as Leigh

Difficulty of the Subject

---

[1] "Wie zeichnet sich .... der Charakter des Schriftstellers in den ihm individuell angehörigen (den nicht incarnirten) Metaphern?" Op. cit. p. 120.

[2] See for example: Servius on Virgil; P. Langen, Die Metapher im lateinschen von Plautus bis Terence (neue Jahrb. f. Phil. und Paedagogik 1882); H. Raeder, Die Tropen und Figuren bei R. Garnier (Kiel 1887); Gummere, The Anglo-Saxon Metaphor (Halle 1881); Degenhardt, Die Metapher bei den Vorläufern Molière's (Marburg 1886); G. Duval, Dictionnaire des Métaphores de Victor Hugo (Paris 1888); etc. See also Professor Jebb's suggestive and valuable study of Homer's similes, in his "Introduction to Homer" (Boston 1893), pp. 26-32.

[3] Das Bild bei Chaucer (Berlin 1893, pp. 450).

Hunt says,[1] and the quality of three-quarters of the imagery of the Elizabethan plays depends, as that of all organic imagery should depend, on the context and the dramatic situation or moment. For purposes of etymology or of phonology or of the study of versification, the method of analysis is appropriate. But the meaning of style and the characteristics of genius are not to be grasped by this process — at least not by this process alone, and in the first approach. One cannot but sympathize with Mr. Swinburne's ridicule of dogmatic and premature, generalization in such matters.[2] But nowhere do the imaginative and poetic quality of an author, the range of his interest, the characteristics of his mind, and the scope of his genius, reveal themselves more certainly than in his imagery, and the closer knowledge of the great masterpieces involves minute as well as free and discursive study. In making any minute study of an author's imagery, accordingly, an analytical subject-index cannot but be of considerable assistance, although as evidence it is of course essentially corroborative, not primary. It is the Bertillon system of mental measurement, and may possibly yield results in the identification of literary aliases.

"The sources of an author's similitudes," wrote Professor Minto,[3] "are often peculiarly interesting, as affording a means of measuring the circumference of his knowledge. We cannot, to be sure, by such means, take a very accurate measure, but we can tell what books a man has dipped into, may discover what writers he has plagiarized from, and may be able to guess how his interests are divided between books and the living world." The essential thing is to guard against the dangers of the arithmetical method. "Non pas, pour nous," as Ferdinand Brunetière writes,[4] apropos of the dictionary of Victor Hugo's metaphors, "que nous ayons une grande confiance dans les applications de la statistique à la littérature. On prouve tout avec des chiffres,

---

[1] Imag. and Fancy, 198.
[2] See his Study of Shakspere, appendix.
[3] Manual of Eng. Prose Lit., p. 13. See, to the same effect, J. A. Symonds, Essays Speculative and Suggestive, 238. Cf. also Hennequin, La Critique Scientifique, 63f.
[4] Nouvelles Questions de Critique, 260.

et même parfois la vérité, quand on sait la manière de s'y prendre. Si cependant il y a quelques objets dont le poète lui-même tire plus souvent ou plus volontiers ses métaphores ou ses comparaisons; s'il y en a quelques'uns qui semblent s'attirer ou s'appeler habituellement l'un l'autre dans ses vers, il sera permis de les compter; et, de la fréquence de certaines images on pourra peut-être conclure à la nature elle-même de son imagination."

In spite however of the endeavor towards an objective and analytical method, such a study as this must be largely subjective.

Method of Observation

No attempt is made to take into consideration all metaphor and simile occurring in the authors studied, nor are metaphor and simile, according to the stricter definitions of some writers upon rhetoric and poetics, alone regarded. All tropes (in the ancient sense of the word), in which imagination is felt to be present, are considered. Incarnate or faded metaphors are generally neglected, except so far as they illustrate the peculiar diction of dramatic poetry at the time. In general only the more striking, individual, and conscious images are fully enumerated. Of course in such a method the personal equation cannot be entirely eliminated. Quotations of striking and significant tropes will be made to as great an extent as the necessary limits of this paper will permit; in order to save space, page references to standard editions (see bibliographical index), rather than to act and scene, are made for all less important tropes. The sums total of the references under each head and under each author are annexed.[1] From the preceding explanations, however, it will be understood that these enumerations are more or less inexact and have no absolute validity; but they should be valid for purposes of comparison and generalization. If the limits of space had permitted it would doubtless have been profitable to continue this study so as to include the entire body of the drama from *Gorboduc* to the closing of the theatres, or at least all the chief dramatists of that period, and to introduce a more constant comparison and reference to Shakspere as the great master of dramatic imagery.

[1] See the table infra, p. 159.

Reference to Shakspere however is not difficult in single metaphors through the concordances or through Schmidt's lexicon.

The classifications employed in analyzing the range and sources of each author's imagery, I have purposely abstained from making minute or thoroughly systematic. It is difficult to see the significance of idiosyncrasies in the use of imagery when the natural groupings of an author's mental pictures are obscured by minute subdivisions. Such subdivisions make a more perfect subject-index, but are otherwise confusing. The more scientific classifications of Aristotle[1] or of Max Müller[2] or Dr Brinkmann,[3] although valuable for other ends, would be here not to the purpose. Dramatic imagery in proportion as it is dramatic, rather than epic or lyric, naturally illustrates human life by human life, and we shall find that the larger part of that which follows is drawn from the field of human life.[4] Accordingly there are two main divisions: tropes drawn from the field of nature and those drawn from the field of human life. Under Nature subdivisions are introduced for (1) Aspects of the Sky, The Elements, etc.; (2) Aspects of Water, the Sea, etc.; (3) Aspects of Earth, Inorganic nature, etc.; (4) The Vegetable World; (5) The Animal World. Under Man and Human Life are grouped (1) The Arts and Learning; (2) Various Occupations; (3) Agriculture, etc.; (4) Trades, etc.; (5) Domestic Life, including Dress and Ornament; (6) Colloquial, Coarse, and Familiar Images; (7) The Body and its Parts, including the Appetites, Senses, etc.; (8) Subjective Life, Religion, etc.; (9) War; (10) Classical and Literary Allusions. Finally, in preference to grouping arbitra-

Plan of Classification.

---

[1] Poetics, c. 21.

[2] Science of Thought, II 480-512.

[3] Die Metaphern, pp. 29-34, viz: (1) The material pictured by the material; (2) The immaterial by the material; (3) The material by the immaterial; (4) The immaterial by the immaterial; etc. Cf. Quintilian VIII vi.

[4] How different is it with Wordsworth, the poet of Nature! A count of the metaphors and similes in Wordsworth's poetry preceding the *Excursion*, made by Mr. Vernon P. Squires of the University of Chicago, shows 258 (or over 50 per cent.) illustrating human things by natural; 46 natural by human; 136 human by human; 59 natural by natural.

rily under any of the preceding heads certain references of doubtful or of double ascription, a small division (11) of miscellaneous or unclassified references has been added.

Complete authors in each case have been studied, with the omission of doubtful plays and plays of composite authorship. I have summarized under each author his chief formal characteristics in the use of tropes, noting generally his observance of essential rhetorical principles, the abundance and vigor of his imagery, the chief cases of borrowed imagery, and the leading figures which he affects, whether simile (and of what sort), metaphor, sententious figures, personification, hyperbole, or whatever else.

I have spoken of the complexity and difficulty of the characteristic figures of the Elizabethan drama. The simile in Homer, or in epic poetry in general, is comparatively easy of study and admits readily of generalized inferences. But the characteristic figurative language of the Elizabethan drama presents very few Homeric similes — almost none of the true type, that is, similes unmixed with metaphor, episodical, and prolonged. Shorter similes, it is true, are frequently used, but they are almost always complicated with metaphor or other figure. Indeed perhaps the most striking feature of the dramatic imagery of this period in its typical writers is the general fusion, the elliptical confusion, of all the more intense and imaginative figures in passages of high excitement or passion.[1] Simile lapses into metaphor, metaphor into allegory, personification, or hyperbole, with kaleidoscopic abruptness. "The compound metaphor, . . . where the analogy is intricate," of Herbert Spencer,[2] is the prevailing, or at

---

[1] These dramatists love to linger over a metaphorical idea and to develop it: Thus in Webster's *White Devil* Vittoria, dying, says:

"My soul, like to a ship in a black storm,
Is driven, I know not whither."

Her brother, the sardonic Flamineo, answers;

"Then *cast anchor*.
Prosperity doth bewitch men, *seeming clear:*
But *seas do laugh, show white, when rocks are near.* . . .
 . . . . Art thou gone?
Art thou *so near the bottom?*"

[2] Phil. of Style, p. 32.

least the characteristic, figure. In a study which is not chiefly a study of words in their metaphorical origins, such figures are difficult of analysis and they do not lend themselves readily to classification.

On the theory of trope, so complicated and still so unsettled, happily it is not a part of my task to linger,—" circa quem," as Quintilian[1] wrote so long ago, "inexplicabilis et grammaticis inter ipsos, et philosophis, pugna est, quae sint genera, quae species, qui numerus, qui cuique subjiciatur." The tripartite division of the ancients into figures of thought, figures of language, and tropes, is still perhaps the best for all practical purposes.[2] [The present study has comprehended the subject of trope alone.] Trope I have used as a generic term comprising the principal aesthetic or imaginative figures, of which metaphor and simile are the leading examples.[3] These figures it is difficult to classify among themselves for the reason that in the complex language of high poetry they seldom are found in their simplicity, but are usually mixed, grading off imperceptibly into one another. They may be legitimately treated together for the reason that a common principle, the principle of imagination, underlies them all. To explain further in given examples the principle of the effect upon the mind usually involves, except in the simplest cases, a separate explanation in each instance. Some classification therefore, such as that of Professor Greene,[4] based on distinctions of degree rather than those

The Theory of Trope

[1] VIII vi 1.

[2] The whole subject is minutely discussed in Gerber, Die Sprache als Kunst (cf. the index under "Figuren," "Tropen," etc.). See also Jebb, Attic Orators, II 60.

[3] It seems to me a mistake to attempt to limit the term as Professor Minto has done (Man. of Eng. Prose Lit. pp. 12-13) to the non-literal use of "single words." Professor Minto cites Quintilian as favoring his definition, but Quintilian says distinctly: "Mihi videntur errasse, qui non alios crediderunt tropos, quam in quibus *verbum pro verbo* poneretur." (VIII, vi 2).

[4] A Grouping of Figures of Speech, Based upon the Principle of their Effectiveness. Based on this principle — that of the degree of imagination present in each figure on the average — Professor Greene groups the various tropes in the following order, proceeding from those nearest to literal statement and ending with those the most highly figurative or symbolical: Synecdoche,

of kind is, it seems to me, the only profitable one. Gerber[1] has pointed out how the principle underlying synecdoche has given rise to other and wider figures (examples, parallels, etc.,—giving a part for the whole); and similarly of metonymy (whence similitude, parable, etc.,—one thing in place of another). "Metaphora brevior est similitudo" is the time-honored definition of metaphor, however probable it may be that metaphor historically precedes simile in actual use.[2] And few can fail to recognize the underlying similarity which has led to the definition of allegory as prolonged metaphor, and which has made apparent in the mythologizing or anthropomorphic tendency that leads to Personification, the very germ and cardinal principle of all primitive thinking and of half the metaphor and imagery in the world.

For these reasons no attempt has been made to classify definitely the various figures used in each author; but any tendency towards the use of a particular form or of particular forms in preference to others has been noted.

The Test of Trope

"The essence of metaphor," says Professor Greene,[3] "is that to the literal understanding it is false, while to the imagination it is true." The same rule, liberally applied, may also be used in the detection of tropes in general. Figures of speech in the ancient sense (antithesis, parallelism, etc.) are too low in the imaginative scale, if indeed they enter it at all, and are Metonymy, Stated Simile, Implied Simile, Metaphor, Personification, Imperfect Allegory, Pure Allegory. Professor Greene writes me as follows on the subject: "It seems to me that there has been too great a tendency .... to draw hard and fast lines between the various figures. To the novice it may have a more learned sound to pronounce dogmatically that a given expression contains this or that figure, but more careful students sometimes see in the same expression a blending of two figures, or, if you choose, a transitional figure. ... It seems to me that the poets themselves, by the readiness with which they pass from one form of language to another, show us that we must not set up hard and fast lines in our classifications, but must admit that one form of language can blend with another."

[1] Die Sprache als Kunst, II 40 f., 66 f.

[2] On the origin of Metaphor cf. Gummere, The Anglo-Saxon Metaphor, pp 11 f: A. H. Tolman, The Style of Anglo-Saxon Poetry, pp. 12 f.; Max Müller Science of Thought, II 480 f.

[3] A Grouping of Figures of Speech, p. 11.

too closely connected with the mere grammatical structure of language to be mistaken for tropes. Figures of thought (irony, hyperbole, etc.) in some cases are and in other cases are not at the same time tropes. The above rule will usually suffice to establish the difference.

Trope, at least in its higher forms, involves imagery, but not all imagery is trope, so that many expressions which, within the conventions of dramatic form, are to be taken literally, are excluded from a study dealing with trope alone. Thus the charming flower passage in Act I, Scene I of Peele's *Arraignment of Paris*, involving as it does several similes and epithets, is not as a whole, a trope. And similarly, Sir Epicure Mammon's glorious imaginings in Act II, Scene 1 of *The Alchemist*,[1] — the passage so admired by Lamb, — are literal in expression, or at best figured forth in a sort of sensuous hyperbole.

Imagery is of the very essence of poetry, and symbol alone is capable of giving to truth that aspect of beauty and that touch of emotion which convey to the mind the subtler implications of thought in a way unattainable to the artifices of circumlocution or the colorless vagueness of abstract terms. "Im Grunde genommen," writes Alfred Biese,[2] "ist jede Dichtung eine Metapher im weitesten Sinne . . . Ohne Symbolisierung entsteht kein Kunstwerk." An investigation of the imagery of the Elizabethan drama is therefore largely an investigation of the poetical quality of that drama. The limitations of the present study, however, are too narrow to admit of complete generalizations on this subject.[1] Shakspere of course is the very type of all that was great and characteristic in Elizabethan poetry, and perhaps the best of the poetic impulse in the strictly Elizabethan drama studied in this essay was communicated after Shakspere to the post-Elizabethan school, to Fletcher, Shirley, and others. I think however it will be found that, except for the lyrical graces of

Significance of the Study of Dramatic Imagery

---

[1] See especially that portion of the extract cited by Lamb, beginning,
 "My meat shall all come in in Indian shells,
 Dishes of agate set in gold," etc.

[2] Das Metaphorische in der dichterischen Phantasie, p. 4. Cf. Dryden, Works, V 120: "Imaging is in itself the very height and life of poetry."

Fletcher, there is a considerable falling off in intensity and power in the imagery of the later drama. In the case of Ford, certainly, I have found this so after a careful study, and Mr. Lowell[1] has noted in Massinger the lack of the inspired word and the picturesque image. In any event the earlier period was the formative period and perhaps on the whole, at least to the student of literary history and development, the more important and interesting one.

[1] Old Eng. Dramatists, 127.

GORBODUC AND THE BEGINNINGS OF THE ELIZABETHAN DRAMA

GORBODUC AND THE BEGINNINGS OF THE ELIZABETHAN DRAMA.

Pre-Elizabethan Dramatic Imagery

THE diction of the earlier English drama, of the miracle plays and the moralities, is generally colorless. Figures, and especially the significant and highly poetical figures of metaphor and simile, are little used. The interest is concentrated on the situation, moral or dramatic, and on the characters of the speakers, types of universal humanity or personifications of fundamental abstractions. The naïve and simple effect of the miracle plays for the modern reader is intensified by the severe and literal plainness of the language employed. One reads on for page after page without encountering a single conscious and literary metaphor. The poet has been taught or he invents for himself the most elaborate and intricate stanzaic and rhyming schemes. But his diction otherwise is singularly unelaborate. Occasionally a comparison illuminates a passage:

Humanum Genus. Whom to folwe wetyn I ne may:
  I stonde in stodye and gynne to rave,
    I wolde be ryche in gret array,
    And fayn I wolde my sowle save.
  I wave *as wynde in watyr.*[1]

Such touches, however, are rare.

In coming to the later moralities and interludes we find no improvement. The dreary didacticism of these pieces is relieved only by the introduction of scriptural phraseology and conventional biblical metaphors. It is a purely national and popular literature, unawakened by foreign influence.[2] Occasionally a con-

---

[1] The Castell of Perseverance, in Pollard, p. 67.

[2] The English ballad literature also is severely plain in its diction. Professor Gummere (Old English Ballads, Boston 1894, p. 309) remarks that in the old ballads "metaphors are rare in any artistic and intentional sort . . . similes

tinental motive appears and lends interest for the moment to a passage, as in the song appended to *The Disobedient Child*,[1] recalling faintly Villon:[2]

> "Where is now Salomon, in wisdom so excellent?
> Where is now Samson, in battle so strong? . . .
> . . . How short *a feast* is this worldly joying?
> Even *as a shadow* it passeth away . . .
> . . . *As a leaf in a stormy weather*,
> So is man's life blowen clean away."

Influence of Foreign Models on Diction and Imagery

The conception of character and the feeling for dramatic situation were present in the English drama before the introduction of Renaissance and Italian influences in the sixteenth century. But the medium of a poetical diction and of adequate form was lacking. This was to be obtained only by recourse to foreign influence and to foreign models. The movement which was going on so rapidly in English poetry during the sixteenth century naturally and inevitably spread. It quickly invaded the field of dramatic writing. At first the foreign influence seizes only upon the learned and cultured classes. The movement is experimental and academic. Popular taste is slow to accept it, and in fact never does completely accept it. Two important things, however, in respect of literary form finally prevail in the national drama as in the national poetry, namely, the foreign ideals of versification, and the impulse toward imagery and poetical ornament. In introducing the first of these reforms into the drama two men rendered preëminent services: Thomas Sackville, who first in *Gorboduc* introduced blank verse into the English drama, and Christopher Marlowe, who first developed the latent capacities of this verse, and established it upon the popular stage. The gradual introduction into the drama of striking and poetical diction is more difficult to trace. There is, however, little signifi-

are few and rarely sustained." Indeed it is safe to say that, with few exceptions, the entire literature of the Middle English period after Chaucer is characterized by poverty of imagery and scanty use of metaphor and simile. Allegory however abounds.

[1] In Hazlitt's Dodsley, II 319-320.
[2] See, on the Ubi Sunt Formula, Modern Lang. Notes, vol. VIII 187.

cant imagery before the plays of the dramatists included in this study.

Foreign influence as affecting the drama in a marked degree first appears in the tragedy of *Gorboduc* (*Ferrex & Porrex*, acted 1561, appearing in its final form in 1570). *Gorboduc* is a highly academic production, written in the atmosphere of court and university, with political moralization for a motive. It is constructed in the main on the Senecan model, and is significant in the history of the dramatic diction of the age of Elizabeth as being practically the first considerable dramatic production to signalize and illustrate the new classical and Italian influence which was to inspire and inform anew the tardy literature of Modern England. This influence at first, and in so far as concerns *Gorboduc* and plays of its class[1] at all times, was mainly formal. There is hardly a touch of the unmistakable and mighty poetic diction of the great Elizabethan drama to be found in *Gorboduc*. Occasionally, it is true, we are reminded of the famous author of the weighty Induction to the Mirror for Magistrates; but the style on the whole is rhetorical and declamatory rather than dramatic. Parallelism and antithesis abound. The classical allusions and the poetical formulæ and phrases are those of the contemporary schools of poets, the school of Tottel's Miscellany, of Gascoigne, and even of Spenser. The mediæval tendency to didactic allegory is prominent in the dumb shows and in the choruses following each act. Personification, not bold and direct, but more or less hidden and conventionalized, is frequent,— e. g., "When time hath taught them," "climbing pride,"[2] etc. Similar abstractions, in the formal poetic diction of the eighteenth century, are written with capital letters and pass as undoubted personifications. The effect is the same in both cases, — to remove the style from prose and create for the author a new and easy pseudo-poetic diction. Formal and direct personification

Gorboduc, its Imagery

[1] Such as *The Misfortunes of Arthur*, and the academic drama of Daniel, Sir Wm. Alexander, etc.

[2] As in this phrase so frequently elsewhere the personification is established by the help of a personifying adjective. Cf. also p. 14 ll. 2-4; p. 22 ll. 5-8; p. 23 l. 15; p. 25 ll. 7-8; p. 41 l. 17.

also is used : p. 6 the classical Aurora, for the dawn ; p. 30 l. 12 ; cf. p. 59 :

> "I think the torment of my mournful case, ...
> Would force even Wrath herself to pity me."

The imagery of the piece in general however is faint and timid.[1] The immaturity of its diction is revealed in the fact that most of the imagery is expressed in adjectives. This is an example of the characteristic style of *Gorboduc*:

> "For cares of kings ....
> Do waste man's life and hasten *crooked* age,
> With *furrowed* face and with *enfeebled* limbs,
> To draw on *creeping* death a *swifter* pace."[2]

> "*Ruthful* remembrance is yet *raw* in mind."[3]

"*black* treason,"[4] etc.

The coloring is mostly classical, although the classical allusions are not numerous: the chief are to Phaeton, pp. 23 and 37; Aurora, p. 6; Tantalus, p. 29; Troy and Priam, p. 44; the Furies, pp. 53 and 70; etc. There are few striking figures. Three formal and expanded similes occur, — the first an example or illustration as much as a simile : See p. 37 ll. 4-9 ; p. 59 ll. 22-24 ; p. 64 ll. 11-14. See also p. 75 l. 10.

It is natural that in an imitative and academic production the imagery should be somewhat stiff and conventional. The imagery of *Gorboduc* accordingly is not organic, but is conscious and ornamental. The frequency of only slightly metaphorical tropes (e. g. "slender quarrels," "to kindle disdain," "heavy care," "decaying years," etc.) of itself connotes a designedly poetic or rhetorical style, as does the undercurrent of personifi-

---

[1] "Sackville écrivait bien, avec éloquence et avec netteté, mais sa langue était plus oratoire que poétique. .... Jamais ... il ne se permettait aucune audace, aucun élan de pure fantaisie ; jamais il ne colorait sa pensée, jamais il ne la revêtait de ces brillantes images, de ces ornements splendides qui, chez les peuples du Nord, constituent l'essence même de la poésie." (Mézières, Pred. et Cont. de Shaks. p. 101).

[2] Sackville's Works, p. 14.

[3] Id. p. 21.

[4] Id. p. 62.

cation throughout the piece. Otherwise there is little that is significant or original in its imagery. In one place there is a reminiscence of Chaucer:

> "Then saw I how he smiled with slaying knife
> Wrapped under cloak."[1]

The most frequent metaphor, extremely common also in the later drama, is that of fire: e. g., p. 48:

> "The secret grudge and malice will remain,
> The fire not quenched, but kept in close restraint,
> Fed still within, breaks forth with double flame."[2]

—an early example also of the "implied simile" common in all the later drama.

On the whole *Gorboduc* seems to have exercised little influence over the diction of the regular Elizabethan drama. It belongs rather with the learned and imitative poetry of the last half of the sixteenth century. Much of the imagery of the Elizabethan drama however is drawn from this poetry and from the imitations of the original sources in classical and Italian literature, as will appear in the study of Peele, Greene, and Marlowe.

[1] Id. p. 63. Cf. Chaucer, Knight's Tale, l. 1141.
[2] Cf. pp. 22, 39, 45, 47, 49, 62, 84.

JOHN LYLY
1554-1606 ?

Acted	Published						Vol.	Pages
1581 ?	1584	Alexander and Campaspe	-		-	-	I	89-151
1582 ?	1584	Sapho and Phao		-	-	-	I	155-214
1588 ?	1591	Endimion	-	-	-	-	I	4- 86
1587 ?	1592	Gallathea		-	-	-	I	217-276
1590 ?	1592	Mydas -	-	-	-	-	II	3- 69
——	1594	Mother Bombie -		-	-	-	II	73-147
1589 ?	1601	Love's Metamorphosis		-	-	-	II	215-259

THE chief importance of *Gorboduc* in the history of the English drama is that it first introduced blank verse as a dramatic medium. Similarly, according to Professor A. W. Ward[1] and to Ulrici,[2] Lyly's chief service was the introduction of an artistic prose as a dramatic medium. Earlier instances of the use of prose in dramatic writing can doubtless be cited, but Lyly was the first to establish the model for such writing in the new drama. "When we consider," says Ulrici, "that Lyly to a certain extent was the creator of dramatic prose, it must be acknowledged that he at that early date handled it with an ingenuity worthy of all praise." For Lyly's prose in a certain sense is a poetical prose. To speak paradoxically his style is not prosaic and pedestrian, like that, for example, of Sir Thomas Wilson in the same half century. It is lucid, it is ornamented, it is often rhythmical,[3] abounding in balance, measure, and antithesis. All this was not without its influence on the dramatic diction of the age. The lightness and the occasional mannerism of Shakspere's prose is suggestive of that of Lyly. Euphuism was symptomatic of the literary tendencies of the time.[4] The Euphuism characteristic of Lyly was naturally subdued in his plays because of the necessities of dramatic form. For this very reason, perhaps, the real characteristics of Lyly's style can better be studied in the plays than in the more exaggerated form of his prose romance.

Lyly's Diction, its Chief Characteristics and Influence

Most of the characteristics of Euphuism pointed out by Landmann[5] and other critics[6] are to be found in the plays, including

Euphuism in the Plays

[1] Hist. Eng. Dram. Lit. (Lond. 1875), p. 159.
[2] Shakespeare's Dramatic Art, Vol. I ch. vii.
[3] See as examples of stichomythy in Lyly I 21, II 227, 250, etc.; of measured prose II 39-40, 225, etc.
[4] Cf. Symonds, Shakspere's Predecessors, ch. xiii.
[5] Landmann, Euphues (Heilbronn 1887).
[6] Minto, Symonds, etc.

(1) Parisonic Antithesis: for example, "Seeing we come out to be merry, let not your jarring mar our jests;"[1] "Bees that die with honey, are buried with harmony."[2] Usually combined with this, as in the two examples just quoted, is

(2) Transverse and simple alliteration: examples,

"To attribute such *lofty titles* to such *love trifles*."[3]
"A dotage no less *miserable* than *monstrous*;"[4]
"I go *ready* to *return* for *advice* before I am *resolved* to *adventure*."[5]

(3) Plays on words and paronomasia: examples,

"Thou to abate the pride of our *affections*, dost detract from thy *perfections;*"[6] "The fee-*simple* of your daughter's *folly;*"[7] "Let me *cross* myself, for I die if I *cross* thee."[8]

(4) The heaping up of illustrations, similes, and examples: as in Act II, Scene I of *Endimion:*

"*Tellus.* Why! is dissembling joined to their sex inseparable? As heat to fire, heaviness to earth, moisture to water, thinness to air?
Endimion. No, but found in their sex, as common as spots upon doves, moles upon faces, caterpillars upon sweet apples, cobwebs upon fair windows."[9]

(5) The abundant introduction of an unnatural natural history.[10] This euphuistic natural history can be traced through all the succeeding dramatists; it derives from *Euphues* directly perhaps as much as from the plays, though of course the fashion was not started by Lyly.

[1] Lyly I 23.
[2] Id. I 179; see also I 18, 20, 112, and passim frequently.
[3] Lyly I 5.
[4] Id. I 6.
[5] Id. I 172.
[6] Id. I 7.
[7] Id. II 78.
[8] Id. I 117; See also I 15, 16, 22, 39, 51, 83, 97, 101, 111, 116, 119, 126, 129, 141, 157, 158, 162, 184, 197, 202, 220, 224, 231, 233, 247, 248, 250-1, 261, 275; II 7, 10, 12, 13, 14, 15, 21, 22, 24, 25, 26, 29, 36, 41, 48, 62, 81, 84, 86, 96, 99, 102, 117, 121, 126, 134, 142, 147, 185, 217, 218, etc.
[9] Lyly I 20-21; see also II 26, 200, and passim.
[10] See infra, p. 17.

Figures of speech, in the stricter sense of the ancient rhetoricians, especially anthithesis, balance, alliteration, and paronomasia, are thus, we see, among the most striking characteristics of Lyly's style. He treats language lightly,[1] deliberately, and with conscious artifice. He is perpetually striving to wrest it into conceits and all sorts of witty perversions. This is a fair specimen of the customary language of his lovers:

"My tears, which have made furrows in my cheeks and in mine eyes fountains; my sighs, which have made of my heart a furnace,[2] and kindled in my head flames; my body that melteth by piecemeal and my mind that pineth at an instant, may witness that my love is both unspotted and unspeakable."[3]

Lyly's sprightly dialogue deals largely in quips, such as he himself has defined in *Alexander and Campaspe:*

"*Psyllus:* What's a quip?
Manes: We great girders call it a short saying of a sharp wit, with a bitter sense in a sweet word."

The manner of Lyly at his best and liveliest is plainly the prototype of Shakspere's lighter manner, as it appears, for instance, in such plays as *Much Ado* and *As You Like It.*

Probably nine-tenths of Lyly's figures are of the nature of conceits.[4] They are intellectual and involve a process of reasoning; rarely are they emotional and imaginative. And so with his style generally, contrasting with the frequently imaginative and "emotional"[5] prose of Sidney. Lyly is not altogether

[1] "Playing with words and idle similes," was Drayton's exact comment on Lyly. ("To Henry Reynolds" — in Chalmer's Poets IV 399).

[2] Cf. *As You Like It.* II vii 148: "The lover, Sighing like furnace." Elsewhere Lyly carries the same metaphor still further and speaks of a heart "*scorcht* with love" (II 170, cf. 251); similarly (I 78): "I *fried* myself . . . in mine affections." This was a favorite in the time of Cowley and somewhat later. A similar conceit however occurs in Chapman's (?) *Alphonsus* (p. 405): "My marrow *fries;*" and in Jonson's *Poetaster* (I 211 a): "When earth and seas in fire and flame shall *fry.*"

[3] Lyly II 17.

[4] For a particularly bad one see II 18: — "Thy effeminate mind, Eristus, whose eyes *are sticht* on Coelia's face." See also for further examples of conceit in Lyly, I 40, 69, 72, 223, 248, 257; II 10, 16, 18, 21, 33, 35, 42, 49, 57 f., 74 f., 113–114, 128, 170, 232, 236, etc.

[5] Cf. Sidney's Defense of Poesy, ed. A. S. Cook, Introd. p. xxvi.

unconscious of the quality of his own style, as a sentence from the Epilogue to *Sapho and Phao* reveals: "We fear we have led you all this while in a labyrinth of conceits." Conceits run well with the antithetical and balanced structure. Both are formal and intellectual. In Aristotle's phrase[1] it is "a style which has a resemblance to a syllogism."

If Lyly has little imagination he has much restless fancy. He is not abundant in metaphor, and such metaphors as he has are conventional and clever rather than intensive. His images are not suggestive and emotional, but are almost always explicit. By way of compensation for his dearth of metaphor his pages swarm with similes. He especially affects the implied simile or imperfect allegory, where the terms of the comparison are either stated without the sign of likeness or one term is omitted entirely. For example:

"Away, peevish boy, a rod were better under thy girdle, than love in thy mouth; it will be a forward cock that croweth in the shell."[2]

This is a favorite form for introducing the illustrations drawn from euphuistic natural history.[3]

Beside their indiscriminate Latin quotation Lyly's plays are streaked throughout with a sort of pseudo-classicism, the overflow of the runlets of mediæval anecdotes from classical sources.[4]

Peele and Greene, however, abound more in this sort of thing than Lyly, who presumably does not go beyond the limits of the court taste.

To sustain his familiar and sprightly style Lyly draws largely for his comparisons upon domestic and colloquial sources.[5] Formal personifications he uses but rarely.[6]

[1] See Aristotle's Rhetoric, bk. III ch. ix on the Antithetical Style; whereunder of Parisosis and Paromoiosis — the very traits of Lyly's style.

[2] Lyly I 22; see also I 32, 79, 89–91, 111, 112, 133, 155, 156, 169, 171, 179, 191, 192, 237, 250, 251, 266; II 11, 118, 230, 231, 232, 250, 255, etc.

[3] E. g. I 89, 127, 178, 179, 182, 183, 192, 255, etc.

[4] E. g. I 89–91, 110 (Hercules' spindle and Achilles' spear), 150 (Demosthenes), 151 (Diomedes); II 68 (Apollo and Aurora), 157 (a conventional series of similes from classical mythology); and many others.

[5] See infra, p. 18.

[6] E. g. I 68 (Ingratitude, Envy, Treachery), 72, 135, 157; II 19, 25 (Ambition, cf. 205), 156, 215, 223.

Out of this incongruous whole there results a certain effect of unity and of charm. It is a Dresden-china world; it is writing of a wholly artificial species; but it has a grace and beauty of its own. Naturally it is not to be subjected to the same analysis that we should apply to a more robust and realistic art. It is a style that depends largely upon figures of speech and upon conscious and formal tropes. Lyly's imagery is entirely ornamental. It matters little where it is introduced. It is adventitious, not a part of the thought. It is largely imitative of foreign models.[1] Its influence, however, appears plainly in the contemporary drama, and it is therefore important to study the sources and range of his imagery somewhat more in detail.

RANGE OF HIS IMAGERY.

Similes and illustrations drawn from a fabulous natural history, it is well known, are the chief characteristics of Lyly's style.[2] Outside of these, however, and within the restrictions of his peculiar manner, the range of his nature imagery is not inconsiderable. Almost everything, it is true, is conventional and courtly, and Lyly doubtless was little observant of nature. But it is the fashion of the Euphuistic school to draw upon nature in one way or another, and the effect is generally pleasing.

NATURE: Aspects of the Sky, the Elements, etc. Of these I have noted some fifty references in the eight plays studied: II 232 (the thousand thoughts of a woman's heart are compared to the infinite stars and to the sundry colors of the rainbow), II 160 ("O, eyes, more fair than is the morning star").[3]

II 176. "Neither Daphne in the spring,
　　Nor glistering Thetis in her orient robe,
　　Nor shame-fast morning girt in silver clouds,
　　Are half so lovely as this earthly saint."

II 189 (the sunshine of her eyes), II 35 (beauty dazzles); II 158 (to darken); Shadows II 228; Storms II 168, 172, 183; Wind I 137, II 182, 159; Stars (cf. I 53 the heavens *tiled* with

---

[1] Cf. Dr. Landmann, Euphues, for a discussion of the sources of Lyly's style.
[2] Symonds, Shaks. Pred. p. 512.
[3] Cf. Greene, 168 b.

stars) I 79, II 42, 158, 164, 172; Moon I 93, II 157; Clouds II 158, 159, 165, 176 (a common metaphor in Chapman, Ben Jonson, etc.); Rainbow I 150; Fire I 48 (to kindle love), 78, 96, 112, 116, 133, 137, 146, 158, 204, 213, 232, 256, II 17, 103, 170, 182, 215, 251—cf. 105, 118, I 91 (torches); Frozen II 131 (frozen conscience), 166; The Seasons II 166 ("Sorrow's winter"), 200.

Aspects of the Water, Seas, etc., appear but little in Lyly: I 45 (the ebb and flow of love), 137, 150, II 26, 167, 231, 235; e. g. II 225 ("Niobe is tender-hearted, whose thoughts are like water, yielding to everything, and nothing to be seen"); Dew I 148; II 201, 231.

Aspects of the Earth: THE METALS: golden is a favorite adjective with Lyly,—I 19 ("My golden years"), 28 (cf. II 82), 44, 256, II 16, 21, 42, 191, 240, 246; Leaden I 44 ("leaden sleep"), II 82, 240; Steel II 27, 250; I 143 (the rust of idleness); Iron I 151; Silver II 189, 194, 246; Dross II 27; Precious stones I 73, 93, 111, 199, 250, II 82, 191; Crystal I 129, II 156; Flint II 209.

The Vegetable World: Growth I 8, 10, 75, II 97, 162; Trees I 22 (cedar), 148, 250, 32 (cf. II 83), I 133, 169, 191; Ivy I 22; Flowers I 29 (Youth the "flowering time"), cf. II 159, 246, I 33, 171, 199; II 20 ("beauty in a minute is both a blossom and a blast"), 241, 256, 160, 178; Hay and grass I 29, II 241; Fruit I 111, 171.

The Animal World is for Lyly a frequent source of similes, but chiefly in the range of a fabulous natural history. Outside of this range the following may be mentioned: Crab I 127, Caterpillars I 21; Spiders I 21 (cobweb); Wasp I 82, cf. 192; Bees I 151 (wax), II 27, 105, 167, 178, 207, 232; Bat I 91; Wings II 197 ("O that thy steeds were winged with my swift thoughts."); II 256 ("A mind lighter than feathers"), II 258; Parrot I 82; Swan I 91; Larks I 133; Pigeons I 184; Serpent I 82, 192; Hare I 90; Lion II 46, 157; Deer I 90, 127; Dog I 108, II 135; Horse II 79 (withers wrung¹), I 241 (unbridled), 253; Ivory II 189; Wolves I 19; Ape II 200, 246; Glowworms II 189:

> "As bright as glow-worms in the night,
> With which the morning decks her lover's hair."

[1] Cf. *Hamlet* III ii, 237.

The **Fabulous Natural History,** as has been noted, is less prominent in Lyly's plays than in his romance of *Euphues*. The chief instances are as follows: Adamant II 23, 170, 192, 219; Asbestos I 203; Origanum I 155; Basel I 89; Ebony I 28; Beet I 144 (of Macedonia); the tree Salurus I 161; Syrian Mud I 169; Various Plants I 170, 171, 190 (Lunary), 192, 240, 244, 250; II 237; Fish I 19, 111, 190; Basilisk II 191; Griffin I 155, 237; Cameleon I 45; Phœnix I 46, 89, cf. 207; Cockatrice I 127; Salamander II 233; Insects I 133, 155, 205, 179, 183, 203 (bite of Tarantula cured by music), II 26; Worms I 45, II 20, I 150, 180, II 26, 94; Serpent I 90, 172, II 26; Birds I 22, 164, 89, 90, 156, 191, 251, 109 (lapwing), II 109, I 179 (swan's song), II 233, I 192 (Halcyon), 251 (Ibis), II 35, 232; Ermine I 111; Bear I 155 (blasts with its breath); Wolf II 230; Polypus II 231; etc.

MAN AND HUMAN LIFE: The Fine Arts, Literature, Learning, etc., naturally appear but little in Lyly's comparisons. Music is mentioned several times: I 40, 108, 125, II 92, 232 (a lady's heart like a lute); Painting I 45 (Time a portrait-painter), 141, 242, II 82, 153, 164 (painted plumes), 200; Similes from the Stage: I 221, II 99, 106, 108, 182; Books I 52, 115, 163, II 25; Law I 59, II 78; II 125 (the rent-racking of wit). 137; Medical: Salve I 112, II 166, 170; Various I 45 ("Thy gray hairs are ambassadors of experience"), II 27 ("to make inclosure of your mind"); I 108 (Money is Diogenes's slave), I 259 (to lackey after); I 128 ("life posting to death, a death galloping from life").

The Practical Arts and Occupations: Agriculture, I 36, 90, 125, II 86 (sow and reap), 92, 166 (harvest of love); II 17 (furrows in cheek); Weaving II 3, 228; Lapidaries I 91; Engraving, printing I 66, 78, 141, 270, 273, II 170; Prentice I 174 (prentice to Fortune), 251, II 255; II 240 (bellows, forge, etc.); 250 (like melting iron); I 34 (rough-hewn soldiers); II 26 ("Is not the country walled with huge waves?");[1] II 89 (head full of hammers).

Amusements and Games: Cards I 123; Hawking II 11, 187, 190, 218; 75 and 91 (mewed up); To angle for I 73.

[1] Cf. Greene, 158ᵃ.

Colloquial and Familiar Images, together with images taken from domestic life, are a specialty in the gentle and courtly style of Lyly. "His comedies were . . . new creations. . . . He invented a species," says Symonds.[1] Lyly's comic power is not great, but one of the elements of comic effect here made use of, the appeal to colloquial, familiar, and domestic life, was afterwards employed by nearly all the writers of comic scenes. Chapman and Ben Jonson are particularly profuse in images of this sort. The chief examples from Lyly are: I 35 (love milks the thoughts); 38 ("He hath taken his thoughts a hole lower"); 40 ("to untrusse the points of his heart"); 59 (commit her tongue prisoner to her mouth); 62 (to "step to age by stairs"); 69 (take the wall of, etc.);[2] 71 (wear the nap of your wit quite off); 70 (chin unfledged); 135 (Truth's face scratched); 141, 178, (to wrastle with love); 249 (thoughts made hailfellows with the gods); II 21 ("gold is but the earth's garbage, a weed"); 86 ("truanted from honesty");[3] 89 (coistrels); 97 ("an idiot of the newest cut"); 219 ("thy words as unkembd as thy locks"); cf. II 107, 110, 91–92 ("this metaphor from ale"); Breeds I 276, II 3, 7, 243.

Domestic Life: I 5 ("my thoughts . . . are stitched to the stars"), cf. 249, II 18, 218; I 156 (a needle's point); Sewing II 82, 85, I 11; Dress I 19 ("as a cloak for mine affections"), 185 (fine ladies—like fine wool which wears quickly); cf. II 44 (to shroud), II 97, 113, 114, 201; Affections II 182 ("the western wind, That kisses flowers, and wantons with their leaves"); Divorcing I 19; I 14 (war "rocks asleep my thoughts"), 158 ("She hath her thoughts in a string"); I 126 (reason must wean what appetite nursed); so I 184, 223; 36 ("that bauble called love"); I 49 ("I have no playfellow but fancy, . . . and make my thoughts my friends"); II 176 ("levity is beauty's waiting maid").

The Body and Its Parts: I 6 ("My thoughts have no veins, and yet unless they be let blood, I shall perish"); I 20 (every vein and sinew of my love), cf. II 228; I 58 (prefers the body of truth to the tomb); I 77 (the wounds of love); cf. 270, 112; I 54 (the

---

[1] Shakspere's Predecessors, pp. 516, 532.
[2] Cf. Ben Jonson, II 408ª.
[3] Cf. Chapman, 304ª.

rheum of love); II 12 (lips are the door of the mouth); II 107 (a body like a cask); II 7 (love is the marrow of the mind); II 19 (the grave's mouth); II 8 ("gold is but the guts of the earth"), cf. II 19, 25, 247, I 267; II 195 (the thunder's teeth); I 19 ("my mangled mind"), cf. I 111 (a crooked mind), cf. I 112 (sighs cleave the heart); 83 (pinched my heart); 112 (wounded thoughts); 128 (the canker of care), cf. II 223 ; II 6, 245 (to tickle the mind); Touch I 64, II 26 ; To creep I 132 ; To pant II 112.

The Senses and Appetites: I 26 ("to glut their eyes"); Surfeit I 27, 44, 68, 112, 156, 181, 183, 192, II 95, 83 ; Food, Eating, etc., I 69 (love's feast), 108, 252, II 19 (eating cares),[1] 215, 35, 81, 86 ; Drinking I 162, 205, 229 (Ship in a storm drinks salt healths) ; I 184 ("Silence shall disgest what folly hath swallowed") ; II 25 (pampered with slaughter); II 47 (to taste war and relish taxes) ; To relish II 83 ; II 167 (honey words, sauced with gall) ; Sugared II 38 ; Spice II 90 ; Sour II 159.

Death and its Surroundings : I 72 (a mouthful of bones [teeth] like a charnel-house) ; I 72 (" go to the sexton and tell him desire is dead, and will him to dig his grave"); I 111 (woman is like a whited sepulchre).

A few commonplace **Images of War** occur in Lyly's plays : I 48 (a war of love in the mind, "instead of sweet parleys"); Armory I 52 ; I 55 (their wits as rusty as their bills); I 60 (the combat of love) cf. I 149, 250; I 81 ("more strength in a true heart than in a walled city") ; I 83 ("let my tongue *ransom* hers ") ; II 96 (the face a *scabbard* of the mind), cf. II 135, 18 ; II 78 (to overshoot oneself).

Subjective Life, Religion, etc.: I 82 (" tell who Eumenides shrineth for his saint"), cf. II 16, 176; Paradise II 174, cf. II 185; Hell II 179 ; Magic I 91 ; Influence of Stars I 221.

A number of **Miscellaneous Metaphors and Similes**, most of which frequently reappear in later writers, remain to be mentioned. Most of these are of the nature of conventional poetical tags and formulæ, although not sufficiently common to fall under the class of faded, or to adopt Max Müller's expression, incarnate metaphors. The more frequently recurring ones are characteristic marks of

[1] Cf. Horace "edaces curae" (*Carm.* 2, 11, 18, etc.).

the poetic diction of the Elizabethan drama: Unspotted I 18 (unspotted love). so I 82, 273, II 17, 258 : cf. I 45, 50, 62, 80 (unspotted thoughts; cf II 234, 254), I 213, 245, 251, II 220; Melt I 28, 37, 40 ("your sad music . . . hath so *melted* my mind") 141, 207, II 17, 27, 250,—cf II 131 (thaw); Quench I 48, 79 ("affection's unquenchable"), II 215, 223 ; Poison I 49, 77, 112 (the poison of love), II 190; Climbing I 157, 178 (mounting), II 7, 19 (to climb the steps of ambition), 25 ; Mirror, Glass, etc. I 181, II 155, 160 ("Thou mirror of dame Nature's cunning work"), 218 (a flatterer is a glass); Mould II 37, 77, cf I 45 (image); Pierce I 58, II 241 ("whose heart no tears could pierce"); Labyrinth I 168, 214; II 24 ("Coelia hath sealed her face in my heart"); Balances, to weigh, etc. I 81, II 7, 9; To whet I 117 (to *whet* one's wits), II 88; II 18 ("thoughts *gyved* to her beauty"); II 35 (thoughts *entangled* by beauty); II 27, 108 (wit of proof); I 182 (filed tongue,—cf II 219); I 241 (thoughts *unknit*); Counterfeit, coin, etc. I 151, II 76, 89, 164, 169; Colors II 11 (black).

GEORGE PEELE

1552?–1598?

Acted	Published		Vol.	Pages
1581?	1584	*The Arraignment of Paris*	I	5– 72
1590?	1593	*Edward the First*	I	85–217
1590?	1594	*The Battle of Alcazar*	I	227–296
——	1595	*The Old Wives' Tale*	I	303–347
1588?	1599	*David and Bethsabe*	II	5– 86

GEORGE PEELE.

PEELE's imagery has received some praise. Hawkins[1] with curiously bad taste called one of his worst metaphors Æschylean.

Opinions of Critics on Peele's Imagery
"There is no such sweetness of versification and imagery to be found in our blank verse anterior to Shakespeare," writes Campbell.[2] Ulrici finds that *David and Bethsabe* recalls *Romeo and Juliet*. "It is more especially the love scenes and the images and similes describing the charms of the beauty of nature, that remind one of those incomparable pictures in *Romeo and Juliet*."[3] Hallam, who is hostile to Peele, says: " Peele has some command of imagery, but in every other quality it seems to me that he has scarce any claim to honor."[4] Peele was in fact a poet rather than a dramatist, and it is by his poetical gifts alone that he attains his slender measure of success. His imagery is seldom condensed and emphatic, and is seen at its best in his two most poetical pieces, the *Arraignment of Paris* and

Nature of his Imagery
David and Bethsabe. When he attempts to be dramatic, as in the *Battle of Alcazar* and *Edward the First*, he becomes strained and turgid. He is fond of simile, and his imagery runs to extended passages rather than to short and burning figures. In his five plays occur over one hundred formal similes, including some seven of the prolonged or so-called Homeric type.[5] This tendency is especially characteristic

---

[1] As quoted in Collier's Hist. of Eng. Dram. Poetry, III 27. The metaphor is contained in the following lines:

"At him the thunder shall discharge his bolt;
And his fair spouse [i. e. the lightning], with bright and fiery wings,
Sit ever burning on his hateful bones."

For somewhat similar metaphors in Peele see II 65, 66, 79, etc.

[2] Specimens of British Poets, page lviii.

[3] Shakspere's Dramatic Art, Vol. I, p. 137.

[4] Lit. of Eur. Pt. II. ch. VI, § 31; see also Ward, Hist. Eng. Dr. Lit. I. 213.

[5] Examples of prolonged metaphorical passages; I 10-11, 205, II 15, 60, and the parables pp. 33 and 45. Prolonged similes: I 10, 96, 203-4, II 12, 29, 42, 80.

of *David and Bethsabe*, where, resulting from the attempt to embody in Elizabethan dramatic form the spirit of the biblical imagery,[1] his language becomes almost a continued series of figures, among which hyperbole[2] and personification[3] especially abound. His imagery is generally extrinsic and ornamental. Where he attempts force and emphasis his language degenerates into rant and extravagance in the vein of *Tamburlaine;* e. g. I 112 (Lluellen's speech on hearing of Elinor's capture), 237, 238, 250, 253, 262 ("a lake of blood and gore"), 280, 288, II 21 (the metaphor which Hawkins so much admired), 40, 60, 63. 66, 82, 83; see especially II 49:

Ahimaas. "O would our eyes were conduits to our hearts,
    And that our hearts were seas of liquid blood,
    To pour in streams upon this holy mount,
    For witness we would die for David's woes.
Jonathan. Then should this Mount of Olives seem a plain,
    Drowned with a sea, that with our sighs should roar" ..

On the other hand, where he writes in his own poetical vein, he is often highly successful. See for example the famous flower passage in the *Arraignment of Paris*,[4] or *Edward I*, sc. V, ll. 109–114:

"What Nell, sweet Nell, do I behold thy face?
Fall heaven, fleet stars, shine Phœbus' lamps no more!
This is the planet lends this world her light;
Star of my fortune this, loadstar of my delight,
Fair mould of beauty, miracle of fame."

and *David and Bethsabe* passim, e. g. sc. xv, ll. 89–90:

"But things to come exceed our human reach,
    And are not painted yet in angels' eyes,"—

and the speech following.

While not strikingly original, Peele's imagery is not, on the other hand, wooden and artificial. His range is not great. Stars, sky, sun, and flowers play the largest part, but are generally used effectively and gracefully. "Painted," "mirror," "mounting,"

---

[1] Most of his borrowings from biblical sources are noticed in Bullen's notes.
[2] E. g. II 19, 21, 49, 54, 60, 63, 65, 66, 76, etc.
[3] E. g. II 7, 8, 11, 13, 17 ("To suffer pale and grisly abstinence, To sit and feed upon his fainting cheeks") 19, 20, 21, 23, 31, 48, 62, 76, 82, 85.
[4] Peele, Works, I pp. 10-11.

and similar poetical catchwords of the day occur frequently. There are a few touches of Euphuistic natural history. And in general Peele does not go far out of the conventional range for his images; there are very few domestic images and few drawn from the arts, from religion, and the like. Two imitations of Spenser[1] and one of Du Bartas[2] occur, while his allusions point to Homer and the classical tradition. His comic and familiar passages Peele usually casts into prose, and in them uses little figure and that almost entirely colloquial and proverbial in nature.[3] The general impression from the *Arraignment of Paris*, *The Old Wife's Tale*, and *David and Bethsabe* is that of sweetness and grace. *The Arraignment of Paris* is practically bare of metaphor and simile save in two or three passages. In Flora's speeches in Act I, scene i, the imagery (referring mostly to flowers) rises and throngs to the expression of lyrical beauty. It is elaborate and conscious poetry but not dramatic. All the strong images in this piece appeal to the sense of sight. The *Old Wife's Tale* contains almost no striking imagery. What there is is colloquial and in keeping. *David and Bethsabe* is Peele's masterpiece. As elsewhere, his genius here is chiefly lyrical: the speeches roll out the beauty of their poetry deliberately, not dramatically, and the imagery is graceful, but not compact with dramatic import. His versification is accordingly fluent and smooth. "Exasperatingly insipid," Mr. Bullen calls the piece, and it is certainly figurative or rather tropical beyond measure. Metaphors, similes, and personification especially abound.

Edward I and *The Battle of Alcazar* are generally strained and stilted. Peele was trying his hand at the extravagant and bloodthirsty rant of the school of Greene, Marlowe and Kyd. There is the usual amount of misplaced classical ornament.[4] These two plays are not important or highly significant.

[1] Cf. II 42, 244; note in I 34-36 the parody of the *Shepherd's Calendar*.
[2] Cf. II 29.
[3] See infra, p. 29.
[4] Classical allusion is frequent in Peele — naturally so in the *Arraignment of Paris*. The Fates (I 6, 71 etc.), the Furies (I 229, 234, 242, 280, 284, 321, 342) and Nemesis (I 229, 241, 242, 280) are particularly prominent, especially in the midst of the hyperbolical rant of the *Battle of Alcazar*. In *David and*

RANGE AND SOURCES OF HIS IMAGERY.

Nature, and especially inanimate nature, affords by far the larger proportion of Peele's metaphors and similes. This fact alone is proof of the non-dramatic character of his mind. The dramatist, alive to all aspects of human life, naturally draws most of his comparisons from human life. Flowers and stars, sun and sunshine, appear more than any other images in Peele, and his touch is often that of a poet.

NATURE   Aspects of the Sky, The Elements, etc.: I 128 (the crystal gates of heaven); cf. I 188, II 9 ("comelier than the silver clouds that dance On Zephyr's wings").

Sun and Clouds: I 87, 162, 291, 293 (sunshine), 112 (cf. II 41):

> "Sun, could'st thou shine, and see my love beset,
> And didst not clothe thy clouds in fiery coats,
> O'er all the heavens, with wingèd sulphur flames?"

Peele is fond of the pathetic fallacy (e. g. I 124, II 19, 50, 54, 76, etc.); II 12 (metaphor of the sun: "heaven's bright eye");[1] II 42 (like the sun dancing forth from the East—after Spenser), 43 (like the sunset), 67, 79.

Stars: I 96, cf. 117 ("The welkin, spangled through with golden spots, Reflects no finer in a frosty night" . . .). 121, 125 ("Edward, *star* of England's globe"), 127, 166, 143:

> "Why should so fair a star [Elinor] stand in a vale,
> And not be seen to sparkle in the sky?"

II 22 ("Making thy forehead, *like a comet*, shine")

> 42 ("Shining in riches like the firmament,
> The starry vault that overhangs the earth.")

> 50 ("That piteous stars may see our miseries,
> And drop their golden tears upon the ground.")

Bethsabe there are (properly) very few. The chief elsewhere in Peele are; Various Gods: I 87, 97, 101, 112, 260, 270, 291, 305, 314, 334; 96 Ops, Ixion, etc.   III Ægeus, 116 Paris, 117 Narcissus, 123 Perseus and the Gorgon; Phlegethon, Avernus, etc., I 140, 209, 235, 230 the Myrmidons, 246 Pompey, 162 the Graces; etc. Cf. I 252 Occasion and her foretop.

[1] Cf. *Comedy of Errors*, II i 16.

Cf. 54, 67 (hyperbole), 86; Comets I 10:

"Nor doth the milk-white way, in frosty night,
Appear so fair and beautiful in sight,
As doen these fields, and groves, and sweetest bowers."

FIRE: I 44 ("Round drops of fiery Phlegethon to *scorch* false hearts"), 61 ("in his bosom carries fire"; cf. 151); 227 ("Honor inflames the Portingal; cf. 272); II 22 ("let hate's fire be kindled in thy heart"), 49 ("the wrath of heaven *inflames* Thy scorched bosom with ambition's heat"), 67 ("all breasts that burn with any griefs").

LIGHT, SHINING, etc.: I 86, 91, 117, II 26 ("his fame may shine in Israel"), II 38, 75, 84.

STORMS: II 41 ("wrathful *storms* of war Have *thundered*").

DEW: II 58 ("So shall we come upon him in our strength, Like to the dew that falls in showers from heaven").

SEASONS: I 336 ("Die in the spring, the April of thy age!")[1]

Aspects of the Sea: I 111 ("the wallowing main"); cf. 259, 203–4 ll. 20–30 (simile of the shepherd who blames the shipwrecked seaman for inaction). Coral I 117 ("coral lips"); so 335; Springs I 210, 212, II 49.

Aspects of the Earth: II 58 ("in number like sea-sands, That nestle close in one another's neck"); Glass I 97; Golden I 290.

FLOWERS: I 10–11 (Flora's speech), 21 ("as fresh as bin the flowers in May"), 31 ("The fairest face, the flower of gallant Greece"), 131, 132, 155, 163 ("And yet is earthly honor but a flower"), 145:

"As when of Leicester's hall and bower,
Thou wert the rose and sweetest flower."

203 ("pale, like mallow flowers"); cf. 204 lines 32–33; 344, II 9 (cf. 10 ll. 67–70), 23 ("Gladsome summer in her shady robes, Crowned with roses and with painted flowers"); 47, 84; I 253 (thorny teeth).

WEED: I 189 ("To spoil the weed [i. e. Lluellen] that chokes fair Cambria"); cf. 198;

FRUIT: I 252, II 19, 68, 77;

TREES: I 90 ("how, like sturdy oaks, Do these thy soldiers circle thee about, To shield and shelter thee from winter's

[1] Cf. II 47.

storms!"), II 9 ("Brighter than inside bark of new-hewn cedar"), II 19 (cedars).

The Animal World enters rather conventionally into Peele's imagery. The traditional "lion-like" is common; I 181 ("to rouse him lion-like"), so 188, 287, 239:

"O fly the sword and fury of the foe,
That rageth as the ramping lioness
In rescue of her younglings from the bear!"

II 32, 57 ("David . . . whose angry heart, Is as a lion's letted of his walk"); Bear II 57 ("Chafing as she-bears robbed of their whelps").

Among **Domestic Animals** appear Dogs, I 125, 126, 139, 251:

"Make the sword and target here my hound
To pull down lions and untamèd beasts."

290, II 15; CATTLE I 183:

"Princes of Scotland and my loving friends,
Whose necks are over wearied with the *yoke*
And servile bondage of these Englishmen,
Lift up your *horns*, and with your *brazen hoofs*,
Spurn at the honor of your enemies."

194: "And heifer-like, sith thou hast past thy bounds,
Thy sturdy neck must stoop to bear this yoke."

SHEEP I 89 (fled "like sheep before the wolves"), 228, II 33.

HORSES II 29 ("Laying his bridle in the neck of sin, Ready to bear him past his grave to hell!"), 30 ("giving lust her rein") 65 (bridle), 78, I 227 (Spur).

BIRDS: I 149, 152, 154; II 29–30 ll. 4–14 (simile from Du Bartas; man flies to sin as the raven to its carrion).[1] The image of wings is a favorite with Peele also: I 195 ("If his wings grow flig, they may be clipt"), 205:

"My soul . . .
Faint [fain?] for to mount the heavens with wings of grace,
Is hinderèd by flocking troops of sin."

II 5, 6, 20, 21 (the winged lightning), 66 ("Then set thy angry soul upon her wings").

[1] Cf. Chapman, 537a.

SERPENTS II 11 : "a hundred streams . . .
Shall, as the serpents fold into their nests,
In oblique turnings, wind their nimble waves,
About the circles of her curious walks."

Fabulous Natural History appears in four or five places: I 35–6: ("like to the stricken deer, Seeks he dictamnum for his wound within our forest here"); 253–4:

"I will provide thee of a princely osprey,
That as she flieth over fish in pools,
The fish shall turn their glistering bellies up,
And thou shalt take thy liberal choice of all."

177 ("His sight to me is like the sight of a cockatrice"), cf. II 48 ("Piercing with venom of thy *poisoned eyes*"), II 80 ll. 119–130 (as the eagle mounts and stares at the sun).

MAN AND HUMAN LIFE. The Arts: I 194 ("Your goodly glosses"); II 61 ("The sins of David, *printed* in his brows"); II 23 (painted flowers); MUSIC II 44; Building II 78 ("for what time shall this round building [the earth] stand"); Prison I 202 ("in this painful prison of my soul"), 290 ("my soul, That breaks from out the prison of my breast"). MEDICINE I 186 (to purge), II 12; AGRICULTURE I 182:

"Why now is England's *harvest* ripe:
Barons, now may you *reap* the rich renown
That . . . *grows* where ensigns wave upon the plains."

II 14 (reaping reward), 86; Wire II 38 ("Thou fair young man, whose hairs shine in mine eye, *Like golden wires* of David's ivory lute"). So 46, cf. 363 ("The Praise of Chastity" l. 73);[1] Hooks and Bait I 273, II 23.

Colloquial, Coarse, and Familiar Images occur in Peele mostly in relief scenes or scenes from low life: I 107 (drawing a pot), 109 ("as plainly seen as a three half-pence through a dish of butter in a sunny day"), 140 (outlawed men like discarded cards),

---

[1] See the same simile in Spenser, *Epithalamion* l. 154 (cf. Todd's note), *F. Q.* III viii 7, IV vi 20, II iv 15, *Ruins of Time* l. 10, *Hymn in Honor of Beauty* l. 97; in Gascoigne "Dan Bartholemew of Bath" stanza 9 (Chalmers Poets, II 501), and in many others. It appears frequently in M. E. poetry; see Shakspere's Sonnet CXXX satirizing the comparison.

168 ("cutting off" the law, as a hangman cuts down his victim), 173 ("the dice, not being *bound prentice* to him"), 191 ("it shall cost me hot water"), 307 (a proverb), 312 ("my first wife, whose tongue . . . sounded in my ears like the clapper of a great bell"), 313 (a series of homely similes). 325, 332, 334 ("He . . . speaks like a drum perished at the west end"), I 125 ("Take that *earnest penny* of thy death" [*stabs him*]), 129, 134, II 30 ("If holy David so *shook hands with sin*").[1]

The Body and its Parts. Entrails and bowels I 57, 250 ("Earthquakes in the entrails of the earth"), II 9, 53, 66, 73 ; cf. 82 ; Veins II 50, 55, 66 : God's finger I 293, II 24, 55 ; I 125 (paws); I 124 (the *thirsty* sword).

Of DOMESTIC IMAGES there are practically none in Peele.

Subjective Life, Religion, etc. Hell and heaven I 131 ("Let me saint or divel be, In that sweet heaven or hell that is in thee"); 262 ("And now doth Spain promise *with holy face*") ; cf. prologue to David and Bethsabe passim ; II 61 ("Even as thy sin hath still importuned heaven") ; 86 :

"Thy soul shall joy the sacred cabinet
Of those divine ideas that present
Thy changed spirit with a heaven of bliss ; "

II 46 (angel).

War. I 182 ("thy treason's fear shall *make the breach*"), 332 ("a woman without a tongue is as a soldier without his weapon"), II 51 ("armed with a humble heart"), I 111 (to dart), II 54 (*dart* plagues at), cf. 85.

A Few Miscellaneous Metaphors are frequent and characteristic tags of Peele's style, especially the image of *piercing* : I 5 ("smoke piercing the skies?"), 42, 234 ("These rites . . . Have pierced by this to Pluto's cave"), 279, 342, II 7 ("Let not my beauty's fire . . . pierce any bright eye"). So 8, 9, 12 (2x), 17, 48, 64, 83 (2x); Climbing, Mounting, etc. I 93 ("thy mounting mind"), 114, 153, cf. 205, 227, 290, II 80 ; Mirror I 19 ("Mirror of virginity"), 344 :

"Whose beauty so reflecteth in my sight
As doth a crystal mirror in the sun."

---

[1] See—with the contrary application of the idea—Webster 77a : "You have shook hands with Reputation "; cf. Ford I 315).

II 63; Mould, Pattern I 127 ("Fair mould of beauty"), 177 (Pattern); Tangle I 282 ("tied and tangled in a dangerous war"), II 11:
"Now comes my lover, tripping like the roe,
And brings my longings *tangled* in her hair."

Cf. 56, 362 (Praise of Chastity l. 51); I 17 (painted paths), II 23 (painted flowers), 8 ("plain *enamelled* with discolored flowers"); Rip I 24 (unrip not so your shames"), II 73; I 46 ("Hard heart, fair face, fraught with disdain"); Poison II 60, 83.

CHRISTOPHER MARLOWE

1564-1593

Acted	Published		Vol.	Pages
1587	1590	*Tamburlaine the Great.* Part I -	I	7–105
——	1590	*Tamburlaine the Great.* Part II -	I	109–206
1588?	1604	*The Tragical History of Doctor Faustus*	I	211–283
1589?	1594	*The Jew of Malta* - - - -	II	5–113
1590	1594	*Edward the Second* - - -	II	119–234
1593?	c. 1595	*The Massacre at Paris* - - -	II	239–298

CHRISTOPHER MARLOWE.

Quality and Value of his Imagery
In the history of English dramatic poetry Marlowe is the first figure of supreme importance. He first established blank verse on the public stage as the principal medium of dramatic expression, and it was he who "first inspired with true poetic passion the form of literature to which his chief efforts were consecrated."[1] The "mighty line" of Marlowe has been felt and applauded by all critics from Ben Jonson down. Connected with his innovation in style, as evidenced by the new music of his verse and the new passion of his thought, the range and character of Marlowe's imagery is also highly significant and worthy of study. The inspiration and Titanic energy of an emancipated genius, qualities so apparent in all his work that they have led most modern critics to rank Marlowe as a dramatic poet next after Shakspere in the Elizabethan circle, are apparent also in the pictures which his imagination bodies forth, in the various forms of figurative language which are woven into the texture of his style. The chief faults as well as the chief merits of this style are displayed in his use of figures. "His poetry [is] strong and weak alike with passionate feeling, and expressed with a turbulent magnificence of words and images."[2] Violence, hyperbole, bombast, the "display of overloaded splendors and colors,"[3] these are the characteristic marks of the two parts of *Tamburlaine*. In his later work the bombast and hyperbole are less apparent, and the color and splendor of the poet's diction are kept more nearly within the bounds of poetic and dramatic decorum.

The condensed metaphor, the brief and pregnant expression of a striking and oftentimes complex metaphorical idea in one

[1] Ward, Engl. Dram. Lit., I 203.
[2] Brooke, Primer of Eng. Lit., § 80.
[3] Taine, Eng. Lit., Bk. II, ch. ii.

short word or phrase, first[1] prominently appears in Marlowe. It accords well at times with his passionate utterance, although it is a form characteristic of the highly elliptical and purely dramatic diction of a poet like Shakspere rather than of the more swelling and lyrical utterance of Marlowe. Examples of this figure in Marlowe are as follows:

Condensed Metaphors in Marlowe

I 50 "Cannons *mouthed* like Orcus' gulf."
156 "Death, why com'st thou not?
    Well, this must be the *messenger* for thee."
                           (*Drawing a dagger.*)
II 15 "Thus *trowls*[2] our fortune in by land and sea."
272 "Her eyes and looks *sow'd seeds* of perjury."
314 "Our *unweapon'd thoughts.*"

While his use of metaphor and simile is not highly literary and conventional like much of the work of Peele and Greene, still Marlowe writes rather as a poet than as a dramatist.[3] In *Tamburlaine*, at least, the imagery is abundant and does not seem to be very much discriminated among the various characters, except that most of the glorious hyperbole is put into the mouth of Tamburlaine himself. It is poetical imagery, seldom existing merely to make clearer or to strengthen the thought, but rather for the sake of hyperbolical magnificence, or to convey and enforce the passion or the pomp of an idea. Thus in the famous description of Tamburlaine,[4]

His Imagery Poetical rather than Dramatic

    "Of stature tall and straightly fashioned,
    Like his desire lift upward and divine," etc.,

all is barbaric hyperbole and ornament. Occasionally the metaphor in its excess of turbulent daring becomes mixed, or as Hazlitt phrased it,[5] "There is a little fustian and incongruity of metaphor now and then, which is not very injurious to the subject." For example:

Mixed Metaphors

[1] Kyd, writing contemporaneously, has some striking examples of the same sort.
[2] A metaphor from drinking. Cf. Nares.
[3] On the lyrical element in Marlowe's drama see J. A. Symonds, In the Key of Blue and Other Prose Essays, pp. 244-246.
[4] Part I, Act II sc. i (I 28).
[5] Age of Eliz., Lecture II.

I 11 (Theridamas is "the very legs Whereon our State doth lean as on a staff").[1]
    I 132: "And jealous anger of His fearful arm
        Be poured with rigor on our sinful heads."
II 244 ("My quenchless *thirst*, whereon I *build*"),
    280 ("Navarre, that *cloaks* them underneath his *wings*").
Cf. II 353 ("Yet Dido casts her eyes, like anchors out"),
    368 ("When Dido's beauty chained thine eyes to her").
But these last may be Nash's conceits.

Tamburlaine of course is the *locus classicus* for magnificent
Hyperbole   hyperbole and glorious extravagance.[2] A characteristic passage may be quoted:

"I will, with engines never exercised,
Conquer, sack, and utterly consume
Your cities and your golden palaces;
And, with the flames that beat against the clouds
Incense the heavens, and make the stars to melt. . . .
. . . . And, till by vision or by speech I hear
Immortal Jove say 'Cease, my Tamburlaine,'
I will persist, a terror to the world,
Making the meteors, that, like armed men,
Are seen to march upon the towers of heaven,
Run tilting round about the firmament,
And break their burning lances in the air,
For honor of my wondrous victories."[3]

Marlowe like Greene is fond of costly passages and gorgeous
Costly Phrases   description: I 14:
    "march in coats of gold,
With costly jewels hanging at their ears,
And shining stones upon their lofty crests."

So 20, 119, 219, II 12, 334, 361, 363, etc. Marlowe has also, like Spenser and Milton, many passages of ethnic pomp and geographic romance. He loves to feed the hunger of
Geographic Romance   his imagination with whole continents. The sounding reports of great conquests are a large part of

---

[1] Cf. II 292 "Sweet Duke of Guise, our prop to lean upon."
[2] The most striking examples are I 18, 23, 35, 36, 50, 60, 70f, 102, 121, 123, 124, 137, 140-141, 147, 173-4, 179, 189, 198. Elsewhere in Marlowe see II 273, 291, 325-6, 348, 351, 353, 357, 358, 369, 373.
[3] I 173.

the poetical motive of *Tamburlaine*. "Give me a map," cries Tamburlaine,[1] "then let me see how much

    Is left for me to conquer all the world."

(*One brings a map*)—And then follows one of those enumerations of mighty empires and far-off regions so dear to the adventurous imagination of the Elizabethan Englishman,—Persia, Armenia, Bithynia, Egypt, Arabia, the Suez Canal by anticipation, Nubia, "the Tropic line of Capricorn," Zanzibar, Græcia, and much else! Note also Faustus' hungry heart for roaming, and the satisfaction with which he recounts his travels.[2]

Marlowe in spite of his strenuous seriousness is not above an occasional play on words, e. g. I 51 ("Which *dyes* my locks so *lifeless.*"), 114

Quibbling

"India, where raging Lantchidol
Beats on the regions with his boisterous *blows.*"

I 196 ("pitch their pitchy tents"), 203 ("Must part, imparting his impressions"), II 43 (foiled), 175 ("The barons overbear me"), 294 (arms).

In the later plays the proportion of tropes is much smaller than in the two parts of *Tamburlaine*.[3] At the same time, while

The earlier and the later work distinguished

much less profuse, the metaphors and similes of the later plays are usually more restrained and effective. Considerable bold personification, of which there is little in the other plays, is furthermore a characteristic of *Tamburlaine*: e. g. I 29 (Honor, Nature, etc.), 46 (Death), cf. 156, 199, 61 (Victory), 95 (Fame, Hunger), 96 (Darkness), 98 (Earth), 137 (The Sun), 144 (Fortune), 170 (a city); cf. the Seven Deadly Sins in *Faustus;* cf. 264 (Time), II 36 (Sleep), 206 (Sorrow). Simile also is frequent in *Tamburlaine;* there are some 75 short similes of one line or less in its two parts,[4] and nearly the same number of similes two lines or more in length,

---

[1] II *Tamburlaine* V iii (Vol. I pp. 201-202; cf. 113-114, 128, 188).

[2] *Faustus* sc. vii (Vol. I, p. 250).

[3] I note some 400 metaphors and similes in *Tamburlaine*, to some 250 in the other four plays taken together.

[4] He is fond of short alternative or cumulative similes: e. g. I 20, 52-3, 60, 115, 119, 183, 218-219, 238, 276; II 41.

including eight prolonged or quasi-Homeric similes, viz.: I 54 (Terror inspired by Tamburlaine's look like that felt by the seaman in the tempest), 89–90 (Zenocrate like Flora, etc.), 151 (a wound like a jewel or ornament), 161 (Tamburlaine like Hector —"I do you honor in the simile"), 173 (torments will make his enemies roar like a herd of bulls);[1] 174 (meteors like armed men), 179 (like "the horse that guide the golden eye of Heaven"), 183 (his plume like an almond tree)[2] Historical example is another form of comparison characteristic of *Tamburlaine*: e. g. I 114;

"As the Romans used,
I here present thee with a naked sword."

34 (Xerxes' host), 42, 61 (Cæsar's host), cf. II 126, 198, 245, 287, etc. Finally, classical allusion, is very frequent in *Tamburlaine*. I note more than 90 instances. There are some 20 instances in *Edward II;* very little in the other plays.[3] The literary and quasi-epical cast of *Tamburlaine* is revealed in its use of trope,—the abundant hyperbole, personification, and simile (all figures of a highly conscious sort), the numerous and forcible metaphors, the borrowings from Spenser and others,[4] and the classical embroidery. But the profusion of *Tamburlaine* in these figures is no more noticeable than is the comparative restraint of the later plays, where significant metaphor is chiefly used in crises and situations of emotional excitement.[5]

[1] Imitated from Spenser, F. Q. I viii 11.
[2] After Spenser F. Q. I vii 32.
[3] References to the classical Inferno, Hades, Avernus, Styx, etc., are common: I 23, 78, 93, 103, 126, 147, 172, 178, 180, 252, II 68, 203, 207; Homer and the Trojan war are frequently mentioned: I 140, 241; Helen II, 140, 270f, 275, II 169; Achilles I 29, 161, II 148; Æneas I 99, 100; Penelope I 238; Œnone I 241; Jove's Adventures and Amours often appear: I 20, 24, 113, 119, 175, 276, II 140, 155, 186; Various Gods I 25, 45, 46, 47, 53, 102, 104, 115, 167, 175, 183, II 34, 122; Phœbus and Cynthia, see infra under "Sun" and "Moon;" Aurora I 31; Hercules I 59, 179, II 125, 148; Atlas I 28, 171, II 178, 307; Phaeton I 72, 205, II 133; The Furies I 78, 126, 147, 178, II 207, 291; Nemesis I 35; The Fates I 157; Fortune and her Wheel I 23, 99, II 214, 232, (cf. I 144, 157); Occasion I 206, II 102; Leander II 119; and many others.
[4] E. g. Ariosto, 177; see elsewhere various quotations or references in Marlowe's text to classical authors, e. g. II 18 (Terence), 154 (Pliny), 201 (Seneca), to Virgil in *Dido* passim, etc.
[5] See examples cited below, p. 174.

Marlowe's epithets and metaphors are often hyperbolical and violent, but seldom conventional or faded, barring the classical allusions, and even these are oftentimes so phrased as to gain a new freshness and beauty, e. g. I 89-90:

> "like to Flora in her morning pride,
> Shaking her silver tresses in the air,
> Rain'st on the earth resolved pearl in showers,
> And sprinklest sapphires on thy shining face."

Or 179:

> "The horse that guide the golden eye of heaven,
> And blow the morning from their nosterils,
> Making their fiery gait above the clouds."

RANGE AND SOURCES OF IMAGERY.

NATURE. Aspects of the Sky, The Elements, etc.: SUN I 35 ("Sun-bright armor"), so 97, cf. 137 (the Sun personified), 171, 183 ("In golden armor like the sun"), II 64, 177: cf. Phœbus I 18, 119, 137, 179, 183, 195, 205, 206, II 38, 193. SHADOWS I 104, 219, II 206:

> "But what are kings, when regiment is gone,
> But perfect shadows in a sunshine day?"

Cf. 246; SUNRISE I 179, II 38 (cf. 307); MOON AND STARS: I 46 ("always moving as the restless spheres"), 92 ("the fiery-spangled veil of Heaven"), 157, 54 ("the furies of his heart That shine as comets"), cf. 71, 146, 174, 189; 276:

> "Oh, thou art fairer than the evening air,
> Clad in the beauty of a thousand stars."

II 37 (Abigail like a star); cf. Cynthia I 71, 134, 136, 137, 157, 175, 196, II 43. CLOUDS I 145:

> "Their ensigns spread
> Look like the parti-colored clouds of heaven."

179 ("My chariot, swifter than the racking clouds"), 195, 201:

> "Thus are the villain cowards fled for fear
> Like summer vapors vanished by the sun."

(cf. II 146), 281, cf. II 54, 271 ("Is Guise's glory but a cloudy mist?"); FIRE I 44 (the flame of ambition; cf. II 243), 68, 130, 137, 145, 166 ("Wrath, kindled in the furnace of his breast").

169, II 120, 239; Lamps (of heaven; — for stars) I 60, 70, 71, 121, 137, 158, 177, 196, 202. Storms, Rain, etc., I 24 (to rain gold), 63, 115 (shower of darts), 127, 133, 144, II 196 (Rain showers of vengeance), 240 ("Guise may storm"), 241, 263, 268; cf. Boreas I 25, 37, 127 : Thunder I 9 (thundering speech), 35 ("bullets like Jove's .... thunderbolts"), 67, 71, 98, 132, 135 ("God hath thundered vengeance"), 166 (cannons thunder), II 158 ("I'll thunder such a peal into his ears"); Snow I 20 ("Fairer than whitest snow on Scythian hills"); Seasons I 45 ("the morning of my happy state"); Night (personified) I 96, II 194.

Aspects of Sea and Water: Tide I 175:

"With thy view my joys are at the full,
And ebb again as thou departest from me."

I 48 (in number as the drops of the sea), 127, 54 (simile of seaman in storm), 76 (simile of pilot in the haven who views the storm).

Aspects of Earth, Minerals, etc.: Adamant II 173; Coal-black I 49, 126; II 227 (a heart "hewn from the Caucasus"), II 273 ("the haughty mountains of my breast"); Golden I 137 (of the sun), II 122 ("hair that gilds the water as it glides"); Silver I 137 ("silver waves"); Leaden II 156 ("Base, leaden earls"); Crystal I 121 (cf. II 363) 157 (a crystal robe), 182 (crystal waves); Diamond II 42–43 (Abigail like a diamond); II 287 (pale as ashes).

The Vegetable World: Trees I 68 (Spearmen "As bristle-pointed as a thorny wood"), 71 (like cedars struck by thunderbolts), 183 (plumes like an almond tree — Spenser's simile), II 154 (emblematic allegory of the cedar-tree and the canker-worm); Branch I 282 ("Cut is the branch," etc), II 181 ("This Spencer, as a putrefying branch, That deads the royal vine"); Leaf I 37 (quivering like an aspen-leaf), 159 (in number like leaves), II 273; Mushroom II 144; Flower II 34 ("A fair young maid .... The sweetest flower in Cytherea's field"); Fruit I 30 ("fall like mellowed fruit with shakes of death"); Seeds II 272 ("Her eyes and looks sow'd seeds of perjury"); I 180 (hedges).

The Animal World: Lion I 18 :

"As princely lions, when they rouse themselves,
Stretching their paws, and threatening herds of beasts,
So in his armor looketh Tamburlaine."

181 (lion-like), II 133, 162, 206, 218; Tiger II 210; Wolf II 207, 212; Fox I 10:

> "Tamburlaine .... like a fox in midst of harvest time,
> Doth prey upon my flocks of passengers,
> And, as I hear, doth mean to pull my plumes."

Deer I 63:

> "Let his foes, like flocks of fearful roes,
> Pursued by hunters, fly his angry looks."

II 248; Porcupine I 121, II 121.

Domestic Animals: Sheep I 169 ("And leads your bodies sheep-like to the sword"), II 41, 207; Bulls I 173 (Spenser's simile); Horses I 180:

> "To bridle their contemptuous, cursing tongues,
> That, like unruly, never-broken jades,
> Break through the hedges of their hateful mouths."

II 66 (ambles); Dogs I 173 ("bark, ye dogs"), II 41 ("We Jews can fawn like spaniels when we please," etc.), 192 (bark).

Birds: Wings I 36 (winged sword, etc.), 115 (feathered steel), 166 (cf. II 35), II 206, 243, 280, 289 ("I'll clip his wings"); Doves I 86 ("What, are the turtles frayed out of their nests?"); Cockerel II 162 ("Shall the crowing of these cockrels affright a lion?"); Lark II 38 (Barabas sings over his gold as the lark over her young); Goose II 121:

> "These words of his move me as much
> As if a goose would play the porcupine,
> And dart her plumes, thinking to pierce my breast."

Wren II 218; Raven II 35 (That "tolls The sick man's passport in her hollow beak"); Partridge II 85 (Barabas hides his gold, "as partridges do their eggs, under the earth").

Fabulous Natural History: Torpedo-fish II 141:

> "Fair queen, forbear to angle for the fish,
> Which being caught, strikes him that takes it dead;
> I mean that vile torpedo, Gaveston."

Allegory of the flying-fish pursued by its enemies II 154; Crocodile I 67 (to lie in sloth,

"As crocodiles that unaffrighted rest,
 While thundering cannons rattle on their skins").

Deer II 205-6 (wounded, seeks a herb for cure).[1]

MAN AND HUMAN LIFE: Arts, Literature, etc.: I 81 (the sword—Tamburlaine's pen with which he draws his map), 90:

 . . . . "thy shining face,
Where beauty, mother to the Muses, sits,
And comments volumes with her ivory pen."

Cf. II 271: "Hath my love been so obscured in thee,
 That others need to comment on my text?"

I 23 ("characters graven in thy brows"), cf. 28, 29, 53; II 228; I 144:

"As all the world should blot his dignities
Out of the book of base-born infamies."

Cf. II 333 ("His looks shall be my only library").

MEDICAL: II 143 ("purging of the realm of such a plague"—i. e. Gaveston), 288 ("This sweet sight is physic to my soul").

MUSIC: II 188 "To think that we can yet be tuned together;
 No, no, we jar too far."

PAINT: I 118 ("to paint in words"), II 87 ("painted carpets," i. e. flowery fields), 156 ("the painted spring").

BUILDING: I 30 (life a palace), 45 ("The wondrous architecture of the world"), 64 (pillars), II 218 ("the closet of my heart").

Prison (of the body) I 175:

"Making a passage for my troubled soul,
Which beats against this prison to get out."

METAL-WORK (I 21): 151 (enamelled), 70, 183 (enchased). II 145:

"My heart is as an anvil unto sorrow,
Which beats upon it like the Cyclops' hammers."

DYEING: I 51 ("Which dyes my locks so lifeless"), 97 (walls dyed with blood), 150.

DRESS, etc.: Cloak or Mantle I 50 ("The ground is mantled with such multitudes"), 90 ("in the mantle of the richest night"), 196 ("Muffle your beauties with eternal clouds"), II 280 (cloak); Veil I 92 ("the fiery-spangled veil of Heaven"), 124,

[1] Cf. Peele, I 356.

134 ("thou shining veil of Cynthia"); Clothe I 121 ("clear the cloudy air, And clothe it in a crystal livery"), cf. Shroud I 170, (II 311. Cf. II 363).

Various: Divorced II 169 (Gaveston "divorced from King Edward's eyes," cf. II 340).

Agriculture: II 156 (like the shepherd); Yoke I 85, 95, II 289; Furrow I 86 ("the folded furrows of his brows"), cf. I 23, II 123, 245 (324, 352).

Amusements and Hunting: I 63, 75, 77:

> "As frolic as the hunters in the chase
> Of savage beasts amid the desert woods."

II 162 ("baited by these peers"), 198 (to start the game), 248 (the deer in the toils).

Dancing I 29 (wind making hair *dance*), 115 ("the cannon shook Vienna wall, And made it *dance*"), cf. 148 ("to undermine a town And make whole cities caper in the air"), 137 (Sun dances on the waves), 183 (plume dancing in the air); Games II 191 (prisoner's base); Cards II 245.

Of Colloquial, Coarse and Familiar Images there are very few in Marlowe: I 57 ("That damned train, the *scum* of Africa"), so 75; I 95 ("*Smeared* with blots of basest drudgery"), II 42 ("The slave looks Like a hog's cheek new singed"), 74 (bells that sound like tinkers' pans), 84 (the hangman's hempen tippet), 84 (mustaches like a raven's wing), 87 (give money as cow gives down milk).

The Body and its Parts: Temples I 137 (of the sun); Eye[1] I 177:

> ... "that bright eye of heaven
> From whence the stars do borrow all their light."

So 179 ("The horse that guide the golden eye of Heaven"), 279; II 38 ("Now Phœbus ope the eyelids of the day"),[2] Brows, etc. I 28 ("in the forehead of his fortune Bears figures of renown"); Stomach II 129 ("All stomach [dislike] him"), so 164; Bowels, Entrails, etc., I 72 (bowels of a cloud), so 133 and 281, 98

---

[1] Metaphors for eyes, see I 28, 95, 140, II 209.
[2] Cf. *Lycidas* l. 26 "Under the opening eyelids of the morn."

(entrails of the earth), so 236, II 15, II 217 ("unbowel straight this breast"), 245 ("the bowels of her treasury"), 280 ("To rip the golden bowels of America"); II 252 ("The head [Coligny] being off, the members [the Huguenots] cannot stand"); Sinews I 133, 143.

VARIOUS HUMAN ATTRIBUTES: Kiss II 136 ("enforce The papal towers to kiss the lowly ground"), so 296; I 114 (to swallow, cf. II 318); Sleep II 123 (sword sleeps in scabbard).

The Senses and Appetites: Thirst I 29 (thirsting for sovereignty), so 35, 44, II 244; Taste II 248; Surfeit I 127 (to surfeit in joy), 212 ("He surfeits upon cursed necromancy"), 216 ("glutted with conceit"), 277 ("A surfeit of deadly sin"), II 285, 294; Feed (II 337, 340).

Subjective Life, Religion, etc.: DEATH I 45 (personified), so 46, 53, 88, 102, 140, 156, 157, 196, 199, II 245; Sepulchre II 59: "These arms of mine shall be thy sepulchre."[1]

HELL I 55 (cf. 135-6), 186 ("More strong than are the gates of death or hell"), II 137 ("this hell of grief"); cf. numerous references to classical Hades, Avernus, Styx, etc.; SPIRITS I 61, 197 (devils and angels), cf. *Faustus* passim, II 260 ("That bell, that to the devil's matins rings"); Heaven I 87, 127, 174 ("the towers of heaven"), II 119:

"The sight of London to my exiled eyes
Is as Elysium to a new-come soul."[2]

II 233 (the undiscovered country). SOUL I 276 ("Her lips sucks forth my soul; see where it flies!"); Preach II 23 ("Preach me not out of my possessions"), 124 ("their heads preach upon poles"), so 176; ALTAR AND SACRIFICE II 60:

---

[1] Dyce compares *III Henry VI*, II v:

"These arms of mine shall be thy winding sheet;
My heart, sweet boy, shall be thy sepulchre."

See further, infra, references on this head under Webster, Chapman and Ford. Cf. in Marlowe II 128, 245 ("in my love entombs the hope of France").

[2] Cf. Mrs. Browning, *Aurora Leigh*, Book II:
"I go hence
To London, to the gathering-place of souls."

Cf. *Two Gentlemen of Verona*, II vii 38.

"Upon which altar I will offer up
My daily sacrifice of sighs and tears."[1]

Influence of the Stars I 29, 44, 57, 71, 86, 94, II 202, 284.

Images of War, etc.: II 273 (Vengeance encamped, shows her gory colors), I 45 ("the breach thy sword hath made"), 90 (Sorrows lay siege to the soul); 174 (meteors tilting like armed men),[2] cf. I 18 ("windy exhalations, Fighting for passage, *till* within the earth"), 54 (Auster and Aquilon *till* about the heavens), cf. II 312 (waves *till* twixt the oaken sides of wrecked vessels); Massacre, kill, etc. I 94 ("That lingering pains may massacre his heart"), 141 ("our murdered hearts") 170, 202 ("bleeding hearts, Wounded and broken"), II 201 (wounds), 247 ("my soul is massacred"), 264 ("thou kill'st thy mother's heart"); Arms II 144 ("'Tis not the king can buckler Gaveston"), so 169, cf. II 314 ("unweaponed thoughts"); ARCHERY I 37:

"Kings are clouts that every man shoots at,
Our crown the pin that thousands seek to cleave."

And see Tamburlaine's discourse (I 148-9) on the art of war—from the sixteenth century standpoint.

The Stage and the Drama: Play a part I 22 ("Our swords shall play the orator for us"), 155 ("Soldiers, play the men"), so 159; I 182 ("make us jesting pageants for their trulls"), II 161 ("thy soldiers marched like players, With garish robes, not armour"); Tragedy II 228 ("I see my tragedy written in thy brows"), so 231, 242, 282, 297.

Miscellaneous: Unspotted I 85 (Unspotted prayers); Melt I 85, II 227 (thy heart will melt); Poison[3] II 129 ("Swoln with venom of pride," cf. II 367); Climbing, Mounting, etc., I 46 ("climbing after knowledge infinite"), II 9 ("My climbing followers"), 156 ("Mounting thoughts"), 243, cf. 283, cf. I 19

---

[1] *Two Gentlemen of Verona*, III ii 73:
"Say that upon the altar of her beauty
You sacrifice your tears."

[2] Cf. The Comedy of Errors IV ii 6: "his heart's meteors tilting in his face."

[3] Poison of a literal sort also appears frequently in Marlowe, e. g. II 49, 55, 67, 163, 221, 242.

("Affecting thoughts coequal with the clouds"), and 28 (" Like his desire lift upward"); Pierce I 27 ("my heart to be with gladness pierced"). 28, 30, 119, 203, II 60, 137 ; Labyrinth II 64 ("The fatal labyrinth of misbelief"); Balance, weigh, etc. I 19 (weigh = esteem), 85 :

> "Your honors, liberties, and lives are weighed
> In equal care and balance with our own."

II 9 ; Fold. Wrap, etc. I 29 ("hair Wrapped in curls"), 35 (bullets enrolled in flame), 53 (" his choler . . . wrapt in silence of his . . . soul"), 72, 86 ("folded furrows of his brows"), 241, II 40 ("bullets wrapt in smoke"); II 124 ("henceforth parley with our naked swords"), 143 (to greet with a poniard); Scourge, Whip I 57 (" I that am termed the scourge and wrath of God"), 75, 123, 144, 160, 182, II 248, 260 (" I'll whip you to death with my poniard's point"), 265 ; Pour I 95, 132, 171, II 177, 182 ("This day I shall pour vengeance with my sword On those proud rebels"); Melt, dissolve I 95, 96 ; Smother I 96, II 54.

Recapitulation When we review these schedules it appears that Marlowe's imagination draws upon no very wide range of sources for its effects. The largest part and the most striking part of the above lists is derived from *Tamburlaine*. But the mature Marlowe is not represented by *Tamburlaine*, and the most remarkable feature of the later plays is the surprisingly small amount of figure employed. Nor can it fairly be said that the range and character of such imagery as therein appears are very great or striking. The effect of *Faustus* and of *Edward II* depends for the greater part on other things. When we consider his imagery as a whole it is noticeable that nature, especially the aspects of the heavens, fire, storms, etc., supply a considerable part. Not only has Marlowe's genius apparently a natural affinity for these images, but they lend themselves more readily to grandiose and hyperbolical effects. Death, hell, and heaven are similarly laid under contribution. Classical allusion, especially in connection with these images

---

[1] " . . . . his raptures were
All ayre and fire." (Drayton, Battle of Agincourt.)

(Phœbus, Cynthia, Avernus, Styx, etc.), is interwoven at all points. Noticeable is the small proportion of comparisons drawn from colloquial and familiar sources, from domestic life, and from the various occupations of men, although the tragic poet and idealist of course has less occasion to draw upon such sources than the realist and the writer of comedy.

THOMAS KYD
1557?–1595?

THOMAS KYD.

IN view of the doubt that involves the authorship of the various plays ascribed to Kyd, it would not here be profitable to attempt an analysis of the range and sources of his imagery. *The First Part of Jeronimo* and *The Spanish Tragedy*,[1] however, seem to have been so important and "epoch making"[2] that it will be well to record here some of the more striking metaphors and similes found in these plays.

Jeronimo, with all its general formlessness and extravagance, has a number of metaphors, including a few striking and effective ones, as will be seen below. The author is fond of strange compound epithets: e. g. 352 *well-strung* speech, 355 *lip-blushing* kiss, 357 honey-damnation, 358 ink-soul, 360 true-breasted.[3] Other noteworthy tropes are: 353: "A melancholy, discontented courtier, Whose famished jaws *look like the chap of death.*" Almost everything in *Jeronimo*, of course, is violent and extravagant. 365:

Striking Metaphors and Similes in Jeronimo

"Then I unclasp[4] the *purple leaves of war;*
Many a new wound must *gasp* through an old scar."

384: "O, in thy heart,
Weigh the dear drops of many a purple part
That must be acted on the field's green stage."[5]

Every subsequent dramatic author will be found drawing metaphors in this way from the stage.

391 "My blood's A-tiptoe;" 351 "*rough-hewn* tyrants;" Melt 354, 359, 375, 383 ("thy court *melt* in luxuriousness"),

---

[1] Both produced between 1584-1589.
[2] Symonds, Shaks. Pred., 487.
[3] Cf. V 352 marrow-burning love.
[4] Cf. Ford, II 47 "unclasp The book of lust."
[5] Cf. also pp. 374, 376, 390 (to play a part).

391, 394; Stamp 353 ("a lad ... of this *stamp*"), 355, 357; Bowels 363 ("in the battle's bowels"), 380;

371: "The badger feeds not, till the lion's served;
   Nor fits it news so soon *kiss* subjects' ears,
   As the fair *cheek* of high authority."

386: "I long to hear the *music* of clashed swords."

387: "Now death doth heap his goods up all at once,
   And crams his storehouse to the top with blood;
   Might I now and Andrea in one fight
   Make up thy wardrobe richer by a knight!"

The Spanish Tragedy is even more extravagant, but it has a few fine passages of hyperbolical passion. It is marred by a superfluity of cheap classical mythology, especially in the way of allusions to Acheron, the Styx, Pluto, Elysium, etc. It has very little striking metaphor, and it is remarkable with how little help of figure are written the one or two stronger passages of the play supposed to be additions by Ben Jonson.

In the Spanish Tragedy

Vol. V. 68: "The night, sad *secretary* to my moans"

101: "Of that thine ivory front, my sorrow's *map*"[1]
   "Wherein I see no haven to rest my hope."

105: "He had not seen *the back* of nineteen years."

111: "Thou hast made me *bankrupt* of my bliss."

115: "Yonder *pale-faced Hecate* there, the moon."

168: "Methinks since I *grew inward* with revenge,
   I cannot look with scorn enough on death."[2]

TROPES COMMON to two or more of the following plays attributed to Kyd:[3] *Jeronimo, The Spanish Tragedy, Cornelia* (translation), *Soliman and Perseda*:

Tropes Common to Various Plays Ascribed to Kyd

Melt IV (as above), V 127, 246; Print, characters, etc. IV 358, 385, V 276; Showers IV 358, V 296; Choke IV 361, 382, V 90; Scabbard, Sheathe IV 361, V 222, 321; Pawn IV 363, 387, V 30; Infect IV 379, V 90, 203; Toad IV 379, V 325;

---

[1] A frequent metaphor in others, e. g. Chapman, 79b, 406b, etc.
[2] Cf. Hazlitt's note, referring to parallels in Marston and Tourneur.
[3] The references are to Hazlitt's Dodsley,—Vol. IV to *Jeronimo*; Vol. V 1–173 to *Sp. Trag.*; 183–252 to *Cornelia*; 257–374 to *Sol. and Pers.*

Adamant IV 372, V 159, 300; Stoop IV 391, V 47, 195, 230; the Stage IV 374, 376, 384, 390, V 41, 305, 358, 364, 373; Pierce IV 387, V 295; Honey IV 351, V 8, 46, 334; Bowels IV 352, 363, V 111, 321, cf. Entrails V 189, 199; Bait IV 353, V 185; Thunder IV 352, 355, 373, V 193; Salve, Balm V 88, 97, 307; Sickle and Harvest V 61, 340; Cloak V 124, 214, 325; Simile of Ship in a Stormy Sea V 43, 185, 259, 349; "translucent breast" V 31, the same 295; Ransom V 67, 288; Lamp V 159, 300, 334.

Little of this can really be called evidence of common authorship in these plays, since almost every one of these metaphors occurs so often throughout the period. Still it may be taken for what it is worth. The resemblances among the last three plays are more noticeable than any that *Jeronimo* bears to the others.

ROBERT GREENE
? 1560-1592

Acted	Published		Pages
1591 ?	1594	*Orlando Furioso* - - -	89–111
1589 ? (Fleay)	1594	*Friar Bacon and Friar Bungay* -	153–181
1592 ?	1598	*James the Fourth* - - -	187–220
1592 ?	1599	*Alphonsus, King of Arragon* -	225–248

ROBERT GREENE.

GREENE, like Peele, is of little account as a dramatist. His faults,— the fustian, the monotonous blank verse, the misplaced and excessive classical allusion[1]— are those of his school.[2] But he has no very striking merits of his own to counterbalance these faults. "Writing in direct competition with Marlowe," says Mr. J. A. Symonds,[3] "and striving to produce 'strong lines,' Greene indulged in extravagant imagery, which, because it lacks the animating fire of Marlowe's rapture, degenerates into mere bombast." Mr. Minto[4] thinks he traces the influence of Greene on Shakspere's diction. The evidence, however, is not very striking. The inferiority of Greene as a dramatic poet appears in the general poverty and commonplaceness of his imagery. Hallam[5] thinks that he is "a little redundant in images," but this criticism can apply only to the *Orlando Furioso*, where Greene's peculiar pseudo-classical imagery is heaped up in superabundant measure.[6] Otherwise his imagery is somewhat scanty. He uses few striking and original metaphors. He is, however, fond of accumulating "gorgeous particulars" and costly descriptions, as has been noted.[7] When he feels prompted to be poetical, as in *Orlando Furioso*, he becomes profuse in two sorts of figures: (1) Sententious tropes, proverb, parable, fable

Quality of his Imagery

His Favorite Forms

---

[1] "His main stylistic defect is the employment of cheap Latin mythology in and out of season" (Symonds, Shaks. Pred., 558).

[2] "En somme, le talent de Greene n'est qu'un pâle reflet de celui de Lyly et de Marlowe" (Mézières Pred. et Cont. de Shaks. 147).

[3] Shaks. Pred., 562.

[4] Char. of Eng. Poets, 242.

[5] Lit. of Eur., Pt. II, ch. vi, § 32.

[6] There are over 100 classical allusions in *Orlando Furioso*; less than 100 in the other three plays taken together.

[7] Minto l. c. 243; Collier II 532. The most striking of these are: Sob, III, 165, 169-170.

and short allegory, (2) short similes, especially those of classical material (e. g. "richer than the plot Hesperides"). There are over one hundred formal similes, including seven prolonged similes, in the four plays, the greater number in *Orlando Furioso*.

His metaphors and similes do not reveal any great degree of imagination. It is true, as Mr. Minto observes,[1] that his classical comparisons are not as generally wooden and perfunctory as those of some of his contemporaries. "He had the notion of giving life to dead names;" e. g. 236:

> "See now he stands as one that lately saw
> Medusa's head or Gorgon's hoary hue;"[2]

89: "Topt high with plumes, like Mars his burgonet,"

90: "The sands of Tagus all of burnished gold
Made Thetis never prouder on the clifts
That overpeer the bright and golden shore,
Than do the rubbish of my country seas."

But his manner on the whole is rhetorical and literate.[3] He has his share of bombast and fustian, especially in *Alphonsus*, which was written "in direct rivalry to *Tamburlaine*."[4] See e. g. 98–106 passim (Orlando's madness) 99, 230, 231, 234. His imagery is literary;[5] it is less original than Peele's even. Greene's nature images are few and are not vividly rendered. There is the usual amount of Euphuistic natural history. He is fond of proverb and sententious comparison.[6] Greene as a dramatic writer as much as Peele fails to leave any very definite

[1] Char. of Eng. Poets, 243.
[2] Cf. Chapman, 170 b.
[3] Greene is very profuse in Classical Allusion. A few of the more striking examples are: 89a Venus' doves; 89-91 Jason, Ulysses, Jupiter and Danae, Hercules and Iole, Thetis, Andromache, Hector and Achilles, etc.; Siege of Troy 92a, 106a; Paris 96a, 158a; 106b, 99a ("like mad Orestes"); Cupid 190b; Nestor 199b; 234b (Midas and Bacchus, Jupiter and Alcmena, Saturn and Tros); of a historical nature: 90 (Caesar in England); Cassius 94b, 164b; Nero's mother 108b; Lucrece 154a; Cleopatra 170a; etc.
[4] Fleay, Chron. Eng. Dr., I 257.
[5] Examples of prolonged similes in Greene are pp. 93b, 95a, 196b, 199b, 228b, 230a.
[6] E. g. 154b, 161b, 173b, 191b, 192a, 193a, 196b, 200, 201b, 204a, 206b, 208a, 213b, 214b, 216a, 226, 228b, 236b, 238a, 246b, etc. Fable 219a.

impression. In *James IV* he has glimpses of character. Dorothea is finely conceived. His plots in two or three instances contain the germ of good dramatic situations ; but his execution is always inferior. Strangely enough, in view of his life and habits, Greene's plays contain little that is coarse or indelicate. He has very few coarse or disgusting images.

RANGE AND SOURCES OF HIS IMAGERY.

Greene's range is narrow and is emphasized in no particular direction. **NATURE** is only slightly represented in his plays.

Aspects of the Sky : The sun shines here and there in Greene, but usually disguised as Phoebus : e. g. 93b. :

" the sparkling light of fame,
Whose glory's brighter than the burnished gates
From whence Latona's lordly son doth march,
When, mounted on his coach tinsell'd with flames,
He triumphs in the beauty of the heavens."

These lines have a certain rhythmic swing and naïve splendor of imagery! Cf. 89a, 90b: 190a ("beauty *shines*"); FIRE: 97a (jealousy like the flames of Ætna), so 107b; 98a, 153b, 191a (the fire of love); the Moon and Stars 93b:

" . . . seest thou not Lycaon's son,
The hardy plough-swain unto mighty Jove,
Hath traced his silver furrows in the heavens,
And turning home his over-watchèd team,
Gives leave unto Apollo's chariot ? "

168b (" Gracious as the morning star of heaven.")[1]

170a : "Margaret, That overshines our damsels as the moon
Darkeneth the brightest sparkles of the night."

Cf. 178b, 194a, 231a ("As clear as Luna in a winter's night").

233a " Ere Cynthia, the shining lamp of night,
Doth scale the heavens with her hornèd head."

Clouds : 94a (" The misty veil strained over Cynthia.")

The Vegetable World : FLOWERS 90b :

" Fairer than was the nymph of Mercury,
Who, when bright Phoebus mounteth up his coach,
And tracts Aurora in her silver steps
[Doth sprinkle] from the folding of her lap
White lilies, roses, and sweet violets."

[1] Cf. Lyly, II 160.

96a : " Sweet crystal springs,
    Wash ye with roses when she longs to drink."
176a : " Thy father's hair, like to the silver blooms,
    That beautify the shrubs of Africa."
179a (Friar Bacon's prophecy of the coming *flower* of England — Queen Elizabeth), 196b :
"Some men like to the rose
Are fashioned fresh ; some in their stalks do close,
And, born, do sudden die ; some are but weeds,
And yet from them a secret good proceeds."

The Animal World, outside of the Euphuistic natural history, is represented by some dozen references in Greene :

SERPENTS : 220a (bad counsellors are vipers).   BIRDS, Wings 177b : " To scud and overscour the earth in post
    Upon the speedy wings of swiftest winds ! "
Eagle 201a, " What, like the eagle then,
    With often flight wilt thou thy feathers loose?
Cf 215a. Peacock 244b (emblem of pride) ; Sheep and wolves 230a (the stock simile of sheep scattering before the wolves : cf 236a) ; Horses 242a (" horses that be free Do need no spurs") ; Dogs 243a ; Grasshoppers 91b :
    " Such a crew of men
As shall so fill the downs of Africa
Like to the plains of watery Thessaly,
Whenas an eastern gale, whistling aloft,
Hath overspread the ground with grasshoppers."[1]
Bees 190b (Love, like a bee, hath a sting).   See the fable of the Hind and the Lion's Whelp 219a.

Under **Fabulous Natural History** come :
Adamant 201b ("The adamant will not be fil'd But by itself ").
Asbestos 232a : " My mind is like to the asbeston-stone,
    Which if it once be heat in flames of fire,
    Denieth to becomen cold again."

Dictamnum[2] 208a (a cure for the wounds of beasts : see Dyce's note p. 208) ; 171b (evanescent as the bloom of the almond-tree, or " the flies hæmeræ ") ; 189b (eagles and their

[1] Cf. Iliad, XXI 12.
[2] Cf. Peele, I 35-6.

young); 228b (long simile of the serpent which, cut in pieces, is revived if its head finds a certain herb); 236b (simile of the echinus, or hedgehog, which keeps her young in her paunch till "their pricks be waxen long and sharp").

MAN AND HUMAN LIFE. Arts and Learning:

168a : " Lordly thou look'st, as if that thou wert learn'd ;
   Thy countenance as if science held her seat
   Between the circled arches of thy brows."

PAINTING: 94b ("paint my grief"), 98a, 154a, 195b, 225a.

PRINT: 94b ("So firmly is Orlando printed in my thoughts").

Law: 91a :   "Venus . . .
   Hath sent proud love to enter such a plea
   As nonsuits all your princely evidence."

91b:

"[Her presence] Prevails with me, as Venus' smiles with Mars,
To set a supersedeas of my wrath."

160b (Bacon's consistory-court wherein the devils plead); 235a ("Naught else but death from prison shall him bail").

Agriculture: 200a (The husbandman does not forsake his field when his crop fails).

Building: 173a :   "Bacon,
   The turrets of thy hope are ruin'd down,
   Thy seven years study lieth in the dust."

Wall 158a :   . . . "the West
   Ringed with the walls of old Oceanus,
   Whose lofty surge is like the battlements
   That compass'd high-built Babel in with towers."

WEAVING : 111b (Silk "from the native looms of laboring worms");

HUNTING: 94a ("To play him hunt's-up with a point of war"), 190b (stales or decoys).

Greene is reported to have studied "physic," and yet I note no tropes drawn from medicine in his plays.

Colloquial and Familiar Images occur mostly in the form of proverbial expressions appearing in the comic scenes: 93a ("to hold the candle before the devil," i. e., to propitiate evil and powerful opponents), 169a (" as serviceable at a table as a sow is under an apple-tree");[1] 173b ("the more the fox is cursed, the better he fares ");[2] 193a (quoted — " No fishing to [= equal to] the sea, nor service to a king"), 200a:

> "Men seek not moss upon a rolling stone,
> Or water from the sieve, or fire from ice,
> Or comfort from a reckless monarch's hands,"

174a (" love together like pig and lamb"), 187b ("I engraved the memory of Bohan on the skin-coat of some of them"), 203a ("this word is like a warm caudle to a cold stomach"), 209b ("like a frog in a parsley-bed; as skittish as an eel "), 196b (the world compared to needlework).

The Body: 89b (bowels of the earth).

War: Shield 234b ("[I] will be thy shield against all men alive"); 243a (Cannon); 246:

> "What, know you not that castles are not won
> At first assault, and women are not woo'd
> When first their suitors proffer love to them?"

Subjective Life: 161b:

> "Love, like a wag, straight div'd into my heart,
> And there did shrine the idea of yourself."

cf. 166b.

Miscellaneous Metaphors: Climbing: 201a (craft climbs high), 220a, 225a: Mirror 241b ("the mirror of mishap"); cf. 215b (lantern i. e. model); Folding 92a ("Folding their wraths in cinders of fair Troy"), 153b:

> "And in her tresses she doth fold the looks
> Of such as gaze upon her golden hair."

154a (" in her shape fast folded up my thoughts"), cf. 161a; Lamps, 96a, 178b ("the crystal lamps of heaven"), 233a; Balance 166a;

> "[Think you] that Margaret's love
> Hangs in the uncertain balance of proud time?"

[1] Cf. Ben Jonson I 114b.
[2] Cf. Jonson, I 390a.

CYRIL TOURNEUR

Acted	Published		Vol.	Pages
1603 ?	1611	*The Atheist's Tragedy*	I	5-155
Entered				
1607	1607	*The Revenger's Tragedy*	II	5-150

TOURNEUR.

THE poetic and imaginative merits of the work of this strange genius have been adequately appreciated by competent critics.[1] After his "acute sense for dramatic situations,"[2]
Dramatic Intensity of his Diction
a quality which he shares in common with Webster, perhaps his most striking characteristic is "the boldness, felicity, and originality of his imagery and trick of putting things."[3] Tourneur first perhaps of the minor Elizabethans satisfies that demand for intense and lurid expression which seems to us to be the dramatic ideal of the period, at least in tragedy. Kyd has gleams of the same thing, and so has Marlowe in a mightier way; but both are marred by mere hyperbole in overmeasure; and even Marlowe only rarely[4] condenses the utterance of passion into single lines and phrases of such burning intensity. "For single lines of that intense and terrible beauty which makes incision in the memory, there is none, after Shakspere, to compare with him but Webster," writes Mr. Swinburne.[5] Crudeness, extravagance, and hyperbole, are among the faults of Tourneur's work; but much of his imagery is comparatively free from these blemishes, and is inspired with imaginative brevity and force. Especially is this true of *The Revenger's Tragedy*, which is distinctly superior to *The Atheist's Tragedy*, and by which Tourneur ought chiefly to be judged.

In its excess Tourneur's imagination descends to such
Hyperbole in Tourneur
examples of hyperbole and extravagance as the following: I 54:

[1] Lamb, Swinburne, J. A. Symonds, J. C. Collins, etc.
[2] Symonds, Introduction to Mermaid ed. of Webster and Tourneur, p. xii.
[3] Tourneur ed. J. C. Collins Introd., p. xlix.
[4] E. g. as in "See where Christ's blood streams in the firmament," etc.
[5] Essays and Studies, p. 310.

> "Drop out
> Mine eyeballs and let envious Fortune play
> At tennis with 'em."

I 119: "I could now commit
A murder, were it but to drink the fresh
Warm blood of him I murder'd to supply
The want and weakness of my own,
'Tis grown so cold and phlegmatic."

I 136: "His gasping sighs are like the falling noise
Of some great building when the groundwork breaks."

Cf. I 115, II 46, 52, 78, 80, 115. Sometimes indeed the originality and power of Tourneur's imagination is characteristically displayed in these very extravagances: e. g. II 54:

> "Hast thou beguiled her of salvation,
> And *rubb'd hell o'er with honey?*"

or II 90:

> "Let our two other hands tear up his lids,
> And make his eyes *like comets shine through blood.*"

Perhaps intense imaginative suggestiveness is the first characteristic of Tourneur's work. Sometimes the effect is produced by the use of a periphrastical image, of an innuendo conveyed through a picture, as, for example, when Castabella says to Rousard: "I'll give you a jewel to hang in your ear.— Hark ye — I can never love you" (I 27); or I 13:

His Imaginative Suggestiveness

"What, ha' you *washed your eyes wi' tears* this morning?

II 70: "Rise my lords, *your knees sign* his release
We freely pardon him."[1]

II 37: "if, at the next sitting,
Judgment *speak all in gold*" [i. e. yield to bribes].

II 84: "Why does yon fellow falsify highways
And *put his life between the judge's lips?*"

II 105: "hoping at last
To pile up all my wishes on his breast"

[i. e. to glut my revenge on him]. See also I 148.

---

[1] Cf. Massinger, *The Duke of Milan*, II i:
> "I am merciful,
> And dotage signs your pardon."

Sometimes it is rather by ellipsis and condensation:

Elliptical Figures

I 29: "Time *cuts off* circumstance; I must be brief."[1]

II 38: "*Wipe your lady from your eyes.*"

II 59 (to be *inward with*—cf. Kyd, Hazlitt's Dodsley V 168); cf. II 130 (to have made my revenge familiar with him;" cf. II 38).

I 9: "the scorn of their discourse
Turns smiling back upon your backwardness."

II 65: Is the day out a' the socket?"[2]

Sometimes, combined with the elliptical swiftness and the periphrastical significance of the figure, the mere vividness or beauty of the comparison, or the ethical impressiveness of its application, explain the secret of its effectiveness:

Striking and Impressive Comparisons

I 34: "Your gravity becomes your perish'd soul
As hoary mouldiness does rotten fruit."

II 51: "Your tongues have struck hot irons on my face."

68: "Thy wrath, like flaming wax, hath spent itself."

85: "Ladies, with false forms
You deceive men, but cannot deceive worms."

120: "Are you so barbarous to set iron nipples—[daggers]
Upon the breast that gave you suck?"

127: "I could scarce
Kneel out my prayers, and had much ado,
In three hours' reading, to untwist so much
Of the black serpent as you wound about me."

139: "to *stab home* their discontents."

Sometimes we meet a subtle introversion of thought phrased in striking form,—what perhaps, with other things, a writer in the *Retrospective Review*[3] had in mind in speaking of the "metaphysical" vein in Tourneur's poetry:

Introspective Conceits

II 24: "Am I far enough from myself?"

51: "Mother, come from that poisonous woman there."

---

[1] Cf. Beaumont and Fletcher, Bonduca, I ii:
"time Cuts off occasions."
[2] Cf. *Romeo and Juliet*, III v 9: "Night's candles are burnt out"
[3] Vol. VII 333.

124: "Joy's a subtile elf.
I think man's happiest when he forgets himself."[1]

It will thus be seen that Tourneur is master of a certain sort of dramatic imagery, and that his power largely depends upon it. His diction is highly metaphorical, but at the same time highly dramatic. Most of the mere machinery of the older poetic diction is abandoned in Tourneur:[2] metaphor and simile become full of meaning at every turn in his lines. Similes of a brief sort are freely employed;[3] personification, both full and concealed, also is used with effect: e. g. II 33: "Sword, I durst make a promise of him to thee," etc.

37: "Step forth, thou bribeless officer" [to his sword].

78: "Grief swum-in their eyes."

Cf. I 9, 17, 40 (the passage quoted in Lamb,—the sea weeping over Charlemont's body), 48, 55, 133; II 8, 10, 14, 24, 25, 35, 52, 67, 69.

RANGE AND SOURCE OF IMAGERY.

NATURE: Aspects of the Sky, The Elements, etc.: I 92 ("this little world of man"); I 17 (the heavens weeping), II 80 ("yon silver ceiling"), 90 (comets), 32 (eclipse), 137 ("I shine in tears like the sun in April;" cf. I 79); Clouds I 94; STORMS I 57 (words a wind laid by a shower of tears) cf. II 122; FIRE I 55 (stars like sparks); II 56 ("the maid, like an unlighted taper, Was cold and chaste"), 62, 65, 68, 126, 139; Thunder I 39; Snow I 50; Ice II 124; Spring I 79.

Aspects of Waters, The Sea, etc.: WATER I 52, 74 (fancy, like troubled waters, reflects brokenly), II 94 ("words spoke in tears, Are like the murmurs of the waters, the sound is loudly heard but cannot be distinguish'd"); RIVERS I 130, 6

---

[1] Cf. Webster, 49b: "There's nothing of so infinite vexation
As man's own thoughts."

[2] He however is not free from occasional conceits and plays on words: e. g. I 79, 118, 129, II 41, 44, 75, 78, 79, 87 (" a grave look"), 92, 101 ("there's a doom would make a woman dumb "), 104, 119, 122, 126. Classical and literary allusion is rare: Tantalus I 32, Pillars of Hercules I 78, Tereus I 115, Occasion II 8, 10; a Latin quotation II 35; Judas II 28.

[3] One or two longer ones appear: I 145 (8 ll.), 146 (5 ll.).

("pleasure only flows Upon the stream of riches"), cf. 28; II 61 (flow); SEA I 40-41 (personified), I 130 (the shipwreck of the vessel of the body"); II 29 ("past my depth"); I 79 (tears like April dew); II 26 ("I have seen patrimonies wash'd a' pieces"); II 44 ("spring with the dew a' the Court"), 137.

Aspects of the Earth, Vegetable World, etc.: METAL II 121, II 14 (gilt); Clay II 102, 105; II 146 (marble impudence); TREES, BRANCHES, etc., I 8 (children like branches and receive sap), 119 (aspen leaf); I 146 (early death like fresh-gathered herbs); Fruit I 34 ("your gravity becomes your perish'd soul As hoary mouldiness does rotten fruit"), 128.

Animal World: BIRDS, etc., II 15 ("That lady's name has spread such a fair wing Over all Italy"); I 42 ("Thou art a screech owl"), so 54; I 58 (raven); II 36 ("fed the ravenous vulture of his lust"); I 47 (goose); SERPENT II 15, 37, 127; Flies II 129; Bees, wax, etc., I 64, II 68, 123; II 36 ("The duchess' youngest son,— that moth to honor"); Dormice I 50; Dogs I 151: Horse II 55 (spur, etc.).

Fabulous Natural History: Phœnix I 78; I 135 (like the cries of mandrakes).

MAN AND HUMAN LIFE. Arts and Learning: I 6 ("Death casts up Our total sum of joy"), 12 ("Shall I serve For nothing but a vain parenthesis I' th' honor'd story of your family?"), 15-16 (Castabella's farewell like the "imperious close Of a most sweet oration," 20 ll.), II 137 ("All sorrows Must run their circles into joys").

MUSIC: I 72, 91, 132, II 100, 106 ("I'll bear me in some strain of melancholy, And string myself with heavy-sounding wire, Like such an instrument that speaks Merry things sadly"), 121 ("quick in tune"), 139.

LAW: I 96 ("We enterchange th' indenture of our loves"), 16 (kissing is the seal of love), 103 ("That fellow's life . . . Like a superfluous letter in the law, Endangers our assurance?— Scrape him out"), 139 ("In yon star-chamber thou shalt answer it"), II 7 ("Vengeance, thou Murder's quit-rent," etc.), 41 ("To be his sin's attorney"),[1] 108, (writ of error, and certiorari), 129 (" 't'as

---

[1] Cf. Webster 31a.

some eight returns like Michaelmas term"), 14 (Law's iron forehead).

MEDICAL: I 82 (pleurisy), 85 (like a tetter), II 12 ("discontent,—the nobleman's consumption"), 69 (purge).

Various Estates and Occupations: GOVERNMENT: I 55 (Stars —viceroys to the King of Nature), 92 (emperor and subjects), 133 (gold a queen), II 49 ("What's honesty? 'Tis but heaven's beggar"), 43 ("that foolish country girl,.. Chastity"); II 7 (tenant), 44; II 11 ("Had his estate been fellow to his mind"), 24 ("That scholar in my cheeks, fool bashfulness"), 21 (a bastard—the thief of nature), II 26 ("Thou hast been scrivener to much knavery"), cf. 105 ("He and his secretary the Devil"), cf. 12.

BUSINESS: I 23 (to engross sin), 19 ("I will take your friendship up at use," etc.), 76 ("Set down the body. Pay Earth what she lent," etc.), II 125 ("put myself to common usury"), 30 ("honesty Is like a stock of money laid to sleep").

AGRICULTURE: II 9 ("he began By policy to open and unhusk me"), cf. 116.

BUILDING: I 43 (foundation, etc.), 46 ("My plot still rises, According to the model of mine own desires"), 118 ("this great chamber of the world"), 136; II 9, 34 ("be sad witnesses Of a fair comely building newly fallen, Being falsely undermined"), 80 (stars and sky = "Yon silver ceiling," cf. Collins' note ad loc.). I 142 ("to paint a rotten post), II 128 ("a virgin's honor is a crystal tower").

Domestic Images: I 30 (courage and love are brother and sister), II 31 ("let thy heart to him, Be as a virgin, close"), 77 ("Your hope's as fruitless as a barren woman"), II 25 ("He is so near kin to this present minute"); Dowry II 36, cf. 39; 120 (iron nipples).

Dress and Ornament: I 20 ("She's like your diamond, a temptation in every man's eye, yet not yielding to any light impression herself"), 27 ("I'll give you a jewel to hang in your ear.— Hark ye—I can never love you"), II 6 (eyes like diamonds); Cloth, etc., II 7 (three-piled flesh), 7 (death's vizard), 117 ("Nay, doubt not 'tis in grain; I warrant it hold color"), 57 (knit and ravel), 123 ("To have her train borne up, and her soul trail I' the dirt").

Colloquial, Coarse, and Familiar Images: Tourneur has many gross comparisons, and a few of a colloquial sort. II 26 ("as familiar as an ague"), 52 ("Wer't not for gold and women there would be no damnation,—Hell would look like a lord's great kitchen without a fire in't"), 13 ("His violent act has . . . Stain'd our honors, Thrown ink upon the forehead of our State"), 34 ("I durst . . . Venture my lands in heaven"), 41 (to take the wall of), 72 ("here is a pin [showing his dagger] Should quickly prick your bladder"), 103 ("Slaves are but nails to drive out one another"), 129 (the fly-flop of vengeance), 132 ("he that dies drunk falls into hell-fire, like a bucket of water, qush, qush!"), 135 ("one of his cast sins"); Birth, etc., I 58, 150, II 36: Bawd. etc., I 99, 118, 153; I 62 (Night—the murderer's mistress).

The Body, Its Parts, Attributes, etc.: I 40 ("the full-stomached sea"); I 92 ("I've lost a signory . . . . A wart upon the body of the world"); II 14 (Law's iron forehead); 46 (heaven's finger); I 115 (the face of heaven); 146 (the canker of sin); II 89 ("Now I'll begin To stick thy soul with ulcers"); II 55 ("How must I blister my soul"); Sleep II 149.

Subjective Life, Religion, etc.: I 11 ("Here are my sons,—There's my eternity"); I 79 ("On the altar of his tomb I sacrifice My tears").[1] Paradise II 47; Devil II 28; Conjuring, spirits, etc., I 52, 87; Influence of the Stars I 133.

Death, the Grave, etc.: I 110 ("this convocation-house of dead men's skulls"), 114 ("The poison of your breath, Evaporated from so foul a soul, Infects the air more than the damps that rise From bodies but half rotten in their graves"), II 37 (monument), 72 ("people's thoughts will soon be buried"), 13 ("The bowel'd corpse May be sear'd in; but . . . The faults of great men through their sear'd clothes break").

War: I 13 ("Shall I . . . . hang but like an empty Scutch-

[1] Cf. Marlowe II 60, Webster 47b.

eon"), cf. II 60 (heraldry); I 76 ("open war with sin"), 145 (like a warlike navy); II 9 ("the insurrection of his lust"), 41 (seige), II 8 ("Thy wrongs and mine are for one scabbard fit"), 62 ("there's gunpowder i' th' court").

The Stage and the Drama: I 57 ("Here's a sweet comedy"), 155 (their tragedies) cf. II 7, 80, 85, 91, 146, II 34 (play a part), II 144 ("Mark, Thunder! Dost know thy cue, thou big voiced crier?"), 52: ("O, Angels, clap your wings upon the skies, And give this virgin crystal plaudites").[1]

Miscellaneous: Melt II 6, 128; Mirror, glass, II 128; Black II 74 ("make him curse and swear, and so die black"); Spot II 122; Poison II 33, 51, 62, 79 ("O let me venom Their souls with curses!"), 120, 127; Instrument I 46, II 31; Coin and Counterfeit II 9, 10, 61, 149; Edge II 45 ("My spirit turns edge"), 72 ("go you before And set an edge upon the executioner"), 103 ("hope of preferment Will grind him to an edge").

Nature plays a comparatively insignificant part in these two tragedies. It is human life in its various aspects which chiefly is used to illustrate human life. Law is well represented. Several domestic and colloquial images are used with much effect. But the morbid and the crudely baleful appear largely in all of Tourneur's work and weaken its effect, so that the vivid originality and the lurid beauty of his imagery cannot save it. This very imagery is infected with the dark and subjective quality of his mind, as appears not only in his various extravagant, gross, and repulsive comparisons, but also in the general tone and the specific application of many others.

[1] Cf. Massinger, *The Duke of Milan*, V ii:
". . . . good angels
Clap their celestial wings to give it plaudits."
Similarly *The Maid of Honor*, V i.

JOHN WEBSTER

Acted		Published		Pages
1607 ? (Fleay)		1612	*The White Devil, or Vittoria Corombona* - -	5– 50
1612 ?	"	1623	*The Duchess of Malfi* -	59–101
1610 ?		1623	*The Devil's Law Case* - -	107–145
1609 ?	"	1654	*Appius and Virginia* - -	149–180

WEBSTER.

Originality and Power of his Dramatic Diction

PERHAPS nothing so much as a close and careful study of his imagery can bring home to one the extraordinary originality and power of Webster in his particular sphere. Webster worked consciously, deliberately, and with a thorough command of his materials. His pages are strewn with tropes,[1] and, in spite of their profusion, such is the keenness of his marvelous "analogical instinct" and the dramatic force of his imagination that scarcely ever do they seem forced or out of keeping. Language here seems to reach the extreme of ruthless and biting intensity. There is scarcely any faded imagery, and there are very few conventional tags;[2] everything stands out in sharp lines, as if etched. The characteristic fault of Webster's imagery, the defect of his peculiar quality, is that he errs if anything on the side of the bizarre,[3] or even of the grotesque.[4] This criticism could be enforced by many citations. Let two or three typical similes, chosen at random, suffice:

9a "'Tis *fixed with nails of diamond* to inevitable necessity."

60b "He runs as if he were ballassed with quicksilver."

80a "A politician is the devil's quilted anvil;
He fashions all sins on him, and the blows
Are never heard."

---

[1] To represent the Range and Sources of the imagery of his four plays, I am compelled to devote thirteen pages, against about four for Greene's four plays, six for Peele's five, and eight for Marlowe's six.

[2] Absence of the usual poetical phrases, of poetical as distinguished from dramatic imagery, is doubtless what the writer of the article on Webster in the *Retrospective Review* (Vol. VII p. 90) means in saying that "in poetical imagery he seldom indulges." See to the same effect, Ward, Hist. Eng. Dram. Lit., II 261.

[3] So Mézières, Contemp. et Succ. de Shaks., 227.

[4] Lowell, Old Eng. Dram., 71.

Not only the analogical but the logical faculty also is incessantly in play in Webster, but the ethical mordacity of his mind is such that he rarely falls into mere intellectualism and conceits.[1] The conceit for the conceit's sake is seldom Webster's fault. It has usually an emotional connotation and seldom is out of keeping. Thus Romelio's bombastic boast:

Dramatic Decorum

> "I cannot set myself so many fathom
> Beneath the height of my true heart as fear,"

is strikingly illustrative of his character, emphasized as it is by Ariosto's dry comment: "Very fine words, I assure you, if they were To any purpose."[2] So the pathetic subtlety of the last words of the worn and tortured Duchess:

> "... Heaven-gates are not so highly arch'd
> As princes' palaces; they that enter there
> Must go upon their knees." [*Kneels.*][3]

And yet the simile, express or implied, the usual mark of the deliberate and self-conscious mind, is perhaps more prevalent in Webster's pages than the metaphor in its various forms. But there is scarcely anything of the relaxed and epical movement of imagery sometimes appearing in Peele and Marlowe.[4] Webster "was the most literary among the Elizabethans, after Jonson."[5] This statement is exemplified not only in Webster's general method of workmanship, but also in the abundance of his historical and literary allusions. Classical ornament also is not rare in Webster, although there is little of that superficial varnish of Latin myth-

The Short Simile his Favorite Form

---

[1] Examples of conceits in Webster are: 152b ("Von great star-chamber;" cf. Tourneur, I p. 139), 132b, 50a. Once or twice Webster falls into mixed metaphor: 160b, 161b ("under his smooth calmness cloaks a tempest"). He is practically free from Euphuism. Examples of Play on Words: 33a, 38b, 62b, 112b, 152b.

[2] *Devil's Law Case*, p. 132b.

[3] *Duchess of Malfi*, p. 89a.

[4] Prolonged similes appear, however, pp. 6a, 11, 37a, 38b, 77a, 78a, 79a, 150a. See also the prolonged metaphorical passages 10b, 21a, 32b, 83b-84a; and similes continued in metaphors 50a, 167b.

[5] Gosse, Seventeenth Century Studies, p. 47.

ology so affected by the earlier school of Lyly, Peele, Greene and Marlowe.¹

Intellect applied to intensely, even remorselessly, tragic emotion, but subtle, swift, and often abrupt in action is the note of Webster's style. Implied simile, where the application is left undefined, to bear itself home with a sudden rush, is a favorite device. Bosola, who is employed for an assassination, is promised attendants to assist him in his bloody deed. He refuses their aid in these terms: "Physicians that apply horse-leeches to any rank swelling used to cut off their tails that the blood may run through them the faster; let me have no train when I go to shed blood, lest it make me have a greater when I ride to the gallows." But the explicit simile is the more common. Note, for example, what effective use Vittoria makes of them in the famous trial scene,—their effect being ironically heightened by the pompous declaration of the lawyer that she

Logical Quality of his Mind

"Knows not her tropes nor figures, nor is perfect
In the academic derivation
Of grammatical elocution." (p. 20.)

Indeed, oftentimes Webster's similes are logical analogies or arguments rather than pictures, e. g. 32a:

"Best natures do commit the grossest faults,
When they're given o'er to jealousy, as best wine,
Dying, makes strongest vinegar."

Or 22b "Condemn you me for that the duke did love me?
So you may blame some fair and crystal river
For that some melancholic distracted man
Hath drown'd himself in 't."

The acrid nature of Webster's genius is everywhere felt in his pungent use of similitudes. The sardonic character of

¹Striking examples of classical allusion are: 31a ("I have drunk Lethe"), 169a; 40a, 83b (Charon's boat), 38a ("Like the two slaughtered sons of Œdipus"), 48b Hypermnestra, 59b Tantalus, 61a Hercules, 63b Vulcan's net, 69a Jupiter and Danae, 75b Venus' doves, 75b Syrinx, Daphne, etc., 76a the Judgment of Paris; The Furies, 35a, 48a, 127b, etc.; 127b Amazons, 150a Briareus, 162b Colossus, 169a Rhadamant, 171b Janus, 173b Actæon, 172b Isis. See also: Æsop 37b, 44a, 133a; Lucian, etc., 48a; Pliny 60b; Tasso 78a; Homer 13a, 30a, 32a; Fortune's wheel 26b, 66b, 83a.

Flamineo in *The White Devil* is heightened by the irony of his incessant similes. So in *The Duchess of Malfi* Antonio's rather colorless virtues are artfully depicted through his fondness for sententious comparisons.

Metaphorical ideas concentrated into a burning word or phrase are not uncommon in Webster and bear a striking resemblance to similar strokes in Tourneur: e. g. 80a, "Your direction shall lead me by the hand;" 85b, "I am full of daggers;" 100b, "I hold my weary soul in my teeth;" 117b, "the stale injury of wine" [insults given in drink]; 74b, "Her guilt treads on Hot burning coulters;"[1] 117b, "I reserve my rage to sit on my sword's point;" cf. 88a, "riot begins to sit on thy forehead;" 125b, "lock'd your poniard in my heart;" 169a, "His memory to virtue and good men Is still carousing Lethe." The poignant intensity, the strange and cogent applicability, of Webster's figures startle us at every turn. All these effects can be illustrated only by reference to the list of tropes cited below ("Range and Sources of Imagery").

Condensed Comparisons

In such a tragic and fearful world as Webster creates the ethical preoccupation of his mind, morbid and excessive as its quality often is, cannot but be prominent at all points.[2] Questions of fate, salvation, sin and repentance are constantly reflected in his imagery:

The Persistently Ethical Motive

97b: "Security some men call the suburbs of hell, Only a dead wall between."

99a: "*Servant.* Where are you, sir? *Antonio* [dying]. Very near my home."

101b: "*Bosola.* Mine is another voyage. [Dies]."

131a: "Such a guilt as would have lain Howling forever at your wounded heart And rose with you to judgment."

cf. 47b: "Millions are now in graves, which last day Like mandrakes shall rise shrieking."

[1] Cf. Tourneur, II 51.

[2] As Lowell remarks (Old Eng. Dram., 69), Webster, like Chapman, is fond of metaphysical apothegms.

And see the references under "Subjective Life, Religion, etc." (p. 117 below). The penchant of his mind for images of death and the grave, so often remarked upon,[1] is largely a part of the same thing, save that it more distinctly emphasizes the morbid quality of his genius.[2]

Hyperbole, except of a purely dramatic sort, is infrequent in Webster.[3] Akin to his metaphysical predilection is his fondness **Sententious-** for sententious figures. These appear especially as **ness** exit lines or ending couplets: e. g. 18a:

"Both flowers and weeds spring when the sun is warm,
And great men do great good or else great harm" (cf. 32a).

27b: "Your flax soon kindles, soon is out again;
But gold slow heats, and long will hot remain."

Cf. also 36a, 39a, 76b, 82a, 97b, 100b, etc.

Proverbial phrases also are not uncommon.[4] There is the usual amount of formal personification in Webster, skilfully managed for dramatic effect; e. g. 12b: "Lust **Personifica-** carries her sharp whip At her own girdle;" 77a **tion** (Apologue of Reputation, Love and Death); 91b "Sacred innocence, that sweetly sleeps On turtles' feathers";

156a: "O Rome, thou'rt grown a most unnatural mother
To those have held thee by the golden locks
From sinking into ruin."

Cf. also 40b, 48, 88a, 100a, 108a, 117b, 152a, 174b, 178a.

[1] E. g. by Taine, Eng. Lit. Bk. II, c. II, Sect. VI ("A sombre man, whose thoughts seem incessantly to be haunting tombs and charnel-houses"); so also J. A. Symonds, Introd. to Ed. of Webster and Tourneur (Mermaid Ser.), p. xxii; Dyce, Introd. to Ed. of Webster, p. xv, and others.

[2] See the examples cited below, p. 119. See especially the series of comparisons, p. 21a; also 37a (simile of the rack), 135b ("to weave seaming-lace With the bones of their husbands that were long since buried"), 139a. Note also the references p. 87 under "Medical."

[3] A few striking examples occur: 15a ("Hell to my affliction Is mere snow-water"), 31b, 73b, 77a, 90a ("Other sins only speak; murder shrieks out; The element of water moistens the earth, But blood flies upwards and bedews the heavens"), 91a, 118b, etc.

[4] E. g. 135a, 136a, 143a, 162b, etc.

Trick of Self-Repetition Webster not infrequently repeats tropes and ideas, sometimes verbatim, in different plays. Numerous examples will be seen below.

Finally it should be noted that *Appius and Virginia* differs largely from the other plays in diction and figure. It is more rhetorical and declamatory, it contains fewer striking and original similitudes; and with a sort of dramatic propriety its language is more latinized and conventional. The attempt is obviously in another vein than the Italianate tragedies of *The White Devil* and *The Duchess of Malfi*.

RANGE AND SOURCES OF IMAGERY.

Mr. Churton Collins'[1] remarks upon "that quick analogical instinct which loads 'Vittoria Corombona' and 'The Duchess of Malfi' with wide-ranging imagery, metaphor, and simile." And Webster's range is wide, although the incisive emphasis and effectiveness and the freedom from conventionality of most of his figurative language is such that we recognize more readily his range and force than we do in the case of more colorless writers.

Inanimate nature does not play so much of a part in his metaphors and similes as does animate nature, while the predominance of allusions to human life and interests is striking evidence of the departure of tragic writing from the more purely poetic traditions of the pre-Shaksperian school.

NATURE. Aspects of the Sky, the Elements, etc.: HEAVENS, 65b ("may our sweet affections, like the spheres, Be still in motion," etc.); SUN AND SUNSHINE, 35b ("In all the weary minutes of my life, Day ne'er broke up till now"), 111a, 149b ("See how your kindred and your friends are muster'd To warm them at your sunshine"); STARS, 5b ("fore-deeming you An idle meteor"), cf. 40b, 48a ("This thy death Shall make me like a blazing ominous star"), 7b, 49b; Eclipse, 76b, 144b; CLOUDS, 108b, 110b, ("this court mist"), 170a, 122a, 150b, 151b, 34b, 88b ("Mist of error"); SHADOW 137b, 140a, 150a, 155b; THUNDER 5a, 12b, 27b; LIGHTNING 6b ("prompt as lightning"), so 71b, 82a ("You see what power Lightens in great men's breath")

[1] In the introduction to his edition of Tourneur, p. xlii.

164b ("This your plot shall burst about your ears Like thunderbolts"); STORMS, SHOWERS, etc., 35a, 111a ("Crying as an April shower i' the sunshine"), 10b (storm), 34b, 88b ("Their death a hideous storm of terror"), 142b, 65b (tempest), so 72b, 74a, 135a, 159a, 160b, 13b (whirlwind), 31a, 82b:

> "Like to calm weather
> At sea before a tempest, false hearts speak fair
> To those they intend most mischief."

Similarly 161b, 50a, 62b: ("What follows? never rained such showers as these Without thunderbolts i' the tail of them; whose throat must I cut?"); 155b (hail); Earthquakes 9b, 177a; Whirlpool 72b; FIRE 44b, 86a (the fire of revenge), 97a, 135a ("no more mercy Than ruinous fires in great tempests"), 139b (wild fire in the blood), 158a (the fire of sedition), 169b, 177b; Heat and Cold 22b ("My frosty answer"), 70a (freeze), 97a (ice), 179b ("This sight hath . . . Ic'd all my blood"); 32a ("Your good heart gathers like a snowball, Now your affection's cold"); 133b; Snow 101b, 169b (snow of age), 172a (laws writ in snow).

SEASONS: 109a (Spring of youth), 107a (the springtide), 109a ("with me 'Tis fall o' the leaf"), 149b ("your stormy winter"), 21a, 169b (winter of age).

Waters, Sea, etc.: 19a (like grasping water), 143b (tide of fortune), 118a:

> "I am pour'd out
> Like water! the greatest rivers i' the world
> Are lost in the sea, and so am I."

11a ("As rivers to find out the ocean"), 22b,
26a: "let the stigmatic wrinkles in thy face,
 Like to the boisterous waves in a rough tide,
 One still overtake another."

32a ("Now the tide's turn'd, the vessel's come about"),

32a: "The sea's more rough and raging than calm rivers,
 But not so sweet nor wholesome. A quiet woman
 Is a still water under a great bridge,
 A man may shoot her safely."

67b: "Say you were lineally descended from King Pepin . . . What of this? Search the heads of the greatest rivers in the world, you shall find them but bubbles of water." 59a ("a prince's court Is like a common fountain," etc.), cf. 10b (Princes compared to dials); cf. 79a; 78b (moisture drawn out of the sea, returns to it).

Aspects of Earth: 64a (wilderness), 11 (policy winds like the crooked path to a mountain's top), 27b ("I'll stand Like a safe valley, which low bends the knee To some aspiring mountain"), 139b (mountain and valley), cf. 165b, 151b (firm as the earth and its poles), 172b ("Thou lov'st me, Appius, as the earth loves rain; Thou fain would'st swallow me"), 27a ("What, are you turn'd all marble?"), 36b ("your iron days"), 60a (rust), 96a ("remove This lead from off your bosom"); cf. 77a, 169a ("False metals bear the touch, but brook not fire"), 176a (Sand; shelf); 31a ("My loose thoughts Scatter like quicksilver"); See "Adamant" below, p. 85.

VARIOUS: 96a (flatterers like echoes); Blasted 10b, 108b; Atom 114a.

The Vegetable World: TREES 6a (bear best fruits, transplanted), 17a (elms), 35a (like the yew tree),

39a ("That tree shall long time keep a steady foot,
 Whose branches spread no wider than the root"),

38a (like a walnut tree cudgelled for its fruit), 59b (like plum trees), 62a ("the oft shaking of the cedar tree Fastens it more at root"), 79a (like a cedar), 66a:

"That we may imitate the loving palms,
 Best emblem of a peaceful marriage,
 That never bore fruit, divided." (Cf. Dyce's note.)

83a ("My laurel is all withered").
120a ("Yield no more light Than rotten trees which shine in the night"), 151b (twig and branches), 159a (branches), 167b (the willow yields to the storm; the oak is overthrown); 178a (To fall like a rotted tree); Vine 29b, 17a:

"Like mistletoe on sear elms spent by weather,
 Let him cleave to her, and both rot together."

cf. 122b ("Wind about a man like rotten ivy"); Leaf 157a (aspen leaf); Roots 70b (to pull up by the roots); FLOWERS 19a ("When age shall turn thee White as a blooming hawthorn"), 82b ("here's another pitfall that's strew'd o'er With roses "); 111b ("Kiss that tear from her lip; you'll find the rose The sweeter for the dew"), 142b (Man's life like that of flowers); Mushroom 25b, so 133a; Fruit 137b ("take from me forty years, And I was such a summer fruit as this"), 138b (the bitter fruit of love); 20b, 47a ("I'll stop your throat With winter-plums").

The Animal World proportionately appears very frequently among Webster's figures. Ben Jonson,—writing mostly in comedy, however, while Webster's genius is tragic and romantic, —alone in our list exceeds this proportion.

FISH, etc.: 81a ("he lifts up's nose, like a foul porpoise before a storm"), 83b-84 (fable of the salmon and the dog-fish), 107b ("whiles he hopes to catch a gilt-head, He may draw up a gudgeon"), 63b (like the crab which goes backward).

REPTILES: 11a ("The way ascends not straight, but imitates The subtle foldings of a winter's snake"), 12a ("Repentance then will follow like the sting Plac'd in the adder's tail"), 43b ("the bed of snakes is broke"), 70b (snake), 85b (vipers), 172a ("Thy violent lust Shall, like the biting of the envenom'd aspic, Steal thee to hell"), Toad 16a (cf. 61a), Cameleon 166b; Tortoise 27b, 31b.

INSECTS: 27b ("Treason, like spiders weaving nets for flies, By her foul work is found, and in it dies"), 61b (the law like a spider's web), 113b ("entangle themselves In their own work like spiders").

36a: "Glories, like glowworms, afar off shine bright,
But look'd to near, have neither heat nor light."

So 88a (verbatim), similarly 133a; 60a (like moths in cloth); cf. 153b ("base moth-eaten peace ");[1] 78b ("these lice," i. e., parasites); 85b:

"Things being at the worst begin to mend ; the bee
When he hath shot his sting into your hand,
May then play with your eyelid."

110a ("For women's resolutions in such deeds,
Like bees, light oft on flowers, and oft on weeds.")

[1] Cf. Tourneur, II 36.

168b ("I am an ant, a gnat, a worm," etc.); 9a (silkworm); Flies 114a.

BIRDS: 38b (fowl); 93b ("Eagles commonly fly alone; they are crows, daws, and starlings that flock together"); 26a (raven), so 41a, 44b, 144b; crow 133a; 39b (screech owl), so 40a, 76b, 119b; 149b;

> "For some suspect of treason, all these swallows
> Would fly your stormy winter; not one sing:
> Their music is the summer and the spring."

46a ("We think cag'd birds sing, when indeed they cry"), 86b ("The robin-red-breast and the nightingale Never live long in cages"), 88a (simile of the lark in cage, 5 ll.), cf. 7a, 83b (birds allured to the net); 76b (to clip wings), 49a:

> "O your gentle pity!
> I have seen a blackbird that would sooner fly
> To a man's bosom, than to stay the gripe
> Of the fierce sparrow-hawk."

See also "Hawking" below, p. 89; 59b ("I will thrive some way; blackbirds fatten best in hard weather"); 64b ("like a taught starling"); 82a ("buntings" depart as soon as fledged); 127b (doves); 13b ("Forward lapwing! He flies with the shell on's head");[1] 150b ("Excellent lapwing! . . . He sings and beats his wings far from his nest"); 133a ("this poor thing Without a name, this cuckoo hatch'd i' the nest Of a hedge-sparrow!"), so 171b; 151a ("never did you see 'Mongst quails or cocks in fight a bloodier heel Than that your brother strikes with"); 44a (fable of the peacock and the eagle).

WILD ANIMALS: 177b (lion-taming), 12b (lion), 83a (tiger), 158a; 73a ("excellent hyena"); 176a ("Never did bear-whelp, tumbling down a hill, With more art shrink his head betwixt his claws Than I will work my safety"), 84b ("Where are your cubs?"); 5a ("Your wolf no longer seems to be a wolf Than when she's hungry"), 22b, 30b, 37b (holding a wolf by the ears), 40b, 44b, 76b, 90a; 94b (fox), 81a, 48a, 165a; 136b ("An old hunted hare; She has all her doubles"), 26a, 31b, 100b: 113b (monkeys); 157a ("You rough porcupine, ha! Do you bristle, do you shoot

[1] Cf. *Hamlet*, V ii 180 and notes.

your quills, you rogue?"); 176a ("I have learnt with the wise hedgehog, To stop my cave that way the tempest drives"); 95b ("like the mice That forsake falling houses"), 74a ("he seems to sleep The tempest out, as dormice do in winter"), 142a; 70a ("This mole does undermine me"); 31b ("be not like A ferret, to let go your hold with blowing"); 11b (pole-cats).

DOMESTIC ANIMALS: Horse 160b ("Let the young man play still upon the bit"); 7a ("Call his wit in question, you shall find it Merely an ass in's foot cloth"); 6a (like shorn sheep to the slaughter); Dogs 7b ("Let her not go to church, but like a hound In lyam [=leash] at your heels"), 9b, 22a ("Cowardly dogs bark loudest"), 34b ("Like dogs that once get blood, they'll ever kill"), 37b (to unkennel), 49a ("Fate's a spaniel, We cannot beat it from us"), 153a ("Make you us dogs, yet not allow us bones?"), 160b, 84a ("Like English mastives that grow fierce with tying"), 82b (bloodhounds), 162b, 37b (Æsop's fable of the dog and the shadow), 71b ("thou wast watch'd Like a tame elephant").

Fabulous Natural History: Adamant 9a, 30b ("We'll be differing as two adamants; The one shall shun the other"), 83a ("Every small thing draws a base mind to fear, As the adamant draws iron"), 96a ("breasts hoop'd with adamant");[1] 143a; 20b (like apples of Sodom), 89a ("Come, violent death, Serve for mandragora to make me sleep!"), mandrake 19a (mistletoe or oak seldom found without a mandrake by it), 47b

> "Millions are now in graves, which at last day,
> Like mandrakes, shall rise shrieking."[2]

So 72b (mandrakes make one mad); 168a (aconite as a remedy against serpents' stings). 177a:

> "What devil
> Did arm thy fury with the lion's paw,
> The dragon's tail, with the bull's double horn,
> The cormorant's beak, the cockatrice's eye,
> The scorpion's teeth?"

76b (the basilisk's eyes), 94b; 81a ("Mark Prince Ferdinand; A very salamander lives in's eye, To mock the eager violence of

---
[1] Cf. in Chapman 158 the same phrase.
[2] Cf. *Romeo and Juliet*, IV iii 47.

86   *METAPHOR AND SIMILE.*

fire "); 172b ("a weeping crocodile "), 32b (fable of the crocodile and the wren — in Herodotus "the trochilus") ; 27b (" patient as the tortoise, let this camel Stalk o'er your back unbruis'd ") ; 27b (the lion and the mice) ; 11b (unicorn's horn as an antidote) ; 12a (eagles that gaze upon the sun) ; 26a ("like your melancholic hare, Feed after midnight "), 44a (" we now, like the partridge, Purge the disease with laurel "); 81a (foxes that carry fire in their tails); 87a (We'll sing, like swans, to welcome death ") ; 9a (the silkworm fasts one day in three).

MAN AND HUMAN LIFE: Arts and Learning: Chronicle 75a (" You are Your own chronicle too much and grossly Flatter yourself "), 128b; 91b (conscience a black register); 84a (" I will no longer study in the book Of another's heart ") ; 112a (" Though I were to wait the time That scholars do in taking their degree In the noble arts "), 119a (" Your patience has not ta'en the right degree Of wearing scarlet," etc.) ;142a (death's lesson); MUSIC 73b (" put yourself in tune "), 71b (like a poor lute player), 79b, 115a, 124a; PAINTING 50b (" I limned this night-piece "), 97a (to " lay fair marble colors " upon), 127b ("As men report of our best picture makers, We love the piece we are in hand with better Than all the excellent work we have done before "), 137b (" Painting and epitaphs are both alike, -- They flatter us and say we have been thus "), Picture 23a, 61b, 86b.

Various Estates and Occupations: 38b (ambassadors), 49b (" I shall welcome death As princes do some great ambassadors; I'll meet thy weapon half way "); 96a (secretary); 155a (miser); 162a (juggler), 28b; 162b (giant); 47b (like ranting preachers); 37b (swear like a falconer, lie like an almanac maker, smell of sweat like an under-tennis-court-keeper), 37b (" Lovers' oaths are like mariners' prayers, uttered in extremity "), 112b (park-keeper), 152b (stewards), 101b (friend), 142b (" is not death A hungry companion?"), 155b, 173a (attendants), 155b (servants), 65a (" I have long serv'd virtue, And ne'er ta'en wages of her"); 86b (" I am acquainted with sad misery As the tann'd galley slave is with his oar"), 18b (prisoner), 155b (jail), 174b; 178a (grief a tell-tale); 110a (to do knight's service).

Law: 31a ("executor To all my sins");[1] 111b (livery and seisin), 65b (debt and discharge—"Quietus est"), 46a, 120a (supersedeas), 123b (caveat), 152a ("The rich fee-simple of Virginia's heart"), 121a (false executors), 173a ("*Virginius*. Thus I surrender her into the court Of all the gods. [*Kills Virginia*]"), 152b ("You great star-chamber;"),[2] 39b (lease of life), 21a.

Medical: 16a ("Look, his eye's bloodshed [bloodshot?], like a needle a chirurgeon stitcheth a wound with"), 60a ("places in the court are but like beds in the hospital, where this man's head lies at that man's foot, and so lower and lower"), 13b ("*Francisco de Medici* . . . Come, you and I are friends. *Brachiano*. Most wishedly: Like bones, which, broke in sunder, and well set, Knit the more strongly"), 31a ("the corrupted limb cut off"), 47b ("These are two cupping glasses [*showing pistols*] that shall draw All my infected blood out"), 62a, 179a ("I'll fetch that shall anatomize his sin"), cf. 21a ("dead bodies . . . wrought upon by surgeons"), 65a (ambition a madness, not kept in chains, but in fair lodgings); Physicians 9b ("You are a sweet physician"), 82a ("physicians thus, With their hands full of money, use to give o'er Their patients"), 97a (as physicians applying horse-leeches, cut off their tails), 119a ("Are you such a leech For patience?"), 120a ("these graves and vaults, Which oft do hide physicians' faults"); Medicines 5b (physic), 11b (unicorn's horn as antidote), 26a ("Physicians that cure poisons, still do work With counter-poisons;" so 168a), 22b (gilded pills; so 84a), 23b (pills), so 47b; Diseases 95b ("Yond's my lingering consumption"), 125b, 71b (wound in the heart, etc.), 8a (Jealousy like the jaundice), 22a (palsy of fear), 24b, 31a, 73b, 31b ("What a damn'd imposthume is a woman's will!"), 81a ("Methinks her fault and beauty, Blended together, show like leprosy, The whiter, the fouler"), 98a (ague), 99b ("Pleasure of life, what is't? Only the good hours Of an ague"), 149b, 166a (plague), 91a.

Agriculture: 22b (vines manured with blood); Scarecrow 38a; 127b (the harvest-home of love), 155b ("We spread the earth like . . . . new reaped corn"); Sow and reap 38b, 42b (harvest),

[1] Cf. Tourneur II 41.
[2] Cf. Tourneur, I 139.

108a ("Virtue is ever sowing of her seeds"), 37a (pigeons and sparrows in harvest time), 63a (pasture).

Trades and Practical Arts: 6b (like a gilder poisoned with his quicksilver), 25a ("We endure the strokes like anvils"), cf. 80a; Weaving 63b; Dyeing 87a (a knave in grain); Glass 71b; 100b ("Whether we fall by ambition, blood or lust, Like diamonds, we are cut with our own dust"); 61b ("You play the wire-drawer"), 83a (like the repairing of a clock or watch), 75b ("Laboring men Count the clock oftenest.... Are glad when their task's ended"), 31b ("Will any mercer take another's ware When once 'tis tous'd and sullied?"), 45b ("Now the wares are gone, we may shut up shop"), 65a (tradesmen and their wiles), 108a (exchange at dear rate), 142a ("The world and I have not made up our accounts yet"), 108a (voyage for a mine), 154b ("Rome, Thou wilt pay use for what thou dost forbear"), 48b (pawn; bill of sale). MINE 65a, 108a.

Ships and Sailing: 9a (shore from ship), 13a ("Should fortune rend his sails and split his mast"), 37a (like ships which seem great upon a river, small upon the seas), 37b (mariner's prayers), 121a ("So sails with fore-winds stretch'd do soonest break"), 142a (" *The Capuchin.* O, you have a dangerous voyage to take. *Romelio.* No matter, I will be mine own pilot"); 32a, 50a, 73a, 83a ("Let us not venture all this poor remainder In one unlucky bottom"); 143a, 149a (steer), 167b, 168a, 176b.

Building: 37a (Men like bricks, alike, but placed high or low by chance); 82a ("Men cease to build when the foundation sinks"), cf. 145b, 89a:
> "I know death hath ten thousand several doors
> For men to take their exits; and 'tis found
> They go on such strange geometrical hinges,
> You may open them both ways."

113b ("As black copartiments show gold more bright"), 153b, 174b; 63b ("footsteps"—stepping stones); 47a (the body the palace of the soul); window 138a; 151b ("Trust my bosom To be the closet of your private griefs: Believe me, I am uncrannied"), cf. 79a (his breast a private whispering-room); 100b ("Thou, which stood'st like a huge pyramid, Begun upon a large and ample base, Shalt end in a little point, a kind of nothing"), 121a (pyramids weakest at the top); Column 108b; Prop 158b.

Sports, Amusements, etc.: 7 (bowling), 28b (juggling), 133a ("he seems A giant in a May-game"), 36b ("strook His soul into the hazard"),[1] 99a ("We are merely the star's tennis-balls, struck and bandied Which way please them"), 120b ("the more spacious that the tennis-court is, The more large is the hazard"), 150a (sprinters who before a race wear shoes of lead); Riding 44b and 67b; Archery 20a ("I am at the mark, sir: I'll give aim to you, And tell you how near you shoot"), 39b ("One arrow's graz'd already"); HAWKING, 12a, 20a, 30b, 38a, 71b, 144b, 160b; Fowling 27b, 37a, 122a; HUNTING 31b, 136b, 165a; Dance (of life) 169a.

Domestic Life: 65b (as children eat sweetmeats), so 149b (verbatim); 49b ("I will be waited on in death"); 83a ("I have seen my little boy oft scourge his top, And compar'd myself to 't; naught made me e'er Go right but heaven's scourge-stick");[2] Relationship 44b ("I have heard grief named the eldest child of sin"), so 100b, cf. 121b, 155b (twins), 86a ("Thy pity is nothing of kin to thee"), 152b ("our mother, Fair Rome"), so 156a.

DRESS AND ADORNMENT: 8b (diamond and its setting), 24a, 63a, cf. 100b, 22a (counterfeit jewels), 46–47 (jewels), 79a, 117b, 124b, 144b; 29b ("this changeable stuff"), 48b ("ere the spider Make a thin curtain for your epitaphs"), cf. 120a; 81a ("Doth she make religion her riding-hood To keep her from the sun and tempest?"), 94a ("Sorrow makes her look Like to an oft-dy'd garment"), 62b ("Your old garb of melancholy"), 117b ("You have not apparelled your fury well") 121a, 140b (veil), 95b ("You shall see me wind my tongue about his heart Like a skein of silk");[3] Wear 154a; Visarded 178b.

Colloquial and Familiar Images: 8a (like images in a basin

[1] Cf. *Henry V*, I ii 263.

[2] See a similar simile in Sidney's *Arcadia* (Poems, ed. Grosart II 163):
"Grief only makes his wretched state to see,
 Even like a top, which nought but whipping moves."

[3] Cf. Chapman, 94a.

of water, broken by bubbles), 9a ("I will put the breese in's tail"), 22a (tell lies like post-boys), 31b (landlady), 32a ("Your little chimneys Do ever cast most smoke!"), 37b ("like a frighted dog with a bottle at's tail"), 43b ("she simpers like the suds A collier hath been wash'd in"), 74b ("he's a mere stick of sugar candy"; so 115b), 77a ("You have shook hands with Reputation"), 163a (a little-timbered fellow), 163b (clerks of the kitchen), 173b ("cheese struck in years"), 173b ("my stomach has struck twelve"). Flamineo in *The White Devil* is particularly fond of colloquial comparisons, which strangely intensify the sardonic irony of his villainy; e. g. 8b, 19b, and passim.

Coarse and Repulsive Images: 5b (vomit), 5b (fleabitings), 78b (lice), 6a ("Make Italian cut-works in their guts"), 22a (to spit in the wind), 37a ("I did never wash my mouth with mine own praise"), 59b (horseleech), 97a; Rotten 97a, 153a, 17a; Dunghill 25b, 133a, 166a, 171a; 5a ("Fortune's a right whore"), 62a, 23b, 92a, 168b; Beget 158a.

The Body and its Parts: 7b (the stars' eyes), 40b (rough-bearded comet), 27b (the valley bends the knee); Sleep 109b, cf. 110b, 171b; 111b (bells tongue-tied); Smother 99a, 135a; To swallow 153b.

The Senses and Appetites: Food and feasting 8b, 17b, 97b, 88b ("A many hungry guests have fed upon me"), 23a, 49b ("You are too few to feed The famine of our vengeance"), 155a, 149b ("To make so many bits of your delight"), 25a (relish like honey); 178a (odors), 6a ("Perfumes the more they are chaf'd, the more they render Their pleasing scents"),[1] so 83a; 47a ("Sins Thrice candied o'er"), so 62b, 115b, cf. 74b.

Subjective Life, Religion, etc.: Heaven 64b, cf. 174b. Hell 64b, 42b, 91a, 97b, 169b; Devil 10a, 21b, 27b, 35a, 41a, 62b, 65a, 67b, 83b, 98b, 142a, 143b, 166b, 172a, 177a, etc.; Witchcraft and Conjuring 19a ("Thou art a soldier, Follow'st the great duke, feed'st his victories, As witches do their serviceable spirits, Even with thy prodigal blood"), 63b, 65a, 75a, 81a, 121a; Perspective Glass 30b, 61b; 85a (an Italian superstition); 91a

[1] Similarly Bacon (cf. Dyce's note ad loc.).

("I stand like one. That long hath ta'en a sweet and golden dream"); Soul 108b; 127a ("mischiefs, Are like the visits of Franciscan friars—They never come to prey upon us single"); Oracles 61b, 92a (heretic), 65b ("I will remain the constant sanctuary Of your good name"), cf. 172a, 30b:

> "Thou hast led me, like a heathen sacrifice,
> With music and with fatal yokes of flowers,
> To my eternal ruin."

94a ("You are all of you like beasts of sacrifice"), 47b ("did make a flaming altar of my heart");[1] 151a ("one whose mind Appears more like a ceremonious chapel Full of sweet music, than a thronging presence"), 83a ("Your kiss is colder Than I have seen a holy anchorite Give to a dead man's skull"), 77a ("be cased up, like a holy relic"), 83a ("In the eternal church, sir, I do hope we shall not part thus").

Death, the Grave, etc.: 10b, 26a ("Misfortune comes, like the coroner's business, Huddle upon huddle"; cf. 127a), 29b (a fowl "coffin'd in a bak'd meat"), 35a (like the yew tree, growing on graves), 48b, 50b ("My life was a black charnel"), 65b, 77a, 89a, 90b ("You have a pair of hearts are hollow graves, Rotten, and rotting others"), 96b, 97a, 101a, 120b, 125a, 128b, 135b, 142b, 166a.

War: Tilting 166a; Siege 27b ("As jealous as a town besieged"), 152a; 153a, 174a; 27b ("undermining more prevails Than doth the cannon"); Cannon 25a, 77a (thy heart is "a hollow bullet, Fill'd with unquenchable wild-fire"), 81a (to laugh "Like a deadly cannon That lightens ere it smokes"), 83b, 91a ("your vengeance, Like two chain'd bullets, still goes arm in arm");[2] Combat 170a, 63b (like men in battle under the influence of fear), 142b ("what is death? The safest trench i' the world to keep man free From fortune's gunshot"); armed 21b, 84b; 70a ("Old friends, like old swords, still are trusted best"); Sheathe 22a.

The Stage and the Drama: 29a ("My tragedy must have some idle mirth in't, Else it will never pass"), 86b, 85b ("I account

[1] Cf. Tourneur I 79.
[2] So Heywood (cf. Dyce's note); cf. Chapman 170a.

this world a tedious theatre, For I do play a part in't 'gainst my will"), 90a ("as we observe in tragedies That a good actor many times is curs'd For playing a villain's part"), 120a (" O look the last act be the best i' the play, And then rest, gentle bones "),[1] 124b ("Are not bad plays The worse for their length?"), 129a, 101a.

Miscellaneous: Melt 101b, 143a, 172a, 179a; Mirror 61b, 124b, 149a; Colors 12a (black slander), 18b, 20a, 22b, 40a, 43b, 46b, 60a, 99a, 165b, 172b, 178b, 179a, 180a; White 82b; Poison 11b, 12a ("there's hemlock in thy breath"), 12b, 15a, 16a, 34a, 40b, 60a, 63a, 64a, 92b, 96b, 122b, 125b, 134b, 157a, 167b, 168a (cf. 36b, 39b, 42a); Instrument, Engine, 19a, 48a, 78a, 79b, 121a ("an engine [that] shall weigh up my losses, Were they sunk as low as hell"), 152a; Coin, Counterfeit, etc., 21a, 133a; Painted 6a ("Leave your painted comforts"), 20b, 32a, 91a, 133a; Drown 34a, 142b; 35b ("He sounds my depth thus with a golden plummet"), 83a; Climbing 178b; 121b ("Sin and shame are ever tied together"); 98a ("a face folded in sorrow") cf. 27a; 48a ("I am caught with a springe"); Watch 69a (like a false rusty watch); to Sift 107b; Weight 82a, 168a; Balance 179b.

Tragedy is ubiquitous in Webster. In his own phrase, he limns night-pieces,[2] and, wide as is his range of imagery, almost everything is hung in black. Take for instance any section in the above list, for example "Insects," and observe the moral connotation of the images cited. Spiders are the emblems of treason 27b, or evil plots 113b, or of the entanglements of the law; glowworms are the type of false glories 36a, 88a, or false honor 133a; moths are types of destructiveness 60a, 153b; parasites are like lice 78b; bees are treacherous 85b, or uncertain of purpose 110a; ants, gnats, worms, etc., are representatives of abjectness 168b; the silkworm's fabulous sagacity and industry is used to point a gross meaning 9a; flies however are nothing worse than emblems of smallness 114a. Such is Webster's world! For results similar, if somewhat less striking, would follow were

Recapitulation

His Morbid Quality

[1] Cf. Jonson, II 379a.
[2] P. 50b.

we to analyze the other fields from which he draws his illustrations. Among stars, meteors are most used. There are two tropes referring to showers, and some twelve to storms and tempests; earthquakes, hail, whirlpools and fire, appear prominently. Nature is not idyllic in Webster. Animal life, and especially birds, he seems to have observed. But mankind was his proper study. The various arts and the estates and occupations of life are laid under endless contribution. Note as characteristic the large number of entries under the rubric "Medical," and also under "Subjective Life."

GEORGE CHAPMAN*
1557 ?–1634

Acted or Entered	Published		Pages
1595–6	1598	*The Blind Beggar of Alexandria*	1– 21
1597 ?	1599	*An Humorous Day's Mirth*	22– 45
1599 ? (1603 Fleay)	1605	*All Fools*	46– 77
1598 ? (1601 ")	1606	*The Gentleman Usher*	78–112
1604 ? (Fleay)	1606	*Monsieur D'Olive*	113–139
1604 ? "	1607	*Bussy D'Ambois*	140–177
1606 ? "	1613	*The Revenge of Bussy D'Ambois*	178–213
1608	1608	*Byron's Conspiracy*	214–242
1608	1608	*The Tragedy of Charles, Duke of Byron*	243–274
1601 ? (Fleay)	1611	*May-Day*	275–306
1605 ? "	1612	*The Widow's Tears*	307–340
1608 ? "	1631	*The Tragedy of Cæsar and Pompey*	351–380

*In the following lists, references to the five tragedies have usually been placed after those to the comedies, except where similarity of the subject or context has brought two or more references together without regard to pagination.

CHAPMAN.

>   GREAT faults counterbalanced by great merits is the judgment rescued from an inappropriate application to Shakspere, and nowadays applied with a greater justice to Chapman.[1]

His Great Faults and Merits

Not only is this apparent in the construction and general purport of his plays, but also and more especially in his diction and use of imagery. For in these respects, while on the one hand it is true that "Chapman abounds in splendid enthusiasms of diction, and now and then dilates our imaginations with suggestions of profound poetic depth,"[2] yet at the same time there are to be found in his plays striking examples of almost all the faults in matters of diction of that most prolific period. Hyperbole of the hugest pretensions, a sort of grandiose magniloquence, which is saved from falling into bombast only by the intellectual passion which inspires it, extraordinary and fantastic conceits, labored and clouded similes, incoherence and obscurity of style,[3] and other similar marks of barbarism are to be found in Chapman's work. The general manner of his imagery has been summed up fully and accurately by Mr. Swinburne:[4] "Few poets . . .

General Manner of his Imagery

have been more unsparing in the use of illustration than Chapman; he flings about similes by the handful, many of them diffuse and elaborate in expression, most of them curiously thoughtful and ingenious, not a few of them eloquent and impressive; but in many cases they tend rather to distract the attention of the reader than to elucidate the matter

---

[1] By Coleridge (Miscellanies, Æsthetic and Literary, p. 289), by Lamb (Specimens of Eng. Dram. Poets, p. 88), and others.

[2] Lowell, Works, I 277.

[3] "A quaint and florid obscurity, rigid with elaborate rhetoric, and tortuous with labyrinthine illustration" (Swinburne on Chapman, Encyclopædia Britannica, 9th ed.).

[4] Introduction to Chapman's Works, Poems and Minor Translations, p. xix.

of his study." The comedies of course differ in these respects from the tragedies, being much lighter and clearer in style. But the characteristic Chapman, the sententious and weighty Chapman, is found in the tragedies. Indeed Chapman the playwright has three distinct styles: (1) What may be termed his High Tragedy Style, an exceedingly undramatic style, in which there is a noticeable straining after the epic manner. The speeches are long and often rhetorical, description and narration are frequently used,[1] the style is exalted, and there are many prolonged or so-called Homeric similes,— though of course Chapman can never let himself down to the quiet pitch and simple manner of the genuinely Homeric simile. (2) His Comedy Style. Here the movement is more dramatic and more colloquial, and the metaphors and similes are shorter and less prominent. (3) Finally, admitting *Alphonsus* and *Revenge for Honor* into the list of his works, we should have to distinguish his Later Tragedy Style, in which few of the characteristics observable in his High Tragedy Style appear. There is little metaphor and simile, the syntax is less involved, and the diction generally is much less abstract and obscure.

His Three Styles

The difficulty and obscurity of Chapman's style is not helped by the manner of his figurative language. Chapman's imagery in some respects is the very opposite of Webster's. Chapman is abstract and often vague,[2] Webster is concrete, vivid, and intense; Chapman is inclined to amplification,[3] Webster to contraction; Chapman is epical, Webster dramatic; both however are highly literary and self-conscious in their methods of workmanship, and

---

[1] See for a striking example the Description of the Duel in Act II, Sc. 1 of *Bussy D'Ambois* (pp. 147–148).

[2] "Often we feel his meaning, rather than apprehend it. The imagery has the indefiniteness of distant objects seen by moonlight" (Whipple, Lit. of Age of Eliz., p. 151).

[3] Some of the more striking prolonged similes are to be found at pp. 48b, 53b, 122b, 126, 140a, 140b, 148a, 150a, 162, 171b, 172a, 175, 176, 185, 189a, 198b, 202a, 204a, 207b, 212b, 219b, 226, 227a, 231a, 239b, 262b, 270a, 352a, 354a, 359b. Prolonged metaphorical passages: pp. 47, 87, 142, 154, 162, 169, 272, 274, 293, 323, 325.

both are sententious[1] and moral in temperament and in the fundamental predilection of their genius.

Chapman's method in tragedy was epical and highly literary. His tragedies accordingly are full of classical and literary allusions and of historical parallels and examples. Homer[2] naturally supplies a large part of the classical allusion, although by no means all.[3] Indeed Chapman is full of literary echoes, which may be considered a note of his style. Even the comedies contain many classical and literary allusions, including various parodies and quotations.[4] In respect to the manner of his classical allusions Chapman has entirely escaped from the facile and superficial mythology of Greene and Peele. His classicisms are not excessive, although occasionally from the dramatic point of view Chapman is somewhat pedantic in his allusions. But within the limits of his peculiar vein of narrative and gnomic tragic writing, they are often used with force and occasionally with veiled and subtle effect. Tamyra's appeal to Montsurry,[5] for example, is aptly enforced by the classical image employed:

<blockquote>
"Oh, kill me, kill me;
Dear husband, be not crueller than death;
You have beheld some Gorgon; feel, oh feel
How you are turned to stone."
</blockquote>

Classical and Literary Ornament in Chapman

Quite in Chapman's more violent vein, again, but not so obvious, is the allusion in Tamyra's earlier speech:

[1] "He is the most sententious of our poets." (Lowell, Old Eng. Dram., p. 91): This appears not only in his great wealth of gnomic verses, but also in his fondness for sententious figures. His similes often have a moralizing turn; he is fond of fable (e. g. 48b, 146, 185b, 189a, 235b); and proverbs and similar figures are not infrequent (e. g. 72a: "extreme diseases Ask extreme remedies;" 161a to swim against the stream, cf. 244a; 188b "Great vessels into less are emptied never;" 197b "Labor with iron flails, to thresh down feathers, Flitting in air;" 259b "This nail is driven already past the head; cf 265a, etc.).

[2] See the references to Homer, 4a, 190a, 196a, 204a, etc.

[3] For example note 140b (Pindar's "dream of a shadow"), 188a (quotation from the *Antigone* of Sophocles), 203a ("this Senecal man"), 80b (Plautus), etc.

[4] E. g. 20b (from Marlowe), 22b ("like an old king in an old-fashion play"), 133a (Parody on Spenser's *Shep. Cal.*), and the (so far as I know) unidentified parodies pp. 80b, 281b, 296a.

[5] *Bussy d'Ambois*, V i (p. 170b); cf Greene, 236a.

> "Come, bring me to him;[1] I will tell the serpent
> Even to his venom'd teeth, from whose cursed seed
> A pitch'd field starts up 'twixt my lord and me,
> That his throat lies."[2]

The strange and bizarre predominate in Chapman's imagery. At times it is even the grotesque. In reading his plays we are repeatedly confronted with the most extraordinary conceptions, which by their very extravagance rise above the level of mere conceits. Passion of a certain high sort, as well as imagination, is present in his tragedies, but it is a passion that cannot abstain from violence at every crisis. The jealous Montsurry[3] cries out,

Excesses of his Diction

> "I know not how I fare; a sudden night
> Flows through my entrails, and a headlong chaos
> Murmurs within me, which I must digest."

The following is from Bussy's dying speech:[4]

[1] Act IV, Sc. i (p. 165a).

[2] Other striking classical allusions are as follows: The Trojan War, etc., 55a, 58b ("to play Menelaus"), 147b, 161b (to "quarrel with sheep and run as mad as Ajax"), 223a, 244a, 285a, etc.; Hero and Leander 5b; to throw in a ball of debate 62b, 217a, 223a; Various Gods 12a, 64b, 157a, etc.; Alcides or Hercules 137a, 281b, 320b, 334b, 176a, 190b, 218b ("like the shaft shot at the sun by angry Hercules"), 224b, 251a, 49b ("like the dragon to the Hesperian fruit"); 69b ("sing to me no more, syren"'), 95b, 169b, 285a, (cf. 243b, 244a); Medea 110b, 201a; Semele 218b; Cyclops 229a; Helicon 202a, 330a, cf. 224b; Actæon and Diana 313a; Gordian knot 292a, 165b; Hermean rod 157a; Lernean fen 162a; Augean stable 165a; Ætna 83a, 157b, 208a; Pandora's box 166a; Occasion and her forelock 123a, 293a; The Wheel of Fortune 142a, 152a. Four or five lines finally may be quoted as an example of Chapman's more poetical manner (p. 175a):

> "Haste thee where the grey-eyed morn perfumes
> Her rosy chariot with Sabæan spices,
> Fly, where the evening from th' Iberian vales
> Takes on her swarthy shoulders Hecate,
> Crown'd with a grove of oaks."

Historical allusion is very frequent in Chapman. A few examples are: 188a (Brutus and Cæsar), 196b (Pompey), 218a (Catiline), 189a ("Domitian-like"), 229a (Curtius), 266b (Manlius), 258 (Alexander and his civilizing mission).

[3] *Bussy D'Ambois*, IV i (p. 164b).

[4] Id. V i (p. 175b).

> "My sun is turn'd to blood, in whose red beams
> Pindus and Ossa hid in drifts of snow,
> Laid on my heart and liver, from their veins
> Melt like two hungry torrents, eating rocks
> Into the ocean of all human life,
> And make it bitter, only with my blood."

This is typical, not exceptional.[1]

The early and distinctly Chapmanesque tragedies are crowded with metaphor and simile. Scarcely a sentence but contains a trope, faded, concealed, or emphatic.[2] Everything **His Profuse Use of Trope** is at the farthest degree from the common, the usual. The vocabulary is full of strange latinized forms, such as prefract (257a), decretal (273b), novation (193a), inclamation (195b), aversation (196a), everted (68a), and the like. He is fond of inversions,—" Her men *ashore go*, for their several ends." (212b);

> " Since he can
> *As good cards show* for it as Cæsar did ; " etc.

He is profuse in illustration, sometimes giving way to a perfect riot of similes and metaphors, as in the interview between Baligny and Clermont in the *Revenge of Bussy D'Ambois* Act II (p. 189). In the same way he is fond of heaping up simile after simile, alternative or cumulative, as in the description of the duel already referred to, or in Henry's invective against La Fin in Act III of *Byron's Conspiracy*.

Chapman in his tragedies is almost as abundant in hyperbole[3] as Marlowe in *Tamburlaine*. Different as they are in essential characteristics, Chapman sometimes strangely **Chapman and Marlowe** recalls Marlowe. Each sympathizes in much the same way with the Titanic spirit, the lust of power, and a sort of hyperbolical pride of soul. The passion of Chap-

---

[1] Note for further example, the accumulation of violent images in the long speeches in which Monsieur and Bussy exchange compliments, Act III near end (pp. 161-162) and see the hyperboles cited below.

[2] It is possible to include only the more striking and significant examples in the lists that follow.

[3] The chief examples are 18a, 109b, 150a, 158b, 162a, 163, 166a, 169a 175b, 176a, 198b, 215b, 217, 229a, 232b, 235b, ("He may drink earthquakes and devour the thunder"), 270b, 368a.

man, however, is less naïve and is more turbulent and turgid than that of Marlowe. It is evident that Chapman in his tragedies, like Marlowe in *Tamburlaine*, is writing in a special vein in conformity to artistic canons of his own. Consequently it is highly uncritical to judge his tragedies simply as tragedies. What their merits are it is more difficult to state than it is to detail in order their defects in style and imagery. Mr. Swinburne has more nearly done justice to them than any other critic. The critics, however, from Dryden to Edmund Gosse, have been curiously contradictory in considering the question of Chapman's bombast and fustian. Mr. Gosse[1] dismisses Chapman's tragedies with the remark that they are "plays that seem bombastic, loose, and incoherent to the last extreme;" and Chapman's bombast seems to be one of the fixed traditions of criticism. Dryden[2] condemned it, and various later critics, Hazlitt,[3] Warton,[4] and Ulrici,[5] for example, have animadverted upon it. Professor Ward, however, in his *History of English Dramatic Literature*,[6] has bestowed high praise upon Chapman's imagery, and Lowell[7] prefers to speak of "an incomparable amplitude in his style."[8] Perhaps E. P. Whipple's defense is the most to the point of any that can be offered: "Pope[9]

The Question of Bombast in Chapman

---

[1] Jacobean Poets, p. 40.

[2] Dedication to the *Spanish Friar*, Works VI 404 (apropos of *Bussy D'Ambois*).

[3] Lit. Age of Eliz., Lect. III ("he often runs into bombast and turgidity — is extravagant and pedantic at one and the same time").

[4] Hist. Eng. Poetry, IV 318 ("His fire is too frequently darkened by that sort of fustian which now disfigured the diction of our tragedy"). See also Hallam, Lit. Eur., pt. III, ch. vi § 103; Campbell's Specimens, p. 130; etc.

[5] Shaks. Dram. Art., Bk. III, ch. ii ("empty pomposity and rhetorical pathos").

[6] Vol. II, pp. 10, 14–15, 19, 21, 35.

[7] Old Eng. Dram., p. 92.

[8] See also the *Retrospective Review*, IV 337: "In no author have we richer contemplations upon the nature of man and the world, where the shrewdness of the remark is ennobled and enforced by *the splendor of imagery and the earnestness of passion*."

[9] Sic Read *Dryden*.

speaks of it [*Bussy D'Ambois*] as full of fustian; but fustian is rant in the words when there is no corresponding rant in the soul, whilst Chapman's tragedy, like Marlowe's *Tamburlaine*, indicates a greater swell in the thoughts and passions of his characters than in their expression."[1] In short, Chapman's passion is real, however confused, perplexed, and turgid in expression; Bussy D'Ambois and Byron are very strenuous figures, and that hyperbole and extravagance abound so much in their speech, granting the conception of the type of character and the peculiar species of poem, is not so unnatural or improbable.

Another fault in Chapman is one allied to his predilection for the bizarre and grotesque heretofore adverted to. This is his fondness for puerile quibbling,[2] and for fantastic conceits.[3] Excuse for the quibbling doubtless is found in the fact that most of it occurs as part of the comic "business" of the comedies; the conceits, not infrequently entangled with his hyperboles, are too often unmeasured, and, as Professor Ward says,[4] recall the conceits of Cowley and the Fantastic School. He is especially fond of that not ungraceful form of conceit in which the sense is, as it were, turned in upon itself, leaving the metaphorical emphasis upon pronoun, preposition or adverb; as in the following examples: 49a ("does he think to rob me of myself?"); 51a ("Up to the heart in love"), 130b ("You know the use of honor, that will ever Retire into itself"), 144a ("Never were men so weary of their skins, And apt to leap out of themselves as they"), 311a ("he is not base that fights as high as your lips"), 328b ("She hath exiled her eyes from sleep"). Another

Quibbling and Conceits

The Introspective Conceit

[1] Lit. of Age of Eliz., p. 153.

[2] See examples of quibbles and plays on words: pp. 4b, 5b, 22b, 24a, 24b, 57b, 63b, 78b, 80a, 118a, 127a, 129a, 135a, 142a, 156a, 201a, 217, 219a, 231a, 254b, 275, 286b, 287b, 289, 292a, 301b, 315b, 319b, 320a.

[3] Examples of conceits: 40, 47 (the opening scene of *All Fools*—a delightful passage in the right Elizabethan vein), 50, 133b, 158b, 165, 175, 177, 207a, 223, 239, 255, 284, 291a, 300, 317, 321, etc. See also the examples of Hyperboles cited above, p. 128*n*.

[4] Hist. Eng. Dram. Lit., II 10.

pretty conceit is somewhat similar: "Her blood went and came of errands betwixt her face and her heart" (317a).

Chapman's epithets are often ingenious, sometimes poetical and noble. Perhaps compound epithets do not occur as often as might be expected in view of his practice in the translation of Homer. A few examples however may be cited: 127b ("stiff-hammed Audacity"). 148a ("the fear-cold earth"), 167a ("black-faced tragedy"), 172b ("music-footed horse"), 175a ("the gray-eyed morn");[1] 194b ("foggy-spirited men"), 249b ("squint-eyed envy"), 266a ("the round-eyed ocean"). Noteworthy single epithets are: 2a ("topless honors"—a favorite epithet with Marlowe, also), 141b ("lean darkness"), 141a ("the waves of glassy glory"), 190b ("the insulting pillars of Alcides"), 180b ("her rosy eyes"), 184b ("steel footsteps"), 215a ("wealthy Autumn"), 353a ("an aspen soul").

Chapman's Epithets

Formal personification is a distinctive mark of Chapman's style in tragedy. Many of his personifications are of classical descent, and many are pure abstraction. The figure of Fortune,[2] usually represented with wings,[3] is a favorite with him. Chapman, like Spenser, loves to elaborate his personifications. Note for example the long description of Envy at the beginning of the second act of *Bussy D'Ambois*,[4] the conception of which is quite in Spenser's manner.

Personification in Chapman

In general Chapman is characterized by abundant and highly conscious and literary use of metaphor and simile. He loves to amplify and pursue his tropes. This tendency, however, does not prevent frequent obscurity in the illustration, due to his theory

---

[1] Cf. *Romeo and Juliet*, II iii 1, etc.

[2] E. g. 142a, 172a, 198a, 224a, 225a, 245a, 308a, 355b, 363b, etc. Other personifications are: of Death 96b, 115a, 162a; Envy 146b, Religion 205a, Despair 215a, Truth 262a; Occasion 293a, 123a; see also 148a, 172b, 175a, 208a, 209a, 229a, 245a, 249b, 268a, 270a, etc.

[3] "The rude Scythians painted blind
Fortune's powerful hands with wings
To show her gifts come swift and suddenly,
Which if her favorite be not swift to take,
He loses them forever." (142a.)

[4] Pp. 146b–147a.

of style[1] in part, and partly also to the naturally involved and abstract character of his genius. Hardly any writer has a manner so personal to himself and so unmistakable as Chapman in his original tragedy style. His range is very wide and miscellaneous but he is also remarkable for a certain stock of favorite illustrations and metaphors which are repeated from play to play, often with only slight variations, as will appear in numerous instances in the following classification of his imagery.[2] His comparisons, however, are mostly his own, and are free from conventionality. Occasionally there is a purely poetical touch, as for example (p. 164a):

Poetical and Vigorous Images

" Here's nought but whispering with us; like a calm
Before a tempest, when the silent air
Lays her soft ear close to the earth to hearken
For that she fears steals on to ravish her."

[1] Mr. Swinburne (Chapman's Minor Poems, Introd. p. l.) notes his "quaint fondness for remote and eccentric illustration." What Chapman's own theory in the matter was may be inferred from one of his own similes (185a):

" As worthiest poets
Shun common and plebeian forms of speech,
Every illiberal and affected phrase
To clothe their matter, and together tie
Matter and form, with art and decency;
So worthiest women should shun vulgar guises."

See also Chapman's Dedication to his poem entitled "Ovid's banquet of Sense" (Minor Poems, p. 21.).

[2] See, for example, 141b (troubled stream, clear fount), so 188a and 247a; 162a and 185a verbatim; 166a and 364a verbatim; 62b (black ball of debate), 217a (balls of dissension); and many others. There are many words and phrases, whether used metaphorically or literally, which occur so often, or in such characteristic collocations that it is almost safe to set them down as hallmarks of Chapman's diction. Most of them, of course, can be paralleled from other Elizabethan dramatists, but the presence of many of them together would, with other things, be strong corroborative evidence of Chapman's handiwork. Such are Finger (God's finger, Nature's finger, etc.); spiced; Drown; Smother; To eat one's heart; Prop; To cut a thread; To sound a depth; the idea of weight superimposed; Shoulders bearing a burden (like Atlas), etc.; Branch; the metaphor of wings, flying, etc. (noted by Mr. Lowell as a favorite image of Spenser's also; cf. Works IV 307n); veins boiling or swelling with poison, etc.; quench; whet; puffed up; blown up; swollen, etc.; infect and taint; shadow; manned (e. g. 59a, 127a, etc.); engender and beget; entrails; chaos; colors (especially

There are also many strong and idiomatic metaphors, brief, compact, and vivid:

"I'll be *hewn* from hence
Before I leave you" (97a);

"Thou *eat'st thy heart in vinegar*" (161b);

"I'll soothe his plots; and *strow my hate with smiles*" (168a);

"Let thy words be *born as naked* as thy thoughts" (182a);

"as if a fierce and fire-given cannon
Had *spit his iron vomit* out amongst them"(198b);

"I would your dagger's point had *kissed* my heart" (256a);

"I .... will not have
Mine ear *blown into flames* with hearing it." (268b)

Finally I may be permitted to quote a somewhat longer, but very noble passage, which will give a more adequate idea of Chapman's thought, style and imagery at his best. It is part of Byron's speech when being led to execution:

"let me alone in peace,
And leave my soul to me, whom it concerns;
You have no charge of it; I feel her *free;*
How she doth rouse, and like a falcon stretch
Her silver wings, as threatening death with death;
At whom I joyfully will cast her off.
I know this body but a sink of folly,
The ground-work and raised frame of woe and frailty;
The bond and bundle of corruption;
A quick corse, only sensible of grief,
A walking sepulchre, or household thief;
A glass of air, broken with less than breath,
A slave bound face to face to death, till death.
And what said all you more? I know, besides
That life is but a dark and stormy night,
Of senseless dreams, terrors and broken sleeps;
A tyranny, devising pains to plague
And make man long in dying, racks his death:
And death is nothing: what can you say more?
I, being a long globe, and a little earth,

black) used in moral sense; gall; to stoop; cement; etc.; and swindge, fautor, noblesse, treacher, and other similar words common in the poetic diction of the early years of Elizabeth. See the references that follow in the analysis of Chapman's imagery.

Am seated like earth, betwixt both the heavens,
That if I rise, to heaven I rise, if fall,
I likewise fall to heaven ; what stronger faith
Hath any of your souls ?"

RANGE AND SOURCES OF IMAGERY.

Mr. Lowell writes in his *Old English Dramatists:* "Sometimes we may draw a pretty infallible inference as to a man's temperament, though not as to his character, from his writings. And this, I think, is the case with Chapman [1] . . . Chapman has some marked peculiarities of thought and style which are unmistakable."[2] The following analysis of Chapman's imagery will perhaps contribute to the more definite understanding of the predilections of his temperament and the scope of his mind.

Chapman's range of imagery is very wide, and his manner very loud and characteristic.

NATURE: Mr. Swinburne[3] has noted the "close and intense observation of nature . . . at all times distinctive of this poet." Inanimate nature, and especially the various aspects of the heavens, the atmosphere, the weather, and the like, are constantly referred to.

Aspects of the Sky. THE SUN : 2a (Cleanthes the sun of Egypt), cf. 151b, 48b ("Love is Nature's second sun," etc., 14 ll.), 141a (men great in state like motes in the sun), cf. 154b, 263a (the sun of royalty); Phœbus, etc., 4a, 4b, 275a ; 219b (to be like the air, dispersing sunlight), 65a, 121a ("joy, sun-like, out of a black cloud shineth "), 332b, 352a, 354a (examples of the rising sun); 332b (knowledge like sunbeams), 191b (false friendship like the sun in mists), 229a (a spirit shines as sun in clouds); 251b ; Shadow 110a, 179b, 191b, 216b, 244b, 327b, 239a; 239b (like the air), 376a (the poles of heaven).

STARS : 12a (like moon and stars reflected in water), 56b ("the sight of such a blazing star as you "), 147b (" like a pointed comet "), cf. 169b, 175b, 207a ; 210a, 215a (like a star from the sea), 319a, 152b (primum mobile), 260b (like an exhalation that would be a star), 188a.

[1] P. 82.   [2] P. 88.
[3] Introd. to Chapman's Minor Poems and Trans., p. lvi.

MOON (cf. Tides): 227a (simile of the moon, stars and winds, 14 ll.); 162b ("the tender moonshine of their beauties"), 238a.

ECLIPSE: 68b, 173b, 227a, 244b, 255b. LIGHT: 165b (shine), 188b, 229a, 255b. FIRE: 4a ("eyes Sparkle with love-fire"), cf. 4b, 9b, 42b, 47a, 68b, 99a, 119b, 120b, 284b, 310a, 317b, 336a, 151b, 164b; 56b (fire of anger), cf. 116a, 134b, 188a, 210a, 370b; 141a, 191b, 205b, 207a, 239b, 244a; 126b, 147a (like bonfires), 147b (like a laurel in fire, like lighted paper, like flame and powder), 169b (like fires in cities), 268b ("I know what it imports, and will not have Mine ear *blown into flames* with hearing it"), 175b ("like a beacon fire"), 177 (love, like a burning taper); 208a ("treason ever *sparkled* in his eyes") cf. 194b (sparks in eyes), 199a, 151b, 254a (furnace of wrath) cf. 169a; 209a ("Melting like snow within me, with cold fire"); 140b ("Man is a torch, borne in the wind"). To QUENCH: 52a, 56b, 191b, 266b, 269b, 380a; As oil quenches fire 56b, 323b. Sulphur and vapor (fumes) 148a, 224a, 232b, 369b, 376b.

CLOUDS: cloudy looks 67b, 79a, 137b; 216b, 325a, cf. 150a ("I see there's change of weather in your looks"), 162b; 204b (clouds of trouble), 226a (clouds of foes), 246b; 122b

"our great men,
Like to a mass of clouds that now seem like
An elephant, and straightways like an ox,
And then a mouse."[1]

194b ("foggy-spirited men"); 252a ("like a cloud That makes a shew as it did hawk at kingdoms," etc.); 245b, 267b (type of instability), 369b; 154b ("Our bodies are but thick clouds to our souls"); 251a.

STORMS, SHOWERS, etc.: 55a ("Till your black anger's storm be over-blown"), 148a ("Storm-like he fell"), 163b (Stormy laws), 164a (like a calm before a tempest), 198b; Tempest 135a, so 292a; 47a (showers of tears), 22b (to rain humors), 238b; 39a (rainbow), cf. 191b; 18a (weather), cf. 168b: Winds 162a, 171b, 232a (like dust before a whirlwind), 251b (as the sun stills the winds), 323a; Thunder and Lightning, 17b ("some monstrous fate Shall fall like thunder"), 67b, 141a, 154a (sin is "Like to the

[1] Cf. 154a; cf. *Hamlet*, III ii 366; *Ant. and Cleop.*, IV xiv 2; Lucretius.

horror of a winter's thunder"); 20b (" As suddenly as lightning, beauty wounds "), 155b (" A prince's love is like the lightning's fume "), 166a, 168b (" A politician must like lightning melt The very marrow and not taint the skin "), 171a, 198b, 205a, 210a.

Time, Seasons, etc.: Morning 5b (" the morning of my love "), 175a (" the grey-eyed morn "); 22a:

" Yet hath the morning sprinkled through the clouds
But half her tincture, and the soil of night
Sticks still upon the bosom of the air."

164b (night); 323b (" Make the noontide of her years the sunset of her pleasures"); Spring 48b; Summer 12b, 91a; 275b (" this January," i. e., this old man); 274a (the seasons return but man never); 270b (" life is but a dark and stormy night "); VARIOUS: 225b (like an echo); Chaos 164b, 245b; Microcosm 61a (" The fair Gratiana, beauty's little world "), 99b, 100b, cf. 170a, 171a, 144a.

Aspects of Water, the Sea, etc.: Tides 145b, 188a (" He is as true as tides " . . .); Sea 63b (women crossed, tempestuous as the sea), 115b (sea of woes), 122b (" our State's rough sea "), 141a (a king's deeds " inimitable, like the sea That shuts still as it opens " . . .), 150a, 159b (" the unsounded sea of women's bloods "), 172a, 209b (" as a rock opposed To all the billows of the churlish sea ;" so 225a), 217b (as the ocean swallows the rivers), 234a, 235a, 259a; Streams 126a (" the affections of the mind drawn forth In many currents "), 141b (" Leave the troubled streams, And live . . . at the well-head "), so 188a, 247a; 226a (like a flood), 227b (" wind about them like a subtle river," etc.), 230b, 239b (false friends like shallow streams reflecting the skies, etc.), 255b, 272b. Flow 67b (" all this plot . . . Flow'd from this fount "), 297a (current), 228a (" All honors flow to me, in you their ocean "), 149b, 239a; 226b (vessels of water); 12a, 215a, 171a (bubble).

Aspects of the Earth: The globe 271a (" seated like earth, betwixt both the heavens "); bog 229a, cf. 31b; 169b (" The errant wilderness of a woman's face "), 219b (like hills piercing above the clouds), 236a (falling great men, like undereaten promontories ; cf. 270b " this declining prominent "), 272b (valleys and mountains, 10 ll.); Dust-like 197a; 68a ("the crater of my heart"); Earthquakes 150a, 163b, cf. 235b.

Inorganic Nature: Metals 324a, 196b; 141b ("thy mettle could let sloth Rust . . . it"), 141b ("like burnished steel, After long use he shined"), 362a (steel toils), 10a ("brazen forehead"); 83b (leaden steps), 223a (leaden rumor); 104b (copper); Golden 356b ("golden speech . . . to gild A copper soul in him"), 9a (hair like gold), so 13a, 61a ("My dearest mine of gold"), 322a ("if she be gold she may abide the test"): To gild 135b; Silver 12a (silver wrists), 87b (silver song); 223a ("harder than Egyptian marble"); Glass 220a (brittle as glass), cf. 251b, 141a ("The waves Of glassy Glory"); Cement 212b, 245b, 251b; Loadstone 67a, cf. 50a (riches a lodestar).

The Vegetable World: TREES 171b, 229b; 174a ("Man is a tree," etc.), 232a (fall of great men like that of topheavy trees before a wind),¹ 140a ("As cedars beaten with continual storms, So great men flourish"), 267a ("like a cedar on Mount Lebanon, I grew, and made my judges show like box-trees"), 276b ("tall and high, like a cedar"), 163b ("so much beneath you, like a box tree"), 148a (like the fall of an oak in Arden), 281a ("hollow and bald like a blasted oak"), 147b ("D'Ambois, that like a laurel put in fire Sparkled and spit"), 154a (aspen leaf), 353a ("an aspen soul"); Branch 14 (i. e. a child), 51b, 249b, 244b ("Cut from thy tree . . . . all traitorous branches"), 315b; 230b ("plants That spring the more for cutting"), 251a (like the blackthorn that puts forth leaf in midst of storms); Mushroom 155a; Fruit 161a, 187a, 202b, 216b, 229b, 254b; cf. 158b, 159a (windfalls). Nipped in the blossom 47a, 18a (like wind-bitten flowers), 245b ("frost-bit in the flower"), 109b, 150b, 321a; Roots 230a, 234b, cf. to root up 217b, 219a; to take root 282a, 323a; Sap 309b; Withered 110b, Ripe 145a ("a courtier rotten before he be ripe").

The Animal World: Paws 59a; 210b ("Like to a savage vermin in a trap"), 200a, 230b.

FISH: 62b ("A man may grope and tickle 'em like a trout"), 84a (gudgeons), 62a, 90a, 133a.

REPTILES: 328a ("What action doth his tongue glide over,

¹ Cf. Webster, 39a.

but it leaves a slime upon 't?"), 352a (flatterers and parasites thrust up like toads and water-snakes in a pool "against great rains"); SERPENTS 14b, 160a, 165a, 169b, 265b, 290a (gentle as a toothless adder), 310a, 26a, 70a ("her serpent noddle," cf. 213b); 287a (Like the sting of a scorpion): 128a (a courtier — like a cameleon); 200b (toads).

INSECTS: 59a ("I 'll smoke the buzzing hornets from their nests"), cf. 278a; 216b ("my court, A hive for drones"), so 217b; 364b (as bees gather sweets), 336a, 24a (stinging wit); 41a (blind as a beetle), cf. 67a, 78a ("as brittle as a beetle"); 204a ("Time's old moth"); 162a (caterpillars); 109b ("glut the mad worm of his wild desires"); 188b (as spiders spin their webs), 330a, 27a (cobwebs), so 154b.

BIRDS: 27b, cf. 45b, 318a, 262b (Byron struggles like an imprisoned bird); Flying, Wings, etc. 1b, 100a ("her winged spirit Is feathered . . . with heavenly words"), 154a, 174a, 184b, 190b, 209a ("The black, soft-footed hour is now on wing"), 209b, 243a, 257b, 268a, 318a ("a flight beyond your wing"), 365b, 371b; Feather 144b, 197b, 337a; note that Fortune, Revenge, etc., are generally personified as winged in Chapman. Eagle 2a, 58a ("puts on eagle's eyes"), 67a, 121b (type of royalty). 155b, 164a, 192b, 207b; 155b ("flatterers are kites That check at sparrows"); 146b, 285a (buzzard); 319b (widgeon); 161b (screech owl), 232b; Turtle-dove 47a ("One like the Turtle all in mournful strains, Wailing his fortune"), 110b, 285a; 158b (peacock); 161a (cuckoo), 228b; 22b, (pigeons); 65b (Like a jackdaw), 129b (dandies like goldfinches), 133a ("a hammer of the right feather"); 47a (like the lark), 156a; 210b ("He will lie like a lapwing, when she flies Far from her sought nest, still 'here 'tis', she cries"), cf. 248a; 332b (the cock); 311b (goose).

WILD ANIMALS: Lion 105a, 189a (as chained lions grow servile, so nobles in peace), 192b, 220a, 230a, 256b, 359b (Simile of the hunted lion, 15 ll.); 145b ("Here's the lion, scared with the throat of a dunghill cock"); 146a (the ass in the lion's skin); Tiger 159b, 161a ("dares as much as a wild horse or tiger"), 176b ("to the open deserts, Like to hunted tigers, I will fly"), 201a; 270a (Simile of the hunted boar, 7 ll.), 320b; 318a ("he has not licked his whelp into full shape yet"), cf. 105a ("Sweet whelps"); Wolf 48a, 161a, 231a; 158b (porcupine); Fox 48b; Ape 23a, 54b, 71b, 59a (baboon), 144b, 92a, 100a.

DOMESTIC ANIMALS—HORSEMANSHIP: 71b ("I have unhorsed them"), 30b ("overthrown both horse and foot"), 80b ("brave prancing words," etc.), cf. 233b, 339a (to bestride the back of authority); Curb 206a; Spur 206a, 221b, 233b; To trot after 277a. HORSES 322a (prolonged metaphor of the unruly colt), 231a ("The stallion power hath such a besom tail That it sweeps all from justice"), 236b (like a lusty courser broken loose, 10 ll.), 256a, 256b; 336b ("that jade falsehood is never sound of all, But halts of one leg still"); Ass 146a, 160a, 308a, 313b; CATTLE 64b ("Is the bull run mad?"), 189b ("Slain bodies are no more than oxen slain"); 273a ("such exemplary and formal sheep"); 224a (Elephant dislikes white); 262b ("And like the camel stoops to take the load, So still he walks"); 146b ("if I thought these perfumed musk-cats . . . durst but once mew at us"), 292b ("Was there ever such a blue kitling?"). DOGS 3b (puppies), 48a (women are "Like hounds, most kind, being beaten and abused"), 278a (like a dog in a furmety-pot), 279b ("be thrust into the kennel," i. e., be put upon), 327b ("the barking of appetite"), 168a (kennel), cf. 255a, 199b ("Some informer, Bloodhound to mischief").

Fabulous Natural History: Adamant 116a, 321b, 158b (heart "hooped with adamant");[1] Laurel 168b ("The stony birth of clouds will touch no laurel"); 239b ("Stygian water [is] . . . to be contained But in the tough hoof of a patient ass"); Phœnix 33b; Cockatrice 65a ("Is this the cockatrice that kills with sight?"), 185a, 301b; Basilisk 169b; Crocodile 132b ("Honor is like . . . a crocodile . . . it flies them that follow it and follows them that fly it"); Halcyon 244b ("like the halcyon's birth, Be thine to bring a calm upon the shore"); Fire-drake 365a ("So have I seen a fire-drake glide at midnight Before a dying man to point his grave"); Unicorn 148a.

MAN AND HUMAN LIFE. The Arts and Learning: 79b ("He is a parcel of unconstrued stuff"), 131b (the Court Accidence),

[1] Cf. Webster, 96a.

163a (high forms in the school of modesty), 127b ("stand aloof, like a scholar"), 129b ("I should plod afore 'em in plain stuff, like a writing-school master before his boys when they go a-feasting"), 141b ("like dame schoolmistresses"); 304a (a truant in the school of friendship); 79b ("a map of baseness"), cf. 118a; 103a (glosses; decipher), 113b (prints), cf. 164b, 278a, 127a ("He that fills a whole page in folio with his style"), 315a (written in lines of fame), 318b (imprinted), 145a ("some knight of the new edition"), 167b (volume), 170b (I'll write in wounds — my wrongs fit characters"), 217b ("those strange characters writ in his face"); 236b (the stars "are divine books to us"), 240a ("He hath talked a volume greater than the Turk's Alcoran"), 262b ("in his looks He comments all, and prints a world of books"); 224b (hieroglyphic), so 236a; 185a ("as poets Shun plebeian forms of speech"), 189a (simile of the foolish poet), 204a (like pedantic critics of Homer), 231a ("as a glorious poem," etc., 15 ll.), 234b ("as a cunning orator," etc., 7 ll.), 142b (rhetoric); Gloss 215b, 265, 370b, 384a; 141a (cipher), 119b (refraction), 169b ("Hereafter? 'Tis a supposed infinite"), 185a (like lines in geometry), 113a ("love is like a circle"), 221b; Sphere 254a.

MUSIC: 9a ("Love . . . tunes the soul in sweetest harmony"); 60a, 78b, 113b, 122b ("we have spurr'd him forward evermore, Letting him know how fit an instrument He was to play upon in stately music"), cf. 104a ("thus you may play on me;"[1] 124a ("like a virginal jack"), 161a ("Still in that discord and ill-taken note"), 172b ("music-footed"), 173a (consort of harmony), 212b (consort), 235b (music), 240a (in tune), 245b; cf. 115b, 48b.

PAINTING AND SCULPTURE: 47b–48a (beauty "like a cozening picture"), 154a (paints), 227b (like Arras pictures); 140a (like unskillful statuaries), 175a ("Here like a Roman statue I will stand Till death hath made me marble"), 193a ("Like statues, much too high made for their bases"), so 236a, cf. 140b.

LAW: cf. 199a, 63b, 193b ("No time occurs to kings"), 267a, 53b (Nature's serjeant John Death), 61a (freehold), 63a ("of counsel with"); 63b (Seal), 148a, 318a, 325b; 66a ("Curses are

[1] Cf. *Hamlet*, III ii 355.

like causes in law," etc., 8 ll.), 68a ("show love's warrant"), 69b (plea to confess action), 96b (bonds), 117b (copy), 314a ("hold thy tenement," etc.), 314b ("enjoy your reversion"), cf. 320b; 339a ("What? shall we have replications, rejoinders?"); 208a ("delays, Bribing the eternal Justice"), 267b, 109b.

GOVERNMENT, etc.: 117a (monopolies and free-trade), cf. 309b; 162b (grief's sceptre), 188a (crown), so 199b, 213b, 220b; 271a (life a tyranny); 121b ("his mind is his kingdom");[1] 372b (the soul empress of the body); to engross 102a, 116a, 286b.

MEDICAL: 6a ("A Spaniard is compared to the great elixir or golden medicine"), 72a ("extreme diseases Ask extreme remedies"), cf. 310a; 96b ("this unmed'cinable balm Of worded breath"), 107a (patience a medicine), 151a (medicine), cf. 215b, 216b ("this physic That I intend to minister"), 195b ("Since 'tis such rhubarb to you"), 238a (balm, etc.), 250b (pills, etc.), 259b ("Where medicines loathe, it irks men to be heal'd"), 267b ("How like a cure, by mere opinion, It works upon our blood!"), 315a (physic), 317b (medicine), 329a (physic); 162b (grief a sickness), 175a ("he dies splinted with his chamber grooms"), 255a (the March sun breeds ague), 313a (like sick men), 339b ("I'll cut off all perished members"), 374b ("As men Healthful through all their lives to grey-haired age, When sickness takes them once, they seldom 'scape; So Cæsar"), 62b ("as fat as a physician"), 368b (physicians); 19a (cankered), so 89a; 66b (salve), so 97a, 298b, 334a, 232b; 183b (tumour), 265a, 376a; Infect 100a, 120a, 309b, 218a, 223a, 224a, 240a; Leprosy 260a; Pleurisy 265b; Purge 116b, 149a, etc.; Wound 1b, 68b, 120a, 277b, 164b, 165b, 238a, 239a, 370a, 376a, 380a.

Various Estates and Occupations: 163b (gardener), 204a (like misers), 204a ("*Chalon.* "How took his noblest mistress your sad message? *Aumale.* As great rich men take sudden poverty"), 223b ("As a city dame, Brought by her jealous husband to the Court," etc.), cf. 253a; 227a, ("like men, that, spirited with wine, Pass dangerous places safe"); 270b ("this body but . . . A slave bound face to face to death, till death"),

---

[1] Cf. Dyer's poem, Ward's English Poets, I 377. This sentiment is traced to Seneca's *Thyestes*, and is frequently employed by Elizabethan writers.

cf. 149a, 209a, 358a; 355b (Fortune Cæsar's page); 156a ("like woodmongers, Piling a stack of billets"); Usher 276b, 231a; Thief 109a; Hangman, Gallows. etc. 195b, 292a; Giant 157b, 207b, 208a, 235b, 378b; 155b ("Worse than the poison of a red-haired man"); Inn 329a.

Trades and Practical Arts: MERCHANTS, SHOPS, etc., 53b (Nature's debt-book), 60a (set his gifts to sale), 236a (bank-rout), cf. 313a, 266b; 284b ("My shop of good fortune," etc.), 325a (the merchant who ventures his all in one bottom), 327b ("To set open a shop of mourning!"), 201a ("our state-merchants"), 225a ("Fortune is so far from his creditress That she owes him much"): Anvil 245b, 260b, 284a ("I have you upon mine anvil"); Forge 134b, 103a, 131b, 221b, etc.; 282a ("this warp of dissembling"), 287a (homespun); 317a (like the needle of a dial); Pawn 69a, 164a. BUILDING: 4b ("Sleep shall not make a closet for these eyes"), 220a (mansions), 270b (the body = the "groundwork and raised frame of woe and frailty"), 284b ("Thus shall I with one trowel daub two walls"), 154b (stone-laying), 236a (foundation and roof), 355a (building on sandy grounds), 376b; Built 326b, 183b, 246a; Fabric 171b, 200b; Wainscot 183a; 336a ("Near-allied trust is but a bridge for treason"); 251b ("hath but two stairs in his high designs; The lowest envy and the highest blood"); Gates 43a; Doors. lock, knock 51a, 128a, 312a, 153b, 217a, 317b; cf. 261b (pull down and repair), and 48a (Women like an Egyptian temple), 9b (Love's temple); 137b (trestles), cf. Prop 175a, 231a, 266a, 376a.

Agriculture: 327a ("As a mower sweeps off th' heads of bents, So did Lysander's sword" . . .); Sowing seed 142a, 201a; 142a (ploughing), 109b; 158b (gathering fruit); Glean 84a.

Mining: 61a, 96b, 233a.

Ships and Sailing: 293b (pinnace), 301b ("we have sailed the man-of-war out of sight, and here we must put into harbor"), cf. 333b; 309b (bore up to, and clapped aboard), 319a ("The shipwreck of her patience"), 223a (sailing), 328a (like seamen's offerings); 122b (to keep wits under hatches), 140b-141a (simile of the seaman and the pilot, 14 ll.), 157b (wind and sails), 158b (voyage), 212b (simile of the ship stopping at a far-removed shore for water, etc., 14 ll.), 233b:

> "Give me a spirit that on this life's rough sea
> Loves to have his sails fill'd with a lusty wind,
> Even till his sail-yards tremble, his masts crack,
> And his rapt ship run on her side so low
> That she drinks water, and her keel plows air."

Sports, Amusements, etc.: 48a (women "inconstant shuttle-cocks"), 203b (like children playing at quoits); Dice 198a ("any die she [Fortune] throws"), 317a, 365a; CARDS 4b (a face like the ace of hearts!), cf. 123b, 258a, 355a ("he can As good cards show for it as Cæsar did"), 311b ("the discarding of such a suitor"); ARCHERY 276b ("Still from the cushion"), 150b ("archers ever Have two strings to a bow"), 202a ("Kings are like archers, etc. 8 ll.), 221b ("to pull shafts home, with a good bow-arm, We thrust hard from us"), 224a ("like to shafts Grown crook'd with standing," etc.); HUNTING 276b, 317a ("I'll retrieve the game"), 326b ("men hunt hares to death for their sports, but the poor beasts die in earnest"), 335a ("I have you in the wind"), 336a (hare and hounds), 157b (hunting the hart), 224a (like the disguise of hunters and fowlers), 270a (like the hunted boar), 359b (simile of the hunted lion; cf. also 165b); HAWKING 114b ("muffled and mew'd up her beauties"), 155b ("like brave falcons," etc.), 194a (to check at), 208b (quarry), 227b ("We must have these lures when we hawk for friends"), 234a (check, and stoop), 252a (like a cloud that hawks at kingdoms), 270b ("leave my soul to me ... I feel her free: How she doth rouse, and like a falcon stretch Her silver wings, as threatening death with death; At whom I joyfully will cast her off").

Domestic Life: 176a ("Virtue imposeth more than any step-dame"), 154a (torture the sire of pleasure), 56a ("the fond world Like to a doting mother glozes over Her children's imperfections with fine terms"), 69a (credulity the younger brother of folly) 220a ("be twins Of either's fortune;" cf. 170a), 308a (the portion of younger brothers,— valor and good clothes), 378a (death and sleep brothers); 315b (changeling); 50a (riches a wife); 199b ("married to the public good"), 238b ("married to victory"); 189a (like children on hobby horses), 203b (like children playing at quoits); 223b (simile of the jealous husband), cf. 253a; 27a ("to make virtue an idle housewife"), 116a ("she's an ill housewife of her honor"), 317b ("these strait-laced ladies"): Dower 109a (of beauty), 49b; 96b ("Pains are like women's clamors, which the less They find men's patience stirr'd, the more they cease").

DRESS AND ORNAMENTS: 3b ("work it in the sampler of your heart"), 5b (to patch up love), 156b ("the outward patches of our frailty. Riches and honor"), cf. 237a: 94a ("he that cannot turn and wind a woman Like silk about his finger, is no man");[1] cf. 99a ("I'll be as apt to govern as this silk"), 317b (spinning); 191b ("the gay rainbow, girdle to a storm"); Veil 67b, 159b, 332a ("the happiest evening. That ever drew her veil before the sun "), 231a; Bombast, Fustian, etc., 79b (a fustian lord . . . a buckram face), 156a. 191b ("bombast polity"), 142a (naps); Cloak 150a, 176b, 181a; 170a ("my breasts, Last night your pillows"); Clothe 212b, 327b; Mask 164b, 184b, 292b, 304a, 309b; Jewels 154a, 155b, 181b. 220a, 221a, 308b; 13a (eyes like diamonds, lips like rubies, etc.), cf. 50b; cf. 321a (shrunk in the wetting); Untruss 233b; Ingrain 308a, cf. 265a; Wear threadbare 340a.

Colloquial and Familiar Images: Chapman's comedies, like Ben Jonson's, abound with images of this sort, in the invention of which he manifests considerable ingenuity. Many of those classified under other headings also are used for comic effect: e. g. 4b (a face like the ace of hearts), cf. 123b; 318a (to lick into shape), 27b (bird), cf. 45b, 62a (gudgeon), 64b (sauce), 71b ("looks much like an ape had swallowed pills"), 79b ("a parcel of unconstrued stuff"), 129b (goldfinches), 278a (like a dog in a furmety pot),[2] 284b, 290b, 304a (truant in the school of friendship), 321a (shrunk in the wetting), 300a (Quintiliano's comparison of a feast and a battle). See also: 87b (the apotheosis of brooms!), 292a (metaphor of gallows and hangman), cf. 195b; 287a ("she nails mine ears to the pillory with it"); 290b ("he

---

[1] Cf. Webster, 95b.
[2] Cf. Massinger, *The Maid of Honor*, V i 14.

drew such a kind of tooth from him indeed"); 291a ("make both their absences *shoeing-horns* to draw on the presence of Æmilia") so 136b, 137b; 304a (skill in baked meats), 311b ("let her pluck the goose"); 317b ("you had almost lifted his wit off the hinges"); 330a ("you women are a kind of spinners; if their legs be plucked off, yet still they'll wag them; so will you your tongues"); 4a ("a face thin like unto water gruel"); 12a (ridicule of various pet names, "cony," "lamb," etc.); 29a ("I have an eye and it were a polecat"); 31b ("quagmired in philosophy"); 32b ("like to cream-bowls, all their virtues swim in their set faces"), cf. 159b; cf. 40a ("Drown'd in the cream-bowls of my mistress' eyes"); 36b ("a proverb hit dead in the neck like a cony"); 53b (distasteful love "is like a smoky fire In a cold morning," etc.); 54b ("to lie at rack and manger"); 63b ("let us endure their [women's] bad qualities for their good; allow the prickle for the rose, the brack for the velvet, the paring for the cheese, and so forth"); 70a ("your wife that keeps the stable of your honor"); 89a (simile of the turnspit — "The most fit simile that ever was"); 100a ("like a Tantalus pig"); 128a ("my ears are double locked"); 132b ("my worth for the time kept its bed"), 135b ("he lay a caterwauling"); 298a ("thus shall his daughter's honor . . . be preserved with the finest sugar of invention"); 315a ("has given me a bone to tire on"); 324a ("I'll be as close as my lady's shoe to her foot"); 338b ("this wooden dagger," i. e. this poor fellow); 145b ("Were not the king here, he should strew the chamber like a rush"); 165a ("Love is a razor," etc.); 173a ("a fit pair of shears"—i. e. Guise and Monsieur; so 319a); 179a ("scarecrow-like"); 180b (haste stands on needles' points), 182a ("emptied even the dregs Of his worst thoughts of me"), 200b (man = a rag of the universe); 158a, 210a (to break the ice); 226b ("I fish'd for this"); 228a (like the weight that draws a door shut).

Coarse and Repulsive Images: Chapman's style is not delicate, and he has an undue proportion of repulsive imagery. The effect sometimes comes from a mere turn of phrase; sometimes from the deliberate coarseness of the comparison. Under other headings the frequent metaphorical use of such words as "entrails," "poison," "snakes," "toads," various diseases and medical terms, and the like, emphasizes this effect.

METAPHORS OF BIRTH, and the like (e. g. To be great with, bring forth, beget, etc.), are very frequent: 80b, 99b ("The ass is great with child of some ill news"), 109b, 114a, 129b, 133b, 134b, 135a, 277b, 319a; 144a, 150a, 151b, 162a (so 185a verbatim), 194b, 248a, 257a, 265a, 378b. Similarly 191a, 157b, 228a, 253a, 79b, cf. 223b ("his state-adultery"), 24a, 116a, 169b, 262a. BAWD, Strumpet etc. 114b, 200a, 233a, 260a, 267a, 271b. In general see also 41a, 182b ("Why have I raked thee Out of the dunghill;" cf. 161b and 266b); 109b ("see how thou hast ripp'd Thy better bosom"), cf. 217b, 233b; 370b ("The rotten-hearted world"), cf. 145a, 376a; 281a (a series of disgusting comparisons); 305b; 315a ("Drunkards, spew'd out of taverns"), cf. 222b ("an expuate humor"), 339b; 146b ("She feeds on outcast entrails like a kite," etc.); 155b ("kings soothed guts"); 372a ("the parings of a . . man").

The Body, its Parts, Functions and Attributes: cf. 229a. Heart 4a ("the heart of heaven, the glorious sun"), 225a, 233b; Bosom, breast, 22a ("bosom of the air"), 212a ("earth's sad bosom"), 215a; 155b ("the brain of truth"); Cheek 200b ("cheek by cheek"), so 216a; Eye 1a ("thy mind's eternal eye"), 244b ("a calm . . . In which the eyes of war may ever sleep"); 172a ("Tumbling her billows in each other's neck"); Gall 211a, 229a; Finger 154b, 183b ("a man Built with God's finger"), 246a, 249b, 365b, 367a; Stomach 365b; 18a (the womb of hell); Entrails 4a, 5b, 61a, 109b, 208a, 210a, 217b, 155b, 163b, 164b, 189b; 205b ("the joints and nerves sustaining nature"); Freckles 148b, 180b ("blood . . . freckling hands and face"); Sweat 142a ("his unsweating thrift"), 217b; and many others.

The Senses and Appetites: Food and Taste, 153b ("your conscience is too nice, And bites too hotly of the Puritan spice"), so 177a, 181a, 195b, 224a, 263a; 64b ("sauce That whets my appetite"); 68a ("such a mess of broth as this"); 8b (love a fig which destroys the taste); 48b ("the sweet taste of love," etc.; cf. 52b); 289a ("help to candy this jest"); 300a (comparison of a feast and a battle); 278b (cloy), 313a; 332b (banquet), cf. 141b; 141a (surfeit), so 166a, 221a, 251b; 182a, 109a, 216a, 286b, 291a; Feed 79b, 115b, 206b; Thirst 167b ("within the thirsty reach of your revenge"), 199b, 215b, 243a, 364b; Drink 96b; Smell 61a ("I smell how this gear will fall out"), 72b, 165b, 190b ("life's dear odors, a good mind and name"); Hearing 239b; Digest 80b ("digest your scoffs"), cf. 205a; Devour 181b, 217b; 220a (eating cares); To eat one's heart 161b, 176b, 217a.

Subjective Life, Religion, etc.: Heaven 48b, 49a, 64a ("this earthly paradise of wedlock"), 187b, 376a; Hell 10a ("a hellish conscience"), 16a, 115a ("this unworthy hell of passionate earth"), 240a, 163b (devil), 335a ("that devil jealousy, hath tossed him hither on his horns"); Angel 33b; 267b (kings are like the ancient gods), 187b (rule of kings like that of God; 20 ll.), 227b (kneeling to king = a superstition); 237a (the ancient Persians and their idols), 328a; 229a (canonize); 48a (Women like Egyptian temples, beautiful without, but with idols inside; 12 ll.); 171a ("as illiterate men say Latin prayers;" 12 ll.); Sect 105a; Rites 58b, 155a, 174b; Votary 137a, 333a, 194b ("a poor woman, votist of revenge"); Shrine 61a, 328a; 123a ("to make his eyes Do penance by their everlasting tears"); Sanctuary 156a (the law = a S.), 156b, 365b; Oracle 172b, 291b; Spirits, Ghosts, etc., 147b (like the wounds of spirits which close at once), 160b ("his advanced valor Is like a spirit raised without a circle, Endangering him that ignorantly raised him"), 163b, 244b, 269b, (cf. 166b); To haunt 146a, 287b; 161b ("like . . . naturals, That have strange gifts in nature, but no soul Diffused quite through"); 230b-231a (omens, spirits, etc.), 365a; Dream 140b ("Man is . . . a dream But of a shadow")[1], 194b, 205b (simile of dreams, 12 ll.), 243b; Astrology and Influence of Stars 233a, 217b, 338b; Alchemy 216a; Magic Glasses 100b, 102b, 141b, 167a, 244a, 370a.

Death, the Grave, etc.: 229a ("all his armies shook, Panted, and fainted, and were ever flying Like wandering pulses spersed through bodies dying"), 297b ("So parts the dying body from the soul As I depart from my Æmilia"), cf. 379; 271a ("like a man Long buried, is a man that long hath lived:

[1] Cf. Pindar, σκιᾶς ὄναρ; cf. Tennyson's Sonnet to W. H. Brookfield.

Touch him, he falls to ashes"); 163b ("like Death Mounted on earthquakes"); 13b ("Having the habit of cold death in me").
329a: "This [the tomb] is the inn where all Deucalion's race,
Sooner or later, must take up their lodging.
No privilege can free us from this prison."
165a (the grave of oblivion); Breathing sepulchres 189a, 270b, 370b; Buried quick[1] 203b, 260a, 270b, 114b, 122b.

War: Siege, Fort, etc., 9a (simile of the fortified town, 8 ll.), 65b, 96b, 216b, 232a, 253a, 261b, 275b, 154a, 156a, 185b (like soldiers capturing a besieged town : 10 ll.); Assault 26b; 9b ("Love that has built his temple on my brows, Out of his battlements into my heart"); 337a (Love "Runs blindfold through an army of misdoubts"); 68a ("Take truce with passion"); 165b (to fire a train) cf. 168a; Powder, Sulphur, etc., 147b, 194b, 208b, 317b, etc; 173b (mustering); 171b (like ships of war); 300a (a feast compared to a field of battle); 105b ("Now must I exercise my timorous lovers, Like fresh-arm'd soldiers, with some false alarms"); 126b (divided affections, like an army disarrayed); 151b ("receive My soul for hostage"); 271a (to die like the captain); 330a (to quit the field); 162b (wars), 164b ("Irish wars, More full of sound than hurt"); cf. also 278a; 284b (to trail a pike under love's colors); Bulwark 17b, 174b, 260a, cf. 376b. ARMS, WEAPONS, etc. 113b (Love's armory) 63a ("the buckler which Nature hath given all women, I mean her tongue"). 174b, 193b (the shield of reason), 203b; 314a ("such a disgrace as is a battered helmet on a soldier's head; it doubles his resolution"), 135a (armed); Cannon 166a (the thunder, Jove's Artillery), so 364a; 198b (cannon spits iron vomit), 170a ("the chain-shot of thy lust");[2] so 205a; 199a ("as a great shot from a town besieged;" 8 ll.); 162a ("like a murthering-piece, making lanes in armies"); 218b ("What force hath any cannon, not being charged, Or being not discharged?"); 226a ("And him he sets on, as he had been shot Out of a cannon"); 175b (a funeral volley of sighs!); Sheathe 259b; To shoot 164b ("You have shot home"), 158a,

---
[1] Cf. Sidney's Arcadia, Lond., 1893, p. 420 "quick buried in a grave of miseries."
[2] Cf. Webster, 91a.

236a, 66b; HERALDRY 215b ("to make my cannons The long-tongued heralds of my hidden drifts"); 291b (rampant and passant): cf. 71b, 30b.

The Stage and the Drama: Tragedy 164a, 167a, 209a, ("Clermont must author this just tragedy"), 360a; 22b ("like an old king in an old-fashion play"); 133b (Plaudite); 285b (satire on artificial disguises); 327a ("act the nuntius;" "a plain acting of an interlude;" "her cue"); To play a part 81a, 165b, 313b, 327a, 339a ("Nay, the Vice must snap his authority at all he meets, how shall't else be known what part he plays?"); 249b (like nuntius and chorus), 145b ("'Tis one of the best jigs that ever was acted").

Miscellaneous: Melt, dissolve 17b, 322a; Mirror, glass 51b, 112b, 309a, 144a, 147a, 162b, 218a, 255b ("for one they'll give us twenty faces, Like to the little specks on sides of glasses"), 167a; Model, pattern, mould, 255b, 323a, 293a, 338b, 316b; COLORS: Black 55a (black anger), 62b, 69a, 167a, 194b, 196b, 202b, 209a, 232b; White 209b (a white pretext); Green 66b (green experience), 1b (a green wound), 238a (so green a brain); 232b (so blue a plague); Poison, venom, etc., 38b, 41a ("the poison of thy tongue"), 232b, 309b, 330a, 165a, 166a ("the poison of a woman's hate"), 174a, 215b, 217a, 221b, 238a, 240a, 247a, 259b, 260b, 368a, 375b, 380b; Instrument, Engine, Organ 56a, 305b, 150a; Coin, counterfeit 79b, 135a, 230a, 323b, 330b; Painted 111b, 189b, 206b, 356b; Swim 234a, 253a; Drown 68b, 40a, 116a, 119b, 126a, 223b, 229a, 232a, 235a, 245a, 255b, 277b, 328a, 142a, 154a, 183b, 370b, 378a, 379a; Pierce 26b, 53a, 109a, ("That makes the news so loth to pierce mine ears"), 110a, 115a, 135a, 308a, 223a; To sound a depth 159b, 194b, 222a, 224a, 227a, 240a, 246b ("you were our golden plummet To sound this gulf of all engratitude"), 356b, 378b; Snare, springe, etc. 159b, 275a; entangle 130a, 281a; To tie 168a ("his dark words have tied my thoughts in knots"), 196b, 311a, 321b; Whet 73a, 133a, 138b, 308a, 323a; Edge 31a, 326b; Scourge, whip 16a ("do but tongue-whip him"), 285b ("be whipped naked with the tongues of scandal and slander"), 19a, 332b, 156a, 246b; To wind into 121a ("with such cunning wind into his heart"), 227b, 368b; To rip, rip up 109b, 147b; To cut the thread (of life, etc.), 67b, 127a, 319a, 320a, cf. 317b, 162a, 173a; Naked 69b ("Time will strip truth into her nakedness"), 293a, 182a, 194b, 244b; To smother 114b, 142a ("thy long-smothered spirit"), 189b, 217a, 223a, 254b; To weigh in balance, etc., 147b, 228b; To bear up a burden (like Atlas, etc.), 115a, 155a, 193b, 260b, cf. 190b; Puff up, blow up 183, 184a, 201a; Sift 254a; Clock 154b ("our false clock of life").

Recapitulation: Nature and human life in all their more prominent aspects are copiously represented in Chapman's imagery.[1]

In the tragedies a good proportion of the more striking images are drawn from nature, and occasionally show a poet's keenness of observation. See for example the brief picture of the lark (p. 47a); the humorous touch upon the habits of the jackdaw (65b); the description of the ill-effect of eastern winds in bringing caterpillars upon the fruits (162a); the very beautiful short simile of the calm before the tempest (164a); the short cloud simile (p. 245b):

His Nature Treatment

"We must ascend to our intention's top,
Like clouds, that be not seen till they be up."

And the simile (207b) of the eagle running on the ground to get a flying start,—Wordsworth has somewhere a few lines describing the same phenomenon of bird life; or finally the simile of the fall of the oak in Arden (p. 148a).

In the comedies, on the other hand, the chief feature is the number of colloquial and idiomatic images, recalling at times the manner of Jonson, the great master in this vein. The comedies, and the tragedies only in a less degree, are unfortunately marred by a large proportion of coarse and repulsive images. Perhaps the segregation of these images in the analysis gives them a worse effect than as they stand in the text, where however they are bad enough.

[1] "His learning was very great and very wide; but he is equally ready to associate his ideas with objects of nature and of daily life." (Ward, Eng. Dram. Lit., II 10).

In review we may note the prominence of the following sorts of images in Chapman: In his Nature imagery, especially in constantly recurring metaphors, clouds, mists, exhalations, vapors, fires, tempests, eclipses, earthquakes, chaos, thunder, meteors, and the like, occur very often and are highly characteristic of Chapman's grandiose manner. Favorites with him also are the images of fount, stream, and sea, of undereaten cliffs and up-piled mountains, of storm-beaten trees and frost-nipped flowers, of eagles, lions, tigers, wolves and serpents. It is the fierce and active, the awe-inspiring and Titanic aspects of Nature that interest him most and seem best to serve his purpose. Many comparisons are drawn from literature, the stage, music, law, and medicine, from the trades and occupations of men; few from agriculture or country life; several excellent ones from ships and sailors' lives, especially in storms; many from hunting and hawking, from domestic life, including dress and ornament, and from religion and the subjective world (dreams, mental operations, spirits, witchcraft, death, etc.). Very significant are the images from war and its surroundings, tending to corroborate the conjecture sometimes advanced that the many years of Chapman's early life, unaccounted for by his biographers, were some of them spent in seeing some sort of military service abroad. Equally striking, however, is the comparative paucity of such similes in Ben Jonson, who is known to have seen such service. Finally there are a number of miscellaneous metaphors highly characteristic of Chapman, but which do not alter essentially the impression of his habits of mind derived from the preceding analysis.

BEN JONSON
1573 ?–1637

Acted	Published	Revised		Vol.	Pages
1598	1600	1616	*Every Man in his Humor* -	I	1– 59
1599	1600		*Every Man out of his Humor* -	I	61–141
1600	1601		*Cynthia's Revels* - - -	I	142–204
1601	1602		*The Poetaster* - - -	I	206–269
1603	1605		*Sejanus, his Fall* - -	I	271–331
1605	1607		*Volpone, or The Fox* - -	I	332–399
1609	1609 ?		*Epicoene, or The Silent Woman*	I	402–462
1610	1612		*The Alchemist* - - -	II	1– 74
1611	1611		*Catiline, his Conspiracy* -	II	76–140
1614	1631		*Bartholomew Fair* - - -	II	141–209
1616	1631		*The Devil is an Ass* - -	II	211–272
1625	1631		*The Staple of News* - - -	II	274–333
1629–30	1631		*The New Inn, or the Light Heart*	II	335–384
1632	1640		*The Magnetic Lady, or Humors Reconciled* - - -	II	391–437
1633	1640		*A Tale of a Tub* - - -	II	439–483
——	1641		*The Sad Shepherd, or a Tale of Robin Hood* - - -	II	484–510
——	1640		*The Fall of Mortimer* - -	II	512–515

BEN JONSON.

Two things in Jonson's use of metaphor and simile stand out prominently, which have not as yet, so far as I know, received due notice. The first and less important is the abundant use made by him of the animal world, fish, reptiles, insects, birds, wild and domestic animals.[1] It is hardly a sympathetic use, since for the most part it is a mere trick of making animals, in every variety of collocation, stand as types of opprobrium, indeed often as mere bearers of billingsgate, as for example, in Corbaccio's little tirade in *Volpone*:

Two Noteworthy Features in Jonson's Imagery

> "I will not hear thee,
> Monster of men, swine, goat, wolf, parricide!
> Speak not, thou viper."[2]

It is a peculiarity which falls in well with Jonson's harsh and satirical vein.

The second trait of note in Jonson's use of trope is his extreme ingenuity and profusion in the invention of colloquial, comic and familiar images.[3] Jonson's comparisons in every vein are endlessly varied, but his colloquial imagery is unique in its extent and comic originality. It is the very salt of his dialogue, and it is evident that he relies on it to a great degree for his comic effects. It is used with characteristic conscientiousness and thoroughness as an aid in the exposition of character[4] and in the enforcement of humors.

[1] See infra, pp. 140–143.

[2] Act IV, Sc. ii, Vol. I, p. 382b.

[3] See infra, pp. 149–151. This reference, however, represents only a small part of the images of Jonson in this sort, which must be sought also under every other head.

[4] As a single example note the characteristic similes put into the mouth of Dame Ursula in *Bartholomew Fair*, coarse, reeking, and unctuous, like the unworthy dame herself! cf. II 167a ("I find by her similes she wanes apace").

Jonson goes about his work deliberately and with full consciousness. He abounds in classical and literary ornament. In spite of the great number of references given below, however, classical allusion is not so obtrusive a feature of his style as it is in Lyly, Greene, Peele, and even Marlowe.[1] He was interested in the theory of his art, and introduces many references to it into the

Self-consciousness in Simile Making

[1] Some of the more striking illustrations occur as follows: Various mention of the Gods I 195b, 357a, 423b, II 19b, 47a, 101b, 187b, 362a; Vulcan I 66b, 298a; Ganymede I 114b; Janus I 76a, 103a; Hercules I 103a, 428b ("I have sold my liberty to a distaff"), 227b ("He cleaves to me like Alcides' shirt"); II 121b; Atlas I 296a, II 121b; Typhœus I 327b; Colossus I 285a; The Hesperides I 86b, 122a, 7a ("play the Hesperian dragon with my fruit"), so I 28a, II 364b; The war of the Giants against the Gods I 310a, 327b, II 101b, 139b; Chimæra I 397b; Centaurs I 444b, II 371a; Medusa and the Gorgon's head I 138a, 418a, 433a, II 139b; The Furies I 364b, II 6b, 160a; The Fates and the thread of life I 90b ("the muffled Fates"), 322b ("I knew the Fates had on their distaff left More of our thread"), 388a ("Is his thread spun?"); Harpies I 259b, 342b, II 297a; Sirens I 93a, 379a, II 171b, 296b; Garden of Adonis I 122a, 201b; Hydra I 227b, II 122b; Ulysses I 349b; Agamemnon I 119a; Medea I 436b; Œdipus and the Sphinx I 295a; Ixion I 244b; Danae II 50a; I 245a ("can becalm All sea of Humor with the marble trident Of their strong spirits"); Cupid I 357b, II 508b ("the delicious Karol That kissed her like a Cupid"); Æsculapius envied by Jove II 49a; Morning in her car II 82b; II 107b ("men made of better clay, Than ever the old potter Titan knew"); II 311b ("They 'll sing like Memnon's statue and be vocal"); II 493b (blue as burning Scamander, etc.). Cf. also II 20b (Sir Epicure Mammon's classical curios!), 165a (Orpheus and Ceres), 343b, 494a ("when Cupid smiled, And Venus led the Graces out to dance"); Labyrinth I 216a, 368b (labyrinth of lust), 395a, II 31a; Wheel of Fortune I 328a; Occasion and her forelock II 380a, I 182a ("let us then take our time by the forehead"); Nectar I 306a, II 81a, 357b; etc.

Some of the more important literary allusions, parodies, quotations, etc., are as follows (I omit more general reference to Jonson's literary quarrels, which are supposed to occupy many passages in his plays:— see the *Poetaster*, etc., passim); I 13 (parody on Kyd); 98a (parody of Daniel), so II 200b, 310b ("Dumb rhetoric and silent eloquence! As the fine poet says"), cf. I 415b; I 88b (as choice figures . . . . as any be in the *Arcadia*,—or rather in Greene's works;" cf. 101b, II 187a); Shakspere I 126b (Justice Silence), 139b (Falstaff); Euphues I 137b; Tom Coryat II 179b; Marlowe's *Hero and Leander* II 199a; The Mirror for Magistrates II 208b; *Lusty Juventus* II 214b; Chaucer II 344a, 353a, 367a, 415. John Heywood II 476b; Skelton II 479b; Jonson (of himself) I 415b, II 417b; II 383a (to venture among savages "like a she-Mandeville"); II

body of his plays.¹ Two of his characters, indeed, are mere personifications of the humor of simile-making. These are Carlo Buffone, in *Every Man out of his Humor*,—"a public, scurrilous, and profane jester, that, more swift than Circe, with absurd similes will transform any person into deformity,"² - and the part is consistently carried out—and Miles Metaphor, in *A Tale of a Tub*. Similarly Jonson tends to insist upon his figures and to make much of them. It is part of his method in art, as has been frequently observed, to leave as little as possible to be inferred, and to develop everything to the height of explicitness. So it is

453a ("Bungy's dog"), cf. 474a; I 31b (Sir Bevis' horse); I 116b ("Sir Dagonet and his squire"), cf. 194a; I 169b (The Knight of the Sun); II 12a (Clim o' the Clough); etc.

Homer II 349a; Plutarch I 406a, II 242a; Lucian I 153a, 387b; II 266b ("gull me with your Æsop's fables"); Plautus I 107b; Tacitus I 444b ("As I hope to finish Tacitus"); Seneca I 448a ("What's six kicks to a man that reads Seneca?"); Ovid II 164b (and see the *Poetaster*, passim); I 410b ("such a Decameron of sport," etc); Don Quixote I 434b, II 61a; Paracelsus I 441b, II 28b; Faustus II 59b, 474a. See also references to various authors I 232f. (parody of "King Darius' doleful strain," *The Battle of Alcazar*, *The Spanish Tragedy* and *The Blind Beggar of Alexandria*), 365b (Plato, Petrarch, Tasso, Dante, "Montagnie," etc.), 415b ("so she may censure poets and authors and styles, and compare them; Daniel with Spenser, Jonson with t' other youth"), 416-417 (Sir John Daw's literary judgments on Plutarch, Seneca, Aristotle, Plato, Homer, Virgil, Horace, Persius, etc.), II 349a (Homer, Virgil, Arthur, Amadis de Gaul, Pantagruel, etc.), I 192b (burlesque of conventional conceits), so 194b; Various allusions: I 62 ("a very Jacob's staff of compliment"), 82b (St. George and the dragon), 117b (Judas, etc.), 174b ("Who answers the brazen head? it spoke to somebody"; cf. Shirley, *Hyde Park* II iv — Mermaid ed. p. 207), 189a ("He makes a face like a stabbed Lucrece"—see Gifford's note); 231a (Howleglas), 429b ("Amazonian impudence"), II 18b ("here's the rich Peru," Solomon's Ophir, etc.), 19a (the Indies); II 40b (Dover pier, etc.), 209a, 296b (London Bridge); etc.

Historical allusions among all the rest are not infrequent in Jonson, e. g. I 371a (Cleopatra's pearl), 435a (the taking of Ostend); II 50a (Nero's Poppæa), I 444a (The Guelphs and Ghibellines), II 208b (Columbus, Magellan, etc.), 301b (Pocahontas); and *Sejanus* and *Catiline*, passim.

¹ See the references to figures and tropes I 9b, 13b (conceit), 14a ("rusty proverb"), 224b; Simile I 48a, 62a, 71b, 79b, 116b, 190b, II 167a, 168b; Metaphor I 9b, 67a, 149a, II 353b, 355b, 439af.; Figures, tropes, etc., I 88b, 386b, 284b, II 221a, 352a, 439, 445b, 475a.

² I 62 ; cf. 71b, 79b, 116b.

with his treatment of character and plot, and so it is in his treatment of metaphor and simile. If a conceit occurs to him, odd or ludicrous in its way, he is not satisfied to suggest it in a brief metaphorical phrase and then to pass on, but the jest must be pursued and exploited to its utmost. Thus, instead of describing a fool's brain with Jacques,[1] as being "as dry as the remainder biscuit after a voyage," we are told that the foolish courtier in *Every Man out of his Humor*[2] among his other affectations,

> ... "now and then breaks a dry biscuit jest,
> Which, that it may be more easily chewed,
> He steeps in his own laughter."[3]

Still in fairness it should be said that Jonson has fewer forced conceits than Shakspere, and that his method in dialogue is on the whole lively and natural, as far as mere wit and comic effect are concerned.

Diction of his Tragedies

The imagery of the two tragedies is totally unlike that of the comedies. It is generally colorless and conventional, and apparently modeled on the style of the Latin orators and historians, much of it, indeed, being directly borrowed from these sources. These two pieces contain considerable hyperbole and personification of the conventional sort.[4] The diction at times remotely suggests that of Chapman's tragedies; not so remotely, however, but that we can conjecture the common models on which both are founded.[5]

---

[1] *As You Like It*, II, vii, 39.

[2] Induction, Vol. I, p. 68a.

[3] See further examples I 71a, 71b, 96b, 108b, 147a, 149a, 431a, etc.

[4] Personification I 310a, II 82b, 83b, 102b, 105a, 109b, 138a, 139, etc. Hyperbole I 280a, 287a, 295a, 308b, 314b, 322a, II 80b, 81a, 81b, 83b, 89a, 99a, 101a, 125b, 128b, 139a, etc.

[5] I find, for example, that the description of Catiline's last fight, in the concluding scene of the play of that name (Vol. II, p. 139), reminds me very strongly of Chapman. Compare, for example, the description of the duel in *Bussy D'Ambois*, Act II, Sc. i (p. 147b–148). Did Jonson have Chapman in mind in writing this scene? A somewhat similar method is exemplified in the description of the battle in Kyd's translation of Garnier's *Cornelia*, Act V (Hazlitt's Dodsley, V 242–245). How far may Chapman have been indebted to French models in his tragedies drawn from French subjects?

Outside of the tragedies, however, the general impression of Jonson's imagery is that of a strong, labored, and varied realism.

Of the Comedies Of poetical imagery there is little, though at times the heat of his satirical mood inspires him with serious and forcible images. And occasionally, also, Jonson's peculiar cumulative and analytical method results in effects equal to the most striking imagery. So Charles Lamb[1] has remarked of Sir Epicure Mammon's glowing daydreams in *The Alchemist:* "If there be no one image which rises to the height of the sublime, yet the confluence and assemblage of them all produces an effect equal to the grandest poetry." Of course the songs and the masques are not considered in these criticisms. In these, as Mézières[2] has observed, a high poetic quality is maintained, and "les images et les métaphores s'y succèdent avec une abondance naturelle." Jonson's aim in comedy is presented with sufficient distinctness in more than one passage in his pro-

Jonson's Restricted Theories of his Art
logues, epilogues, and by-plays or critical passages within the scene. A portion of the passage in *The Magnetic Lady*,[3] with its suggestions at a distance of *Hamlet*,[4] exhibits the realistic aim he held before himself. "If I see a thing vively presented on the stage, that the glass of custom, which is comedy, is so held up to me by the poet, as I can therein view the daily examples of men's lives, and images of truth in their manners, so drawn, for my delight or profit, as I may either way use them" . . . And Jonson is indeed constantly preoccupied with the examples of men's daily lives and the images of truth in their manners. His range of allusion nevertheless is wider than that of any other dramatist included in our study, but his allusions are characteristically those of the learned man[5] and the encyclopædic observer rather than those of the idealist and the poet. His interest, strictly, is in human life and

[1] Specimens, 283.

[2] Pred. et Cont. de Shaks., p. 363.

[3] Act II. Sc. ii (Vol. II, p. 410a).

[4] Act III, sc. ii.

[5] "The literature of the Renaissance, Erasmus and Rabelais, the literature of the Middle Ages, books on sports and hunting, books on alchemy, books on

manners. He refuses to adopt in comedy the grandiloquent or the romantic manner. His imagery correspondingly is subdued and colloquial in matter and manner. "We do not meet on our way," says Taine,[1] "extraordinary, sudden, brilliant images, which might dazzle or delay us; we travel on enlightened by moderate and sustained metaphors." Jonson's comedies are a mine of idiomatic English. He catches and records the current phrases and metaphors of common life. Almost nothing of the conventionally poetic invalidates his realistic diction. He is full of the homely sententiousness of daily life.[2] Proverbs and proverbial phrases are constantly employed.[3] Historical similes and examples, familiar and local allusions abound.[4] But above all Jonson relies upon ludicrous and colloquial similitudes for comic and realistic effect.

Jonson's pages are not so thickly sown with metaphor as are Chapman's and those of many others. His language is too realistic for that. There are almost no prolonged similes[5] and few

natural history, books on Rosicrucian mysticism, furnish unexpected illustrations of the commonest, most vulgar incidents." (J. A. Symonds, Ben Jonson, p. 51.)

"Son érudition lui présente sans cesse des images, des expressions, et des idées empruntées à l'antiquité." (Mézierès, Pred. et Cont. de Shaks., p. 186.)

[1] Eng. Lit., Bk. II, ch. iii. (p. 271).

[2] Sententious figures of a different, a Latin type, abound in the tragedies: e. g. I 289a, 290a, 293b, 304b, 307a, 314b, 326a, II 122a.

[3] For example, I 16b (to have the wrong sow by the ear), 16b (claps his dish at the wrong man's door), 18a ("As he brews so shall he drink"), 41a ("Whose cow has calved?"), 49a (Fair hides may have foul hearts), 347a ("Pour oil into their ears"), 390a ("The fox fares ever best when he is curst." cf. Greene, 173b), 447b (Strike while the iron is hot); II 69a ("I'll pluck his bird as bare as I can"), 108a (Still waters run deepest), 150a ("You have a hot coal in your mouth now, you cannot hold"), 153b ("He has a head full of bees"), 180b (sits the wind in that quarter), 328a (a tub without a bottom), 328b (" a rat behind the hangings "—for eaves-dropping), 403a (Call a spade a spade), 407a (a bird in the hand), 473b (for the black ox to tread on one's foot). And see *A Tale of a Tub*, passim, where the rustic dialogue is liberally sprinkled with proverbs. See also I 303b (the fable of the Fox and the Raven). And see further I 59a, 350a, 439b, II 117b, 151a, 153a, 176b, 180a, 180b, 218a, 251a, 344b, 345 with note, 376a, 406b, 425b, 430b, 436a, 443a, 445a, 448a, 453b, 454a, 465b, etc.

[4] See infra, pp. 203-204.

[5] See however I 246b, 247a, II 88b.

prolonged metaphorical passages.[1] Short similes, however, are very frequently employed.

In the effort for wit and comic effect it was inevitable that many of Jonson's colloquialisms should partake of the nature of conceits. But he does not search out conceits and load his style with them, as did Lyly and later the poets of the "metaphysical" school. Indeed Jonson like Shakspere[2] has burlesqued the conceited style of the earlier school of poetry. In the fantastic contest of courtship in *Cynthia's Revels*[3] Mercury is made to utter a long rhapsody in the Euphuistic vein on woman's beauty: "You are the lively image of Venus throughout; all the graces smile in your cheeks; . . . you have a tongue steeped in honey, and a breath like a panther; your breasts and forehead are whiter than goat's milk or May blossoms,"—and more to the same effect. Jonson's impulse to satire and parody gets the better of him again in a similar passage with burlesque touches[4] immediately preceding the beautiful lyric "Do but look on her eyes, they do light All that love's world compriseth!" Personification and hyperbole also are not wanting in the comedies as well as in the tragedies, though they are used with little serious import.[5] In fact, Jon-

Conceits in Jonson

---

[1] See I 28a, 122a, 132a, 279b, 319b, II 99a, etc.

[2] In his 130th Sonnet.

[3] Act V Sc. ii (vol. I p. 192b).

[4] In *The Devil is an Ass* Act II Sc. ii (II 237b). See further also I 83b, 211a:

"Then shall Lucretius' lofty numbers die,
When earth and seas in fire and flame shall *fry*."

an unhappy metaphor which becomes a favorite with the poets of the next age! Add II 317b (a passage of burlesque like the two referred to in the text above), 353b, 377a, 379b (burlesque of the conventional poetical hyperbole), 501b ("I weep and *boil* away myself in tears"); and see the attempts of Miles Metaphor in *A Tale of a Tub*, passim. Jonson's similes, moreover, occasionally fall into ineptitudes of the worst sort. See, for example, I 140a (Elizabeth, the Thames, and the London sewers), 195a (the hills of tyranny, cast on virtue, etc.), and II 96b (kisses close as cockles—the same simile occurs in *The Masque of Hymen*, III 28b, where Mr. Swinburne has singled it out for ridicule. Cf. his "Study of Ben Jonson" p. 47). Jonson too is an inveterate punster.

[5] For examples of Personifications (in addition to those in the tragedies cited in note 4, p. 130, above) see I 90b, 140b, 244b, 249a, 253a, 335 (Poetry),

son's spirit of burlesque seizes upon these two respectable and time-honored figures also and makes them serve the ends of comedy. Pug, the unhappy devil, in shackles and waiting impatiently for the termination of his period of earthly torment, exclaims: "I think Time be drunk and sleeps, He is so still and moves not!"[1] I cannot but think also, in spite of the romantic tone of the speech, that there is an intention of burlesque concealed under the hyperbole of Lady Frampul's confession of love in *The New Inn*:[2]

"Thou dost not know my sufferings, what I feel:
My fires and fears are met; I burn and freeze,
My liver's one great coal, my heart shrunk up,
With all the fibres, and the mass of blood
Within me is a standing lake of fire,
Curled with the cold wind of my gelid sighs,
That drive a drift of sleet through all my body,
And shoot a February through my veins."

This is either the worst of Jonson's dotages, or the very midsummer madness of feminine wits and the best of burlesque!

But Jonson could not escape the influence of his age in spite of the most resolute theories, and there are touches in his work which bear the characteristic Elizabethan accent. Condensed and rapid images weighty with meaning and poetry sometimes occur. Lovell in *The New Inn*[3] says:

Pregnant Metaphors

"As it is not the mere punishment,
But cause that makes a martyr,[4] so it is not
Fighting or dying, but the manner of it,
Renders a man himself."

Volpone, in *The Fox*,[5] exclaims (of the disappointed would-be heirs): "Now their hopes Are *at the gasp*." Arruntius in *Sejanus*[6] comments on a specious promise of Tiberius:

II 279a, 349a (The Hours), 508a. Examples [of Hyperbole I 65a, 72a, 78b, 93a, 216a, 237a, 248b, 393b, II 58b, 349b, 376b, 379b, etc.
[1] II 267b, similarly 376b; cf. II 155a.
[2] Act V Sc. i (II 379b).
[3] Act IV Sc. iii (II 374b).
[4] This identical sentiment has also been attributed to Napoleon.
[5] Act V Sc. i (I 388b).
[6] Act III Sc. i (I 295b).

"If this were true now! but *the space, the space,
Between the breast and lips* — Tiberius' heart
Lies a thought farther than another man's."[1]

Equally subtle is Catiline's sinister threat,[2] on hearing of the decrees against him, "I will not burn Without my funeral pile." See also I 227b ("Never was man *So left under the axe*"), 299a ("His thoughts *look through* his words"), I 303b ("a quiet and retired life, *Larded* with ease and pleasure"). Jonson is fond of condensing a metaphor into a verb, as in the last two examples. See also I 201b (Niobe "was *trophæed* into stone"), 250a (poesy *rammed with* life), 309a (*bogged* in lust), 315b ("croaking ravens *Flagged* up and down"). There

His Epithets are also many striking epithets in Jonson: I 65a (sail-stretched wings), 70b (grey-headed ceremonies), 107b ("this green and soggy multitude"), 140b (turtle-footed Peace), 116b ("your stabbing similes"), 138b (wrinkled fortunes) 149a ("your skipping tongue"; cf. 157a "your capering humor"), 156b (muffled thought), 211a (frost-fearing myrtle), 239a (thorny-toothed), 249b ("pathless moorish minds"), 338a ("the furrow-faced sea"), II 107a (a sulphurous spirit), 125a ("your cobweb bosoms"), 288b ("stall-fed doctors") 414b (silken phrases).

Jonson was town-bred and by choice and temperament a realist. Nevertheless Nature was not a sealed book to him. There are

Nature in Jonson touches in the *Sad Shepherd* and elsewhere[3] which show the germs of a delicate feeling for some of her forms; and his observation of nature so far as

it went was as keen as his observation of man. Significant illustrations from nature are not infrequently used:

I 291b: "The way to put
A prince in blood, is to present the shapes
Of dangers greater than they are, *like late
Or early shadows.*"

[1] Cf. Chapman, 158b.
[2] Act IV Sc. iv. (II 122a).
[3] E. g. I 248a ("the loving air, That closed her body in silken arms"); II 317b ("A hair Large as the morning's, and her breath as sweet As meadows after rain, and but new mown!"); etc.

I 362a "*Turn short as doth a swallow.*"
II 300a "I shook for fear, and yet I danced for joy;
I had *such motions as the sunbeams make*
Against a wall or playing on a water."[1]

II 489a: "like the soft west wind she shot along,"—and see the whole of the opening speech of Æglamour in the *Sad Shepherd*. Of course in his lyrics there are many such touches.[2] But in order to determine the extent to which nature enters into Jonson's habitual imagery, an inspection should be made of the following analysis.

RANGE AND SOURCES OF IMAGERY.

Mr. Swinburne[3] has remarked upon "the vast range of Ben Jonson's interest and observation." In so far as embodied in metaphor and simile the most striking results of that interest and observation are displayed and classified in the following lists:

NATURE. Aspect of the Sky, The Elements, etc.: THE SUN: I 308a (fires of liberty like the sun), I 140a ("she hath chased all black thoughts from my bosom, Like as the sun doth darkness from the world). II 317b ("Yourself who drink my blood up with your beams, As doth the sun the sea!"); Sunrise I 343b (the rising sun=the new heir), I 328a ("He that this morn rose proudly as the sun," etc.), cf. II 82b, II 81a ("Appear and break like day, my beauty, to this circle"), Sunset I 370b ("Suns that set may rise again. But if once we lose this light, 'Tis with us perpetual night,"—from Catullus), II 84a ("Cinna and Sylla are set and gone; and we must turn our eyes On him that is, and shines"); Sunshine, etc., I 24a ("the sunshine of reputation"), II 300a ("I had such motions as the sunbeams make Against a wall, or playing on a water").

LIGHT: II 3 (shines greater by contrast of a thick darkness), I 251a (shine). Shade, Shadow II 84a, 300b, 464b.

[1] This simile, it is true, is borrowed from Virgil (Æneid VIII 25), but is none the less apt for the borrowing.

[2] See especially the song "Have you seen but a bright lily grow," in *The Devil is an Ass*, Act II Sc. ii (II 238a).

[3] A Study of Ben Jonson, p. 77.

STARS: I 88b ("our court-star there, that planet of wit"); cf. I 237a, 349a, 249b ("Bearing the nature and similitude Of a right heavenly body"), I 362a ("Your fine elegant rascal, that can ... Shoot through the air as nimbly as a star"), II 238a ("Do but look on her hair, it is bright As love's star when it riseth!"), II 376a ("A wise man never goes the people's way; But as the planets still move contrary To the world's motion, so doth he to opinion"),[1] II 293a ("Move orderly In our own orbs"), I 371b ("When she came in like star-light"); Comet, meteor, etc.; I 110a, 247b ("for me, a falling star"), II 371b ("His rapier was a meteor, and he waved it Over them like a comet");[2]

MOON: I 24b ("that thought is like the moon in her last quarter, 'twill change shortly"), I 286a ("such a spirit as yours Was ... created ... to shine Bright as the moon among the lesser lights").

FIRE: I 4b ("while you affect To make a blaze of gentry to the world, A little puff of scorn extinguish it"), I 25b (sparks of wit), 92a ("I am like ... fire, that burns much wood, yet still one flame"), 286a (love, "like the fire which more It mounts it trembles"), II 50a (beauty to set the eyes afire), 349b (the fires of love, 8 ll.; cf. I 357b); I 139a (the flame of humor), 277b (the fire of a great spirit), 310a ("the pitchy blazes of impiety," etc.), 337b (gold that shows "like a flame by night"), 157a (phrases that "sparkle like salt in fire"), 168a (to throw away money like burning coals), 308a (like fools who puff at a dying coal), II 97a ("Cruel, A lady is a fire; gentle, a light"); I 101b (affections= false fires), 72a ("Mine eyeballs, like two globes of wild-fire"); Furnace I 357b (Cupid's flame rages "As in a furnace an ambitious fire, Whose vent is stopt"), II 332b (an enraged man like a furnace); Taper I 150b ("thy youth's dear sweets here spent untasted, Like a fair taper, with his own flame wasted"), II 183b (like a candle); Sulphur, fumes, etc., II 107a ("She has a sulphurous spirit, and will take Light at a spark"), cf. 115a.

HEAT AND COLD: I 17b (heat of humor); 304a (fury boils, heat with ambition), cf. 310a; Ice II 83a ("We are spirit-bound

[1] Cf. Shirley, *The Traitor* I ii (Mermaid Series p. 97).
[2] Cf. Chapman 147b: "D'Ambois' sword ... Shot like a pointed comet."

In ribs of ice "), 493b ("stand curled up like images of ice"), II 88b ("Sealed up and silent, as when rigid frosts Have bound up brooks and rivers," etc.), I 72a

"Made my cold passion stand upon my face
Like drops of dew on a stiff cake of ice ".

CLOUDS : I 19b ("this black cloud," i. e., of suspicion), so 135b; II 159a ("this the cloud that hides me," i. e., his disguise), cf. 230a; II 357b (clouded brows); II 509b; I 249a (Kings "Sit in their height, like clouds before the sun "); Mist, Vapor, etc.; I 19b; I 152b ("the least steam or fume of a reason "), 386b ("I was a little in a mist "), cf. II 127b, 108b ("Our hate is spent, and fumed away in vapor"). Humor I 17b, 67a, etc.

STORMS : II 333b ("the weather of your looks may change"); I 120b (" The just storm of a wretched life "), II 195b ("cloud-like, I will break out in rain and hail, lightning and thunder, upon the head of enormity"); Tempest I 364b; Shower I 289a (shower of tears), II 349a (to shower bounties); Thunder I 287a ("the thunder of Sejanus "), 289a ("thunder speaks not till it hit. Be not secure "), 418a, cf. II 6b (to thunder at), 103b, 121a (" He has strove to emulate this morning's thunder, With his prodigious rhetoric"); LIGHTNING II 84b (" You are too full of lightning, noble Caius "), 108b, 371b; Hail I 366b (a hail of words); WINDS I 311b (Sejanus, like a whirlwind), 326a, II 109b, 180b, 359a (as the winds shift, so a decree may be altered), I 314b ("Winds lose their strength, when they do empty fly, Unmet of woods or buildings"), II 489a ; ECHO I 150b, 458a.

Aspects of Water, The Sea, etc. SEA : I 66a ("conscience Is vaster than the ocean "), 431a (a sea and flood of noise); Tide I 110a (ebb and flow of humor), cf. II 68a, 262b ("such tides of business"), 282a (" The powers of one and twenty, like a tide, Flow in upon me "); II 317b ("my princess draws me with her looks, And hales me in, as eddies draw in boats," etc.); I 183a (good men, like the sea, always salt), 295b (" all my streams of grief are lost, No less than are land waters in the sea, Or showers in rivers"); POOL, SINK, etc. I 92a, II 119a, etc. SPRING I 143 (the Court the spring which waters England), II 351a ("a fountain of sport "); RIVER, STREAM I 92a (" I am like a pure

and sprightly river, That moves forever, and yet still the same "),
115b ("the stream of her humor "), 248b (the streams of poesy),
I 160b (an overflowing face), 440a (youth like rivers that cannot
be called back); Torrent II 102a ("Ambition, like a torrent, ne'er
looks back "), I 386a, II 128b; Flood I 31a (the flood of passion),
85a, 124a ("you shall see the very torrent of his envy break forth
like a land-flood "), 310b, 352a, II 88b (" break Upon them like
a deluge "), 96a.

Aspects of the Earth: Cf. II 237b. Precipice (of sin, etc.)
I 22b, II 259b (" My fortunes standing in this precipice "), 346b;
Mountains I 108b (to stand " before their Maker, like impudent
mountains "), II 113b ("the mountain of our faults"); Earth-
quake I 431a, II 326a; Bog, quagmire I 28a (" give you oppor-
tunity, no quicksand Devours or swallows swifter "), 108b, 309a
(bogged in lust), II 166a; Dirt, clod, dust, etc.; I 75b (" to be
enamoured on this dusty turf, This clod!"), 135b (dust of sus-
picion), 162a (dust and whirlwind), so 311b, II 370b ("thou
glorious dirt!"); Path, highway, etc., I 148a, 182a, 305b, 398a,
II 37b, 98a (to cut a way), 401b.

Inorganic Nature: METALS I 23b ("the metal of your minds
Is eaten with the rust of idleness"), 183b, II 243b ("I am not
So utterly of an ore un-to-be-melted "), 451b; I 28a (leaden
sleep), 248b (leaden souls), I 157a ("Act freely, carelessly, and
capriciously, as if our veins ran with quicksilver"), II 328a
(" Forehead of steel and mouth of brass!"); Glass I 188b; I 28a
(as a jet draws straws); Caract' I 28a, II 223a, 395b, 401b; Salt
I 82a, cf. 157a, 183a, 349b, 380a, II 149b, 374b, 446a.

Time, Seasons, etc.: I 162a ("Today you shall have her look
as clear and fresh as the morning, and tomorrow as melancholic
as midnight "), 290a (the night of ambition), 321a ("About the
noon of night ");[2] I 394a (" it is summer with you now ;' Your
winter will come on "), I 95a (" look not like winter thus "), 307b
(" the winter of their fate "); I 393a (autumn), 406b (" her autum-
nal face "); II 224a (" ere your spring be gone, enjoy it "), 489a
("the world may find the Spring by following her "); I 414b ("as

[1] See Gifford's note.
[2] Cf. Whalley's note.

proud as May and humorous as April"), II 441b ("he'll weep you like all April").[1]

The Vegetable World: II 120b (the weed of evil, etc.), cf. 66b, 208b; TREES I 124a (like the chopping-down of a full-grown tree), 307a ("a fortune sent to exercise Your virtue, as the wind doth try strong trees, Who by vexation grow more sound and firm"); 319b (Germanicus, "the lofty cedar of the world," Drusus, "that upright elm," etc. 12 ll.), 383a ("that piece of cedar, That fine well-timbered gallant"), II 361a ("his tall And growing gravity, so cedar-like), 333b; I 326a (leaves); Seeds I 277b, II 79b (the seeds of treason), 128a, 272b, 330b; I 305a ("greatness hath his cankers. Worms and moths Breed out of too much humor"); FLOWERS II 507b (she is the "crown and garland of the wood"), I 201b (roses and thorns, beauty and its guardians), cf. 372a; II 224a ("Flowers, Though fair, are oft but of one morning"), cf. 489a, II 238a (white as a lily), 505a ("His lip is softer, sweeter than the rose"); Blossom and fruit I 367a (of hope); FRUIT I 349b ("All her looks are sweet As the first grapes or cherries"), 28a ("To taste the fruit of beauty's golden tree"), 252a, 277b, 371a, II 10a ("A fine young quodling," cf. Gifford's note), II 149b (the garden and fruits of beauty), cf. 230b; II 327a ("Hang him, an austere grape," etc.); I 290b ("Let him grow awhile, His fate is not yet ripe"), 349a; I 407a (a well-dressed woman is "like a delicate garden"), II 416b ("France, that garden of humanity, The very seed-plot of all courtesies"); I 117a ("O, that such muddy flags . . . should achieve The name of manhood"); Mushroom I 75b, 419b, II 417a, etc.

The Animal World is used in Jonson largely to supply opprobrious epithets. Beasts I 24b, 283a ("Of all wild beasts preserve me from a tyrant"), I 398b ("Mischiefs feed Like beasts till they be fat, and then they bleed"), II 114a, 128b, 174b; Animal I 171b, II 376a; Vermin II 152b, 279b, 426b; To hatch II 27a ("hatch gold in a furnace . . . As they do eggs in Egypt!"), 280b, 459a. FISH: Sponge I 68a (spongy souls), 324a ("how the sponges open and take in, And shut again!"); I 209b ("Howe'er that common spawn of ignorance, Our fry of writers, may

[1] Cf. *Ant. and Cleop.*, III ii 43 "The April's in her eyes."

beslime his fame"), II 309a ("as dumb as a fish"); Shark I 64, 254b, 443a, II 9b; Whale I 77b ("like a boisterous whale swallowing the poor, Still swim in wealth and pleasure"), II 167a ("they'll kill the poor whale and make oil of her!"); Porpoise I 326b (cf. Gifford's note), 443a; Flounder I 103a; Pike II 332a; Carp I 188b; Smelt I 161a; Rochet I 369a; I 164a ("they are all ... no better than a few trouts cast ashore, or a dish of eels in a sand-bag").

REPTILES: Crocodile I 133b, 292b, 461a; Serpent I 76b, 78b, 289b (rear Their forces, like seen snakes, that else would lie Rolled in their circles, close"), II 122b; Viper I 106b, 300a, II 298b, 422b; I 361b ("I could skip Out of my skin now, like a subtle snake"), II 105a ("their snaky ways," etc.); II 83a (tortoise speed); Cameleon I 383b, II 304a. Snail I 275a ("We have ... No soft and glutinous bodies that can stick, Like snails on painted walls").

INSECTS: I 462a ("Take heed of such insectæ hereafter"); Flies I 172b ("all the gallants came about you like flies"), 315b, 394a, 414b, II 83a, 125b, 156a, 227b ("blow them off again, Like so many dead flies"), II 342a, 431a, II 238a ("At this window She shall no more be buzzed at"), I 226b ("This brize has pricked my patience") Flyblown II 275b, 353a; Bees I 350a, II 41a ("till he be tame As ... bees are with a besom"), 505a; Drone II 348b; Swarm I 35b, II 320a; Wasps II 448b; Hornets I 265b, 266b; Sting II 264a; Butterflies I 154a; Grasshoppers I 266b ("like so many screaming grasshoppers Held by the wings, fill every ear with noise ;"—so 364b, where see Gifford's note; also II 406b), II 160b ("your grasshopper's thighs"), 332a ("he will live like a grasshopper On dew"); Locust I 369b; Beetle II 6b (scarab), I 246a ("They are the moths and scarabs of a state"); I 49b, 183a (dor); Moth I 246a, 461b, II 324a; Gnats I 328a ("They that ... like gnats, played in his beams"); Ants I 45b ("they will be doing with the pismire, raising a hill a man may spurn abroad with his foot at pleasure"), 145a (Emmet); Earwig I 458b; Caterpillar I 106b; Worm II 233a, II 329a ("your worming brain"); Silkworm II 148b ("to spin out these fine things still, and, like a silkworm, out of myself"), so 281b; Cobweb I 168b, 251a, 294a, II 6b, 125b.

BIRDS (cf. also Hawking p. 148 infra): I 149a ("your hooked talons"), 364a (bird-eyed), II 72a ("*Mammon*. The whole nest are fled! *Lovewit*. What sort of birds were they?" etc.), 238b, 226a (bird and cage; so 379b), 332b ("the whole covey is scattered;" cf. 409b); Birds of Prey I 342a, II 295b; Wildfowl II 67a; Eagle I 247a ("Virtue, whose brave eagle's wings, With every stroke blow stars in burning heaven"), cf. II 19b; Vulture I 237b ("to be tired on by yond vulture"), 259b, 308a II 329a; Kestrel II 293a; Hawk II 332b, 279b ("like a tame hernsew"), 164b (goshawk); Rook I 67a, 72a, 425b; Jackdaw I 190b; Raven I 283a; Crow I 428b, II 95a, 403b; Buzzard II 355a; Owl I 428b, II 100b, 342b; Screech owl II 122a, 364b; Peacock II 337 (cock-brained); Dove I 428b, II 73b, 379b, 495a; Lapwing I 246a, 325a, II 309a; Partridge I 382b; II 185a ("Was there ever green plover so pulled!"); II 52a ("a delicate dabchick"); Cuckoo I 461b; Sparrow II 333a; Wren I 145b; Goldfinch I 180a; Swallow I 247a ("that virtue . . . . Should, like a swallow, preying towards storms, Fly close to earth, and with an eager plume, Pursue those objects which none else can see," etc.), 362a ("Turn short as doth a swallow").

WILD ANIMALS : II 514b (To affect meekness among enemies is "As if with lions, Bears, tigers, wolves, and all those beasts of prey, He would affect to be a sheep!"); Lion I 304b, II 139b ("ran . . . Into our battle, like a Libyan lion Upon his hunters"), II 53b; Bear II 332a ("he will live like . . . a bear, with licking his own claws"); Hyena I 383b; Wolf I 246a, 290a (Sir, wolves do change their hair, but not their hearts"), 298a, 299b ("Excellent wolf! Now he is full, he howls"), 310b, 387a, 398a; Fox I 23b, 325b II 395b ("your fox [i. e. your sword] there, Unkennelled with a choleric, ghastly aspect, . . . Would run their fears to any hole of shelter"); Buffalo I 380b; Rhinoceros I 152a; Camel I 24b, 67b ('They, "like galled camels, kick at every touch"), 285a; Monkey, Ape, etc. I 40b, 209b, 363b, II 240b; Marmoset I 168a, 171b; Baboon I 189a, 443b, II 9b; Polecat II 26a, 165b, (cf. 446b); Mammet II 73b; Stote II 446b; Squirrel I 80a ("they'll leap from one thing to another like a squirrel"); Mole I 195a, 419b; Bat II 363b; Mouse II

83a (dormice), 348b, 342b (reremice), 363b; Rat II 291a, 328b, I 283a (courtiers=palace-rats; so II 324a); Cormorant I 124b.

DOMESTIC ANIMALS: Cat I 318b, II 122b, 329b ("She is cat-lived and squirrel-limbed"); Goat I 358b ("goatish eyes"); Swine I 114b, II 166a (sow); Sheep I 59a, II 155a (cosset), 164b (lamb), 442b (bellwether), 486 (wool from English flocks); Cattle I 164a ("all the ladies and gallants lie languishing upon the rushes, like so many pounded cattle in the midst of harvest"), I 246a (bellow), 421a (heifer), 453b (ox), II 380a, 318a ("He's chewing his muses' cud"), II 453a (calf); Cream II 369b; Milk I 342b, 432a, II 53b, 327b; Yoke II 85b, 113b; Ass I 225a, 253b, II 180a, 224b, 327a; Mule I 394a, II 295b; Horses and horsemanship (see in general the part of Knockem in *Barth. Fair*): I 440a ("What a neighing hobby-horse is this!") 32b ("have translated begging out of the old hackney-pace to a fine easy amble"), II 262b (gallop), I 65a ("check his spirit, or rein his tongue"), 302a (reins), 335 (snaffle); I 91b (husbands to treat their wives like their horses), 112a ("his head hangs so heavily over a woman's manger"), 148b ("as tender as the foot of a foundered nag"), 171b (a swaggering coach-horse, etc.), 215a ("jaded wits that run a broken pace for common hire," etc.), Stallion I 436b, II 167b, II 206b ("hinnying sophistry"), 169b ("a dull malt-horse"), 235b (harnessed), 469b (weary as a mill-horse); Spur II 9b; Dogs I 90b ("that dog called chance"), II 449a, I 72a (the belly barks), 167a ("Traduce by custom as most dogs do bark"), 258b ("buffoon barking wits"), II 8b ("Leave off your barking"), II 321a (kennel); Mongrel, cur, etc. I 76a, 76b, 134a, 189b, 312a, II 5b; Beagles I 128a, II 430a; I 7b ("Like to the eager but the generous greyhound, Who ne'er so little from his game withheld, Turns head and leaps at his holder's throat"), I 62a (Carlo Buffone is "a good feast-hound, or banquet-beagle, that will scent you out a supper some three miles off"), 115a ("a good bloodhound, a close-mouthed dog, he follows the scent well"), 300a ("Two of Sejanus' bloodhounds, whom he breeds With human flesh, to bay at citizens"); Ban-dogs I 86a, 228b; Mastiffs I 329a ("like so many mastiffs, biting stones"), II 9a.

Fabulous Natural History: Adamant I 93a, II 49b; Aconite I 304a; I 276a ("true as turquoise in the dear lord's ring, Look well or ill with him"); Phœnix II 48b ("To burn in this sweet flame [of love]; The phœnix never knew a nobler death"), so 349b; Salamander I 110a; Basilisk I 209a, 394a; Cockatrice I 76a, II 346b; I 244a ("a panther whose unnatural eyes Will strike thee dead"), 372a (panther's breath; so I 192b); Crocodile's tears I 369b, II 377a; II 19b ("renew him, like an eagle"); Unicorn's horn I 133a (cf. 372a); II 107a ("A serpent, ere he comes to be a dragon, Does eat a bat;" cf. Gifford's note), 212 ("must all run into one, Like the young adders, at the old one's mouth!") I 227b ("I am seized on here By a land remora; I cannot stir"), so II 403b.

MAN AND HUMAN LIFE: I 357a (Life a pilgrimage).

The Arts and Learning: I 372b ("to score up sums of pleasure"); II 257a ("hell is A grammar-school to this"), Grammar and logic II 51b, 52a ("the grammar and logic And rhetoric of quarrelling"), 375a ("Most manly uttered all! As if Achilles had the chair in valor, And Hercules were but a lecturer"), 396a (grammarians' souls are nought but a syntaxis of words); I 199a ("like a circle bounded in itself"), II 353b ("I fear a taint here in the mathematics. They say lines parallel do never meet; He has met his parallel in wit and schoolcraft"),[1] 508b ("Why do you so survey and circumscribe me, As if you stuck one eye into my breast, And with the other took my whole dimensions?"), Burning glass II 50a. Books and printing I 93b (a fashion "of the last edition"), 96a ("a whole volume of humor, and worthy the unclasping"), 161a ("all his behaviors are printed, his face is another volume of essays"), 323a, II 373a ("A printed book without a blot"); I 109a (tobacco taken as a parenthesis); II 344a (degree at Tyburn, laureate, etc.), II 377b (to read and decipher).

Music: I 48a (musicians); II 375a (music); In tune, harmony, etc. I 70b, I 118a, 195b, 216a, 386a, II 261a, 343b; To play on I 27a, 70b; Chime II 350b, 355a; To run division I 110a; II 267a ("You had some strain 'Bove e-la?"), I 430a

[1] Cf. Hazlitt's Dodsley, V 335.

(barber's citterns); I 25a ("my wind-instruments"), I 70b ("yond sackbut"), 159a (sackbut); Music of the spheres I 151, II 508a.

PAINTING AND SCULPTURE: I 65a ("my soul Was never ground into such oily colors To flatter vice and daub iniquity"), I 188a (to play the painter), 289b ("darkly set As shadows are in pictures, to give height And lustre to themselves"), I 248b ("hollow statues which the best men are"), I 407b (the city statues).

LAW: I 215b ("There's . . . A *supersedeas* to your melancholy"), 216a ("Julia's love Shall be a law," etc.), 444a ("take the mortgage of my wit"), II 12b (assumpsit), 342a (libel), 328b (conscience=a thousand witnesses); Seal I 197a ("Thy presence broad-seals our delights"), II 85a, 225a; I 372b ("that unhappy crime of nature, Which you miscall my beauty"); Rack and torture I 67a, 321b, II 196a.

GOVERNMENT, etc. I 453a ("the kingdom or commonwealth of ladies' affections"); I 373a (rebellion of the blood); State I 195b, Empire II 243b.

MEDICAL: I 395b ("he must now Help to sear up this vein, or we bleed dead"), II 374a (remedy), 495a (dose); Medicine, physic, etc. I 387b, II 4b, 37a, 254a, I 67b ("all physic of the mind"), 219b, 282a, 345b, II 493a, I 68b (pills), 78a, 122a (drug); Cure I 71b, II 4b, 377b; Purge I 68b, II 101b ("to purge sick Rome"), 295a; Diseases and Wounds I 338a (wound), so 71b, 441a, II 86a, 95a, 413a, I 220a (to search a wound), so II 490b, II 268b ("a scar upon our names"); II 176a (to be infected with the disease of poetry), I 222a, 258b, 344b, II 374a; I 19b (like a pestilence), II 105a (sickness); Fever I 227b, 364a, 398a ("These possess wealth as sick men possess fevers"), II 120b; Ulcers I 202b, II 324a; Leprosy I 66b ("Plagued with an itching leprosy of wit;" cf. 156b), 262a; I 123b ("his disease is nothing but the flux of apparel"); Itch I 414a, 418b; I 202a (medicines, maladies, etc.); Physician and patient I 68b, 167a; Infect I 19b, II 176a, 324a; Anatomy I 115a, 67b, 98a; Horse-leech I 239b, 311b, II 162b, 289b.

Various Estates and Occupations: I 111b ("he's like the zany to a tumbler"); Slave I 246b, 276b, II 84b, I 320a (captive); Rebel II 102a; Thief I 197a, II 94a; Picklock II 180a, 410a;

Usher I 242b ; Rabbi II 368b ; Heirs II 84a ; Prodigals II 127a ; Barber I 425a ; II 374b (Patience, magnanimity, etc., are the waiting-maids of valor);[1] II 504b (the nightingale = the angel, i. e. messenger of spring — from Sappho); II 173b (husbandman, pilot, shepherd, constable, etc.); I 407b ("gilders will not work, but inclosed "); II 94a (beauty locked up " Like a fool's treasure"); 118a ("The shop and mint of your conspiracy "); 469b (" We are like men that wander in strange woods ").

Trades and Practical Arts: II 107b (" I'll trust you with the stuff you have to work on ; You'll form it").

MERCHANTS, TRADE, etc.: I 4b ("Oft sells his reputation at cheap market"), 51b (" have I forstalled your honest market ?"), 419b (" Was there ever such a two yards of knighthood measured out by time, to be sold to laughter ?"); Buy I 156a, II 115b ; II 247a (to put out to use); II 392a (" the poetic shop "), 118a ; II 422a (" a wife Which since is proved a cracked commodity ; She hath broke bulk too soon ").

BUILDING : I 19b ("The houses of the brain ");[2] 284a (" Temples and statues, reared in your minds "); To build II 48b, 80a, 113b ; II 81a (" He that, building, stays at one Floor, or the second, hath erected none "), 83b (" the porch of life "), 366a (simile of the traveler and the palace— 6 ll.), 393b (the portal or entry, " according to Vitruvius "); 101a (a bridge of " the heads Of men struck down like piles "), 129b (the bridge of state); Hinge I 397a (" All's on the hinge "), 424b, II 54a, 114b. Well-timbered I 71a (" a well-timbered fellow, he would have made a good column, an he had been thought on, when the house was a building "), 155b, 383a ; Cabinet I 281a, II 401b ; Closet II 471a (" ope the closet Of his devices "). WEAVING : I 32b (" a weaver of language "), 294a (" Their faces run like shittles ; they are weaving Some curious cobweb to catch flies "), 304a (" thou art . . . Woven in our design "), II 501a (" I hae that wark in hand, That web upon the luime "); Spin II 418a. THE POTTER'S ART II 427b ; METAL WORK II 258b (" melt, cast, and form her," cf. II 87a); Forge I 132a, 293b, 303b, II 423a ; I 36a ("hammering

[1] Cf. Lyly, II 176.
[2] Cf. the *Fairy Queen*, II ix,—The House of Alma.

revenge"); MINE I 450a, cf. 362b; DYEING I 22a ("This dye [of sin] goes deeper than the coat, Or shirt, or skin," etc.); I 44b ("make grist of you").

Agriculture: Harvest I 349a ("a beauty ripe as harvest"); Crop I 380b, II 93a; Sow and Reap II 299a ("My man of law . . . sows all my strifes, And reaps them too"), 328a, 97a (to sow and reap kisses), so 238a ("plant and gather kisses"); I 436a ("be like a barren field that yields little"), 440a, 386b (a fruitful glebe); II 247b; II 226a ("I lie fallow"), 281a; II 472a ("I am not for your mowing"), I 445b ("to mow you off at the knees"), II 109b ("all else cut off As . . . mowers A field of thistles; or else up, as plows do barren lands, and strike together flints And clods, th' ungrateful senate and the people"); 173b ("The husbandman ought not, for one unthankful year, to forsake the plough"); II 241b ("Our shop-books are our pastures, our corn-grounds"); II 227a ("I have considered you As a fit stock to graft honors upon"); I 338a (simile of the thresher—from Horace); Furrows I 338a.

Ships and Sailors: Ship of State II 97b, 99a (10 ll.), 128a; II 277 ("steer the souls of men As with a rudder"); I 68b ("bear this peremptory sail"), 71a ("when his belly is well ballaced, and his brain rigged a little, he sails away withal"), 76a ("to sink this hulk of ignorance"), cf. 96b, 230b; I 4b ("Not that your sail be bigger than your boat; But moderate your expenses"); To sail II 184b ("he comes down sailing that way all alone"), 222b, 232b; II 107a ("wings as large as sails"); II 300a ("She is not rigged, sir; setting forth some lady Will cost as much as furnishing a fleet. Here she is come at last, and like a galley, Gilt in the prow"), 372b ("Let his wife be stript. Blow off her upper deck. Tear all her tackle"), cf. 404a; II 509b ("You must be wary, and pull in your sails"), 379a ("She is set forth in't, rigged for some employment . . . . 'Tis a fine tack about?"); II 120b ("shipwrecked minds"); II 423b ("I have run my bark On a sweet rock . . . And must get off again, or dash in pieces"); Pilot II 173b ("the pilot ought not, for one leak in the poop, to quit the helm"), 510a; Embark II 103b, 260a; I 103a ("He may hap lose his tide").

Sports, Amusements, etc.: GAMES, etc. I 112a ("like a pawn at chess; [he] fills up a room"); Primero I 165a, 367a II 261a; Gambling I 393a, 436a, II 261b; Dice II 138a, 149a; Cards II 183b, 166b, 302b ("like the knave of clubs"), 316a, 344b (the world like a game of cards, 5 ll.); II 237b (a well-torned chin, like a billiard ball); I 455a (jugglers); Leap-frog II 149a; Wrestling II 190b; Tennis II 316a; Level coil II 461a (cf. Gifford's note); ANGLING II 31b ("Has he bit? . . . And swallowed too . . . I have given him line, and now he plays," etc.), 326a, 428b; Bait and Hook I 238b, 292a, 346b, 310b, II 306b, 471a, 171b. HUNTING, etc. (cf. "Dogs," above p. 143) I 19a ("She has me in the wind"), so 292a; II 150b ("Have you ta'en soil here?"); I 292a ("They hunt. There is some game here lodged," etc.), II 303b ("You hunt upon a wrong scent still"), 455b ("to hunt counter thus, and make these doubles"); To decoy, to stalk, etc. I 302a, II 231b; I 27b (tracking hares), II 26a (snaring hares), 469b; To lime twigs I 190b, II 187b; I 22b ("I am fleshed now"), so 384b; HAWKING AND FALCONRY I 443b (to hawk at), II 355b; Seeled II 84b, 95a; To stoop at, to souse II 73b, 261a ("I think I soused him, And ravished her away out of his pounces"), 371b ("every stoop he made Was like an eagle's at a flight of cranes"), 440b; To fly to mark, to fly at, II 179b, 304b, 342b, 361a, 376b, 413a, 514a.

Domestic Life: Nurse II 34b ("deal like a rough nurse, and fright Those that are froward, to an appetite"), 120b, 154b; II 286a ("it shows Wit had married Order"); II 375b ("like children We are made afraid with vizors"); Relationship II 407b ("My monies are my blood, my parents, kindred"); Child or Infant I 334, II 341a (brain-child); Daughter II 477b; Mother I 363b ("Admit your fool's face be the mother of laughter"), II 103b, 104a, 105a; Step-dame II 48b (Nature a step-dame), 80b, 87b; Father II 318b; Dowry I 409b ("her silence is dowry enough"), 421a, 441a, II 383b; Wean I 3a, 175b.

DRESS AND ORNAMENT: I 88b ("she speaks as she goes tired, in cobweb-lawn, light, thin"), 198b (folds, plaits, etc.), 165b (a grogran rascal); II 394b ("a good play is like a skein of silk," etc.), cf. 373a, 328a ("the unwinding this so knotted skein"); II

344b ("To be wrapt soft and warm in fortune's smock"); I 170b (to embroider discourse); Apparel I 170b; To clothe I 151b ("I have but one poor thought to clothe In airy garments"), 156b (muffled thought); Fustian I 70b, 99a, 144b, 147b; To truss points I 184a ("trussing all the points of this action"), 190b; Cosmetics and toilet I 148b; Mask, vizor, etc. I 290a, 381b, 418a, II 38b. 100b, 375b, 377b; Veil I 195a, 246b; Rags I 335, II 194a, 349b ("Be still that rag of love You are; burn on till you turn tinder"), 415b (clouts); Starched I 73a, 168a; Strait-laced II 156b.

JEWELS, GEMS, etc. I 15b, 69a, 125a, 216a, 222b, 453b, II 401a ("A chrysolite, a gem, the very agate Of state and policy, cut from the quar Of Machiavel," etc.), 454a; Brooch I 213b, so II 310b, 256a; Foil, Lustre, etc., I 28a, 305b, 453b.

Colloquial and Familiar Images are very frequent in Jonson's comedies. The most noteworthy are as follows: I 4b ("to be left like an unsavory snuff"), 9b ("this man! so graced, gilded, or, to use a more fit metaphor, so tin-foiled by nature," etc.), 27a (Stephen is like a drum or child's whistle, "every one may play upon him"), 32b ("made it run as smooth off the tongue as a shove-groat shilling"),¹ 42b ("it vanished away like the smoke of tobacco"), 54a (like an artichoke), 68a ("now and then breaks a dry biscuit jest," etc.), cf. 130a ("like a dry crust"), 72b ("I am like your tailor's needle"), 73a ("look with a good starched face, and ruffle your brow like a new boot"), 76a ("he looks like a musty bottle new wickered, his head's the cork, light, light!"— cf. 147b), 79b ("He looks like . . . one of these motions [puppets] in a great antique clock"); 80a ("will run over a bog like your wild Irish"); 82a ("he looks like a fresh salmon kept in a tub; he'll be spent shortly"), 82b ("When he is mounted he looks like the sign of the George"),² 84b ("as it he went in a frame or had a suit of wainscot on"), 90a ("the actors come in one by one, as if they were dropt down with a feather into the eye of the spectators"), 114b ("holding his snout up like a sow under an apple tree"),³ 115a ("he walks up and down like a charged musket"), 132b

¹ Cf. *II. Henry IV*, II iv 182.
² Cf. Chapman, 83a.
³ Cf. Greene, 169a.

("lean ribs . . . like ragged laths"), 133b ("he looks like an image carved out of box, full of knots; his face is, for all the world, like a Dutch purse, with the mouth downward, his beard the tassels"), 161a ("He speaks all cream skimmed" . . . "He is no great shifter; once a year his apparel is ready to revolt"), 157b (a crowd greater "than come to the launching of some three ships"), 161b ("His eyes and his raiment confer much together as he goes in the street. He treads nicely like the fellow that walks upon ropes"), 168b ("Then walks off melancholic, and stands wreathed, As he were pinned up to the arras"), 172a ("there's one speaks in a key, like the opening of some justice's gate, or a postboy's horn"), 172a (a face like a sea-monster), 172b ("His face is like a squeezed orange"), 195a ("What mere gilt blocks You are"), 225a ("jests As hard as stones") 236b ("you shall have kisses from them, go pit-pat, pit-pat, pit-pat, upon your lips, as thick as stones out of slings at the assault of a city"), 283a ("he permits himself Be carried like a pitcher by the ears, To every act of vice"), 338a ("swallow A melting heir as glibly as your Dutch Will pills of butter"), 342b ("I have milked their hopes"), 357a ("seats your teeth, did they dance like virginal jacks");[1] 366b ("The bells in time of pestilence, ne'er made Like noise"), 379b ("your husband told me you were fair, And so you are; only your nose inclines, That side that's next the sun, to the queen-apple"), 393a ("some would swell now, like a wine-fat, With such an autumn"), 396b ("his eyes are set, Like a dead hare's hung in a poulter's shop"), 438a ("She takes herself asunder still when she goes to bed, into some twenty boxes; and about next day noon is put together again, like a great German clock," etc.), 441b ("labor not to stop her. She is like a conduit pipe, that will gush out with more force when she opens again"), cf. 23b. Vol. II pp. 12a ("spit out secrets like hot custard"), 40b ("six great slops Bigger than three Dutch boys"), 46a ("What shall we do with this same puffin here Now he's on the spit?"), 53a ("He looks in that deep ruff like a head in a platter," etc.), 122b (to ring hollow), 169a (a loud voice like the "mouth of a peck"), 166b ("Every rib of them is like the tooth of a saw" cf. I 132b), 205b ("I have gaped as the oyster

---

[1] Cf. Chapman, 124a.

for the tide "),¹ 238b ("Away, you broker's block, you property !"), 255a ("keeps the skin ... ever bright and smooth As any looking-glass "), 255b (" I saw in the court of Spain once, A lady fall in the king's sight along, And there she lay, flat spread, as an umbrella "), 257a ("laugh as loud as a larum "), 283b (" there the molten silver Runs out like cream on cakes of gold, And rubies do grow like strawberries "), 300b (" Thy beard is like a broom "), 304a (" I move upon my axle like a turnpike "), 308a (" There is a ninepence, I will shed no more "), 329a(" I shall see you quoited Over the bar, as bargemen do their billets "), 332a (" as thin as a lanthorn, we shall see through him "), 342b (" He prates Latin An it were a parrot or a play boy "), 353b (" Spins like the parish top "), cf. 463b; 379a (clothes that fit " Like a caparison for a sow "), 380a (" Sheelee-nien Thomas Runs like a heifer bitten with the brize "), 406b (" I find where your shoe wrings you "), 408a (" Wealth . . . makes a trade to take the wall of virtue ");² see also I 48a, 71a, 159a, 164a, 166a, 425a, II 38b, 151b, 160b, 161b 166b, 179a, 183b, 188a, 276b, 293b, 300, 318a, 343a, 345b, 373a, 444b, 463b, 474b, 498b, etc. I 6b (batch), 393a (leaven), II 117b.

Note also the Puritan cant of Ananias, Tribulation, etc., e. g. II 71b, 150 f., 181, etc., passim.

Coarse and Repulsive Images are frequent in Ben Jonson as in Chapman.

METAPHORS OF BIRTH and the like : I 44a, 75a, 104b, 128a, 150a, 171a, 174b, 200a, 292b, II 84a, 223b, 276a, 464b. Similarly I 31a, 341b, 389b, II 183a; I 181b, 283a, II 276a, 286b; I 407a (the adulteries of art); II 215a, 344a; 325a.

BAWD, strumpet, etc., I 76a, II 85b, 285b; I 156b, II 226b; 316a (" That money-bawd "), Fortune a bawd I 76b, II 355b, 455a.

In general see also : I 265b (garbage), 282b (slime); Dunghill, etc., I 23a, 78b, 106b, 249b, 265b, 312b, II 27b, 323b; I 108a (" rince his cammy guts in beer "), II 110b (dregs), I 140a (the

---

¹ Cf. Beaumont and Fletcher *Bonduca* I ii :

"Did I not find thee gaping like an oyster
For a new tide ? "

² Cf. Lyly I 69.

London sewer), 212a ("blow your ears with these untrue reports), 236b (ears *furred* with the breath of compliments), 445b ("that sword hath spawned such a dagger"), II 24b ("somewhat costive of belief;" so 295a); 409a (bugs); see also I 348b, II 21a, 37a, 151b, 245b, 281a, 316a. See also various passages of billingsgate and opprobrious epithets, passim, e. g. I 75b, 76, 106b, 130b, 145, 214a, 382b, II 61a, 296b, 353b, 381a, etc.

The Body, its Parts, Functions, and Attributes: Bosom I 77b ("lies he hid Within the wrinkled bosom of the world"), cf. II 508a ("in the lap of listening nature"); I 280a (the heart and face of his designs); II 120b ("veins and bowels of the state"); II 279a ("Thy pulse hath beat enough" [to his watch]); Womb II 302a; Bowels, etc. I 140a ("The hallowed bowels of the silver Thames"), II 80b, 86a, 100a (to stomach), 120b; Head II 136a; Eye I 317b, 412a (London the eye of England); Face I 280a, 288a; Finger I 418b ("Fortune had not a finger in't"); Throat I 438b (the brazen throat of a trumpet); Sinews II 97b; Ribs II 83a (of ice), 86a; Wrinkle I 77b, 149b; Hug II 367b (to hug time); Kiss I 237a ("kiss heaven with their titles"), II 507b; Lame I 165a; Sleep II 105a, 369b.

The Senses and Appetites: II 508b ("the touches or soft strokes of reason"), cf. I 277a, Tickle I 109b, 289a; Scents, Odors, etc. I 298a, 313a, 384a, 386a, II 152a; Food and Taste I 23a, 83b (the syrup of the jest), 237b (sugared), 172b ("The very march-pane of the court"), 44b, 71b, 145b, 147a, 151a, 150b, (hunger), II 283b (strawberries, cakes and cream), 340; I 387b ("a rare meal of laughter"), 404a; Feast, Banquet, etc. I 300a, 390a, 420b, II 9b, 359a, 367a, 515a; Diet II 345b; Batten I 347a, II 464a (fatted); Surfeit, glut, etc. I 91b, 250b, 289b, II 367a; Eat II 89b, 109b, I 459b (to eat one's words); Digest I 258b; Vomit I 159b, 246a, II 8a; Thirst I 151a, 289b; Drink I 71a; Spice and seasoning II 374b (salt and its savor), I 244b, 318b, 398b, II 344a, 374b.

Subjective Life, Religion, etc. Heaven I 173a, 370a; Purgatory I 433b; Hell I 173a, 363b, II 280a; Devil I 116b, 188b, 389a; Spirits, to haunt, etc. I 38a (they haunt him like spirits), 100a ("his familiar that haunts him"), 147a; Conjuring, witchcraft, etc. I 94b ("your good face is the witch and your apparel the spells, that bring all the pleasures of the world into their circle"), 179a, 246b:

> "As in a circle, a magician then
> Is safe against the spirit he excites;
> But, out of it, is subject to his rage,
> And loseth all the virtue of his art:
> So I, exiled the circle of the court,
> Lose all the good gifts that in it I 'joyed,"

cf. 248a, 359a, II 41b, 223b, 282a, II 348b ("Stalk like a ghost, that haunted 'bout a treasure"), 509b; Superstitions I 138a ("has the wolf seen you"), II 19a (fire-drake), 347b (fern-seed); Fairy-lore I 140b, 149a (charm), 454a, II 448b ("Dance o'er the fields like faies"); Incubus II 161a; Prodigy I 227b; Alchemy (cf. *The Alchemist*, passim) I 72b, 95a ("play the alchemist"), II 6b (projection), 366b; Perspective Glass, etc. II 212, 237b, (cf. 341b); Influence of the Stars I 213a, 410a, II 317a.

Religion, etc. II 376a:

> "There's nought so sacred with us but may find
> A sacrilegious person, yet the thing is
> No less divine, 'cause the profane can reach it." . . .
> "They that do pull down churches, and deface
> The holiest altars, cannot hurt the Godhead."

II 367a ("Where have I lived in heresy so long Out of the congregation of love, And stood irregular by all his canons?"), II 361b (horses = "poor dumb Christians"), II 379a (hallowed), II 411a ("a recusant In sack"); cf. 412a, II 422b (Eve and the Apple); Heresy I 25b ("self-love burnt for her heresy"), 435a, II 229b, 367a; I 31b ("martyrs o' the girdiron"); Sacrilege I 195b; Sacrifice I 279b; Shrine I 337a; Altar and Idol I 373a, II 38b, 55b, 373b; Miracle I 370a, II 50a; Oracle II 295b, 376a, 406a; Saint I 337, II 220b; Soul I 337a.

DEATH, THE GRAVE, etc. Death I 388b ("Now their hopes Are at the gasp"); Buried I 30b, 334, 249b ("this grave of sin"), 306b, 338a (coffin), II 383a (coffined); I 375a (sepulchre), 391b ("the funeral of your notes"); I 156b ("Floats, like a dead drowned body, on the stream Of vulgar humour"), II 122a (*Cat-iline*—"I will not burn Without my funeral pile").

War: cf. II 317a. See the parts of Bobadil, Captain Tucca, etc. passim. Siege, Fort, etc. I 201b ("thorns lie in garrison about the roses"), 236b, 282b, II 282b, 283a; II 94a (artillery), 126b ("the train hath taken"); Civil War II 6b, 139a; II 41a (entrenched), 156b ("suffer not the enemy to enter you"), 376a ("He is shot-free in battle is not hurt, Not he that is not hit"); I 128b ("at the tilt of all the court-wits"); I 18b ("such strong motives muster and make head"), 24a ("faces about to some other discourse"), 76a ("you should have turned your broadside . . . to sink this hulk of ignorance . . ."), 76a ("his spirit is like powder, quick, violent; I fear him worse than a rotten wall does the cannon—shake an hour after at the report"); Arms, etc. I 131b–132a ("three of our ordnance are burst," etc.), 313b (armed), 253a; I 149a-b (a duel of wit). HERALDRY I 162a ("What, lay color upon color! that affords but an ill blazon"). ARCHERY, etc. II 350b ("shoot bolts and sentences To affright babies with!"), I 108b ("her brain's a very quiver of jests," etc.); 213a, 362a, II 333b, 359a; I 162a (to dart).

The Stage and the Drama: Tragedy I 74b, 240a, 312a, II 58b; Motion or Puppet Show I 68a, 156b, 234b ("What's he . . . that salutes us out of his cloak, like a motion, ha?"), 255a, cf. 79b, II 12b, 460b; I 444a ("here will I act such a tragi-comedy" . . . etc.); I 296b ("The curtain's drawing"); Epilogue I 358a; Prologue I 168a ("repeats, Like an imperfect prologue, at third music. His part of speeches" . . .), II 171a ("We had wonderful ill luck, to miss this prologue o' the purse; but the best is, we shall have five acts of him ere night"); I 366b (noisy as the Cockpit); II 376b ("how like A court removing, or an ended play, Shews my abrupt, precipitate estate"); II 379a ("like a noble poet, to have had My last act best");[1] II 43b ("You shall have your ordinaries bid for him As play-houses for a poet"); II 82a ("be thrown by, or let fall, As is a veil put off, a visor changed, Or the scene shifted in our theatres"); II 99b ("Would you have Such an Herculean actor in the scene, And not his hydra? they must sweat no less, To fit their properties, than to express their parts"); II 342b ("he prates Latin An it were a parrot, or a play-boy"); II

---

[1] Cf. Webster 120a.

102b ("it so far exceeds All insolent fictions of the tragic scene"); II 345a ("All the world's a play"—simile, 8 ll.),¹ so II 350a; 425b ("No theatres are more cheated with appearances").

Miscellaneous: Melt, dissolve, etc. I 4b, 66a, 69a, II 51b, 441b ("melting as the weather in a thaw!"); Mirror, Glass, etc. I 67b, 143, 150b, II 255a, 325b, 348b, 365b, 410a ("the glass of custom, which is comedy," etc.); Mould II 465b, cf. 87a, I 66a, 85a; COLORS: I 37a; Motley I 95b, 154b; Black I 19b, 120b, 149b, 275b, 330b, II 115a, 118a, 139a; White I 92b ("as white as innocence"), 255b; Red I 253a; Green II 337b; Poison I 19b, ("black poison of suspect"), 96a, 166b, 212b, 296a, 304b, II 24a, 81b, 95a, 100b, 128b, 135b; Instrument, Engine, Organ, I 72a, 107b, 275a, 285b, 290a, 298a, 302a, 304a, 305b, 327a, 391a; II 111b ("The enginers I told you of are working, The machine 'gins to move"), 232b ("It creaks his engine"), 305a, 328a, 329a, 352b; Coin, Counterfeit I 24a, 69a, II 286a, 383b, 419b ("light gold—And cracked within the ring"); Painted I 244b, 306a; Swim I 77b, 344a; Drown I 295a, II 105a, 368a, 493a; To sound a depth I 291b; Snare, Springe, Trap, etc., II 357b (net), 231b, 436a, I 309b, 395b, II 175a (springe), 471a, II 41a (fettered), so 317b; Tie, Tangle, Knot II 9b, 427b, 243b; Whet, Edge, etc. I 23a, 149a ("the edge of my wit is clean taken off with the . . . stroke of your thin-ground tongue"), 193a, 387b, II 117a ("This twenty days of that decree We have let dull and rust," etc.), 154b, 498a; Scourge, whip, etc., I 65b, 123b, 259a (a bastinado of words), 328b; Rip I 275b; Smother II 333a, 461b; To weigh in balance, etc. I 454b, II 109b ("No rage . . . May weigh with yours, though Horror leaped herself Into the scale"); Weight, Burden, etc. I 296a, II 98a, I 161b, 307a; I 197a ("our unspotted fame"); Dial I 83b, Clock I 161a ("he will lie louder than most clocks"), 194b, 276a ("Observe him, as his watch observes his clock"), 438a, II 402a; Hourglass I 28b ("My brain, methinks, is like an hour-glass, Wherein my imaginations run like sands, Filling up time," etc.); Borrow ("Convey, the wise it call"), I 149a ("to speak by metaphor, you borrowed a girdle of hers"); Beam II 205a (metaphorical uses of the word distinguished); Fireworks,

¹ Cf. Jonson's "Discoveries" (Works, III 404).

crackers, etc. I 130b, 179b, II 12b, Squib I 189a, II 53a; Distil I 250a, II 357b, 495b; Height I 331b (pinnacles of state), II 136a; II 349a ("thereon hangs a history"); Prop I 246a, 291a; To piece I 406b, II 251b ("I will have all pieced, And friends again — It will be but ill-soldered!"), 411a.

Almost every prominent domain of nature and of human life is drawn upon in Ben Jonson's use of figure. He is not a deeply metaphorical writer, nor on the other side does he fall into the conventional manner of using imagery; but with an even-handed realism, if also somewhat through the spectacle of books, he sees life steadily and he sees it whole. Certain sides of nature and of human life, it has already been noted, he emphasizes to a high degree. Fire is often used by him in a metaphorical sense, the animal world constantly appears, all aspects of common human life are presented; agriculture, ships and sailing, sports, amusements, and hunting, domestic life, dress and ornament, colloquial images without end, a large number of coarse and repulsive images, man with his body and its senses and appetites, devils, witchcraft and conjuring, religion, classical and literary coloring in profusion, many references to the stage and the drama, — all these things are largely represented in Ben Jonson's pages. It is the complete life of the times in its humbler and more familiar phases. Nowhere, outside of Dickens, is there so encyclopædic an array for any period.

Recapitulation

TABLE OF TROPES INDEXED

TABLE BY AUTHORS AND BY TOPICS OF TROPES INDEXED.

	LYLY.	PEELE.	MARLOWE.	GREENE.	TOURNEUR.	WEBSTER.	CHAPMAN.	JONSON.	TOTALS.
No. of Plays Indexed	7	5	6	4	2	4	12	16	56
Total number of pages (approximate)	446	393	549	212	295	322	718	1892	4827
Aspects of Sky, etc	50	50	93	17	21	69	155	100	555
Aspects of Waters	11	8	5	—	14	13	34	28	113
Aspects of Earth	32	3	14	—	5	19	39	46	158
Various: Times, Seasons, etc	2	1	3	—	—	6	20	12	44
Vegetable World	29	26	14	5	5	30	44	41	194
Animal World	36	36	36	12	17	105	158	276	676
Fabulous Nat. History	67	5	4	7	2	26	14	23	148
Total Nature	227	129	169	41	64	268	464	526	1888
Arts and Learning	16	4	14	7	11	19	66	44	181
Law and Government	4	2	1	4	12	12	36	17	88
Medical	3	2	2	—	4	37	56	62	166
Various Occupations	5	—	—	—	10	24	24	23	86
Trades, Practical Arts, etc.	17	2	8	1	5	20	25	27	105
Building, etc	—	1	4	2	9	16	31	21	84
Agriculture	7	3	8	1	2	9	7	21	58
Ships and Sailors	Cf.	above	"Aspe	cts of	Waters"	15	13	26	54
Sports and Amusements	8	2	13	2	—	25	33	61	144
Domestic Life	{ 25	—	2	—	7	11	22	22	89
Dress and Adornment	{	—	9	—	8	22	41	48	128
Colloquial, Comic, and Familiar Tropes	} 24	16	8	10	17	16	61	100	252
Coarse & Repulsive Images	(	—	—	—	—	21	55	72	148
The Body, its Parts, etc.	31	{ 15	24	{ 1	9	10	39	29	158
The Senses and Appetites	30	{	11	} —	—	15	48	53	157
Subjective Life, Religion, etc	8	5	36	2	7	45	60	68	231
Death, the Grave, etc	3	—	—	—	5	20	16	11	55
War, Arms, etc	12	6	18	3	8	18	64	30	159
The Stage and the Drama	5	—	10	—	10	8	15	27	75
Miscellaneous	67	36	50	13	20	70	154	133	543
Total Man	265	94	218	46	144	433	866	895	2961
Grand Totals	492	223	387	87	208	701	1330	1421	4849

NOTE:—This table is merely for purposes of general comparison. The enumerations are not complete under each head, and must be taken to represent only roughly the average from author to author.

SUMMARY AND CONCLUSIONS

III. SUMMARY AND CONCLUSIONS.

Chief Forms of Trope in the Elizabethan Drama: The Elizabethan Drama is fundamentally national, complex, and passionate. Its imagery therefore is generally original, varied, and intense. All varieties of trope in infinite complexity are in constant use. Shakspere, of course, is the great type and name of the period, and Shakspere's usage largely determines our judgment of the general characteristics of Elizabethan diction and imagery.

General Value and Quality of Elizabethan Dramatic Imagery

The present study, however, prosecuted without reference to Shakspere, must present its results independently, and not attempt a correction from the standard of Shakspere for the statement of the entire period and the literary species as a whole. The other dramatic poets of the period, it need hardly be said, cannot abide the touchstone of Shakspere. A few supreme passages in Marlowe, some of Chapman's obscured but colossal metaphors, and now and then a brief and passionate simile in Webster or Tourneur, have the Shaksperian, or, in other words, the ideal Elizabethan dramatic quality. But no such level of performance in every variation and modulation of passion and beauty as that of Shakspere in a score of masterpieces is long kept up. Webster's searching similes, to my mind, approach nearest to it, but Webster lacks precisely variety and modulation. Indeed, deep and pregnant metaphor, adequate to the highest reaches of dramatic or poetic passion, is rare in the world's literature. Pindar, Æschylus, and Shakspere represent a certain type of imagery, present, perhaps, in no others to the same degree; and concentrative and illuminative flashes of metaphor only less intense or subtle are sometimes found in modern poets such as Tennyson, Browning, and Victor Hugo. But the list is not long.

The imagery of the Elizabethan drama outside of Shakspere is not then of the highest rank. Great passages and poetical pictures there are, however, and it is largely for these occasional beauties and excellences that this drama remains one of the most interesting and important sections of the world's minor literature. "It is," as Mr. Lowell writes,[1] "for their poetical qualities, for their gleams of imagination, for their quaint and subtle fancies, for their tender sentiment, and for their charm of diction, that these old playwrights are worth reading."

These playwrights work as a rule hastily and almost impersonally or with little thought of Fame's eternal beadroll.

Method of Workmanship of the Dramatists

Their imagery was designed for direct dramatic effect. It is daring, and seldom regards the censor. Nevertheless, it is not by any means naïve and artless. They are strong and self-conscious craftsmen, well aware of the task that they are about, and continually casting about for new devices and literary effects. The university wits bring with them to the stage all the figures of rhetoric. "Art thou a scholar, Don Horatio?" Jeronimo says to his son,[2]

"And canst not aim at figurative speech?"

"Use all the tropes
And schemes that Prince Quintilian can afford you;
And much good do your rhetoric's heart,"

says Fitzdottrel in *The Devil is an Ass*.[3] And references of a similar sort abound in all the dramatists.[4] The newly imported rhetoric and poetics of Italy and of the ancient writers were operant in English poetry and prose[5] before the revival of the

[1] Old Eng. Dram., p. 26.
[2] *First Part of Jeronimo* (Hazlitt's Dodsley, IV 368).
[3] Jonson, II 221a.
[4] See for example: Lyly, II 91-92, 230; Marlowe, I 161; Webster, 12a, 33a ("a dried sentence, stuft with sage"); Chapman, 78, 83, 89, 93, 117, 142, 187, 189, 226, 231, 234, 256, 329; and see the references under Ben Jonson, supra, p. 129 note 1.
[5] Cf. Sir Thomas Wilson, the Arte of Rhetorique, 1553 and later editions. Sir Thomas writes comprehensively of the theory of metaphor, as follows:

"Men count it a point of wit to pass over such words as are at hand, and to use such as are far fetcht and translated [i. e., metaphorical, *Lat.* translatio]: or else it is because the hearer is led by cogitation upon rehearsal of a metaphor, and thinketh more by remembrance of a word translated than is there expressly

drama, but the drama more than any other agency perhaps helped to popularize and diffuse the new literary diction, or at least such parts of it as were available for popular and dramatic use. Without the drama the breach between literary and popular speech might never have been mended. Vital, condensed, and infinitely varied figure was an outcome of the drama.

In imagery as in other things there is observable a rapid development from Greene and Peele to Webster and Tourneur. The work of the early university wits is predominatingly literary and imitative. Lyly, Peele, Greene, and Marlowe are full of classical imagery. The manner of contemporary poetry is frequently followed. There is an epical expansiveness of diction throughout the most dramatic passages and situations of Peele and Greene, and much of Marlowe, especially in *Tamburlaine*. Prolonged similes of an epical type are not infrequent;[1] and several of them are borrowed directly from Spenser,[2] and other contemporary poets. The style is poetical rather than dramatic.

The Evolution of Dramatic Imagery

Lyric interludes, the "lyrical interbreathings" alluded to by Coleridge, are not infrequent, and include not only the interpolated songs, characteristic of the Elizabethan drama in all its stages, but also passages in the body of the text which in movement and diction are lyrical rather than dramatic.[3] There are numerous touches of this sort in Greene and Peele, and many also in Marlowe. Lyrical is

Lyric Interludes

spoken; or else because the whole matter seemeth by a similitude to be opened : or, last of all, because every translation is commonly and for the most part referred to the senses of the body, and especially to the sense of seeing, which is the sharpest and quickest above all other." (Fol. 91a. I quote, modernizing the spelling, from a copy of the first edition now in my possession, and formerly belonging to J. P. Collier.) Note the reference to "far fetcht and translated" words, such words as were in one sense to become the very life of the diction of the succeeding age. Note also Ben Jonson's objection to "far-fet" metaphors many years later in his *Discoveries* (Works III 413b).

[1] See the references on this head under Greene, Peele, and Marlowe, above, pp. 23, note 5, 38-39, 58, note 5.

[2] E. g. Peele, II 42; Marlowe, I 173, 183.

[3] Cf. J. A. Symonds, Essays Speculative and Suggestive, 409. Mr. Symonds has developed this topic at considerable length and with his usual felicity of

nearly the whole of Peele's *Arraignment of Paris*, which in fact is a masque rather than a play, and most of *David and Bethsabe*. Miles, Friar Bacon's servant, in Greene's *Friar Bacon and Friar Bungay*, not without decorum is made to talk in Skeltonian verse. In Act IV, scene ii, of *James IV* there is a passage of rhymed lyric dialogue between the huntsmen and the ladies. Lyrical in movement and imagery also is Tamburlaine's descant at the opening of Act II, scene iv, of the Second Part of Marlowe's play of that name, with its regularly repeated refrain,

"'To entertain divine Zenocrate."

So in *The Jew of Malta*, Act IV, scene iv, Ithamore, not without parody, one must believe, addressing the precious Bellamira, drops into poetry, like Silas Wegg:

"Content, but we will leave this paltry land,
And sail from hence to Greece, to lovely Greece.
I'll be thy Jason, thou my golden fleece;
Where painted carpets o'er the meads are hurled,
And Bacchus' vineyards overspread the world;"—

ending his little madrigal with the refrain from Marlowe's own poem of "The Passionate Shepherd to his Love,"—

"Thou in those groves, by Dis above,
Shalt live with me, and be my love."[1]

Indeed, so thoroughly was the poetical tradition established that Chapman, with his literary and classical prepossessions, although writing contemporaneously with Shakspere, was unable to shake off the epical conception of tragic style, and accordingly produced tragedies as destitute of dramatic movement and structure as Kyd's translation of Garnier's *Cornelia*, or as the academic tragedies of Sir William Alexander or of Lord Brooke. Characteristic of the pre-Shaksperian school also is the abundance of personification of the formal type, and of hyperbole passing over into bombast.

critical touch and charm of illustration, in an essay on "The Lyrism of the English Romantic Drama" contained in his volume entitled "In the Key of Blue."

[1] See Lyric Movements in Webster, 88b, 142b-143a, 144b, etc.

In the later dramatists included in this study these characteristics give way in large measure to others. Prolonged similes seldom occur, although short and pregnant similes become more common, at least in Webster and Jonson. Formal and abstract personification is less frequently resorted to and is less frequently sustained, while a subtler and swifter incomplete or quasi-personification takes its place. Hyperbole also becomes less frequent, and after Chapman is seldom found assuming the Titanic airs of Tamburlaine and Bussy D'Ambois. Classical allusion also becomes less profuse, and the conventional and poetical manner yields to the dramatic and direct. There is a decided increase in complexity of style and diction, passion grows less grandiose and more introspective in its utterance, and there is a deepening intensity of speech and of imagination, until the dry and terrible manner of Webster and Tourneur is reached. The dramatic type of figure and diction, superseding the lyrical and the epical, is finally established.

<small>Characteristics of the later Elizabethan Drama</small>

Among the tropes of high imaginative value which are especially available for dramatic use, and of which therefore we may expect to find striking and frequent illustrations in the Elizabethan drama, metonymy and synecdoche can hardly be ranked. Yet, as Professor Greene has said[1] "Some instances of metonymy manifest more imagination than do some instances of metaphor," and examples of this sort occur now and then in the dramatists. Thus, in *The Revenger's Tragedy*,[2] the Duchess' youngest son says of Antonio's wife, "her beauty was ordained to be my *scaffold*,"—where evidently the particular form of means of death is suggested in place of the general term "death" itself, for the sake of greater force and vividness. Later in the same play occurs a

<small>Metonymy and Syndecdoche in the Drama</small>

---

[1] A Grouping of Figures of Speech, p. 19.

[2] Tourneur, II, p. 16; cf. Webster 80b ("ere you attained This reverend garment"); Kyd, in Hazlitt's Dodsley, IV 357, 360 ("O my *true-breasted* father.... Had not your reverend *years* been present...."), 364 ("worthy my *sword's* society with thee"); Jonson I 308a (shield and sword), 414b ("all the yellow doublets and great roses in the town will be there"), II 85b (axes), 104b ("this good shame"); etc.

phrase which may no doubt be interpreted as a mere ellipsis, but which carries the effect of intense metaphor conjoined with metonymy,—"My Lord Antonio, for this time *wipe your lady from your eyes.*"

Simile as a Dramatic Figure

The commonplace of the rhetorics that simile is a non-dramatic figure is hardly borne out by the facts of the case in the Elizabethan drama. The prolonged and elaborate simile is doubtless always the mark of the non-dramatic style, and the metaphor *per se* is a more intense and dramatic figure; but the short simile in itself is not undramatic; at most it can be called a neutral figure. Striking examples of short similes in the most dramatic collocations exist without number throughout the drama. Indeed it can be said that the form of the short simile, with its slightly deliberate and intellectual cast, often lends itself to the expression of sardonic and tragic irony and similar emotions with startling effect. This appears in Webster in numberless instances:

> .... "like to calm weather
> At sea before a tempest, false hearts speak fair
> To those they intend most mischief"[1]

> "your good heart gathers like a snow-ball
> Now your affection's cold."[2]

> "Like mistletoe on sear elms spent by weather,
> Let him cleave to her, and both rot together."[3]

> "Thou hast led me, like a heathen sacrifice,
> With music and with fatal yokes of flowers,
> To my eternal ruin."[4]

Of course, the context here, as almost everywhere in dramatic writing, is indispensable for grasping the emotional connotation of the simile.

The Simile of Action

Another highly dramatic and effective form of simile, a favorite with Elizabethan playwrights, is what may be termed the Simile of Action. The illustration that will occur at once is Othello's last speech:

[1] Webster, 82b.
[2] Id. 32a.
[3] Id. 17a.
[4] Id. 30b.

> "Set you down this;
> And say besides, that in Aleppo once,
> Where a malignant and a turban'd Turk
> Beat a Venetian and traduc'd the state,
> I took by the throat the circumcised dog,
> And smote him — thus." [*Stabs himself.*][1]

—although this particular instance technically would be called Example rather than Simile, if either, by the rhetoricians.

So the Duchess of Malfi, kneeling to her execution, exclaims:

> "heaven-gates are not so highly arch'd
> As princes' palaces; they that enter there
> *Must go upon their knees.*"[2]

And Virginius, as he kills Virginia, says:

> "Thus I surrender her into the court
> Of all the gods."[3]

An earlier instance occurs in Kyd's *Spanish Tragedy*,[4] where Hieronimo, holding in his hand papers entrusted to him by the citizens, promises

"Revenge on them that murdered my son," when he has them in his toils,—

> "Then will I rent and tear them thus and thus,
> Shivering their limbs in pieces with my teeth."
> [*Tears the papers.*]

This is the sign-language of simile and often excels elaborate diction in effectiveness.

Implied simile, omitting the terms of comparison,—the figure intermediate between full simile and metaphor,— is naturally a frequent form. Complex and sometimes fantastic in structure, it is especially a favorite in the highly undramatic style of Lyly. Passing into the higher forms of imperfect allegory, parable, fable, and similar sententious forms, it is also a favorite with

---

[1] *Othello*, Act V, sc. ii. Cf. Chapman 441b.
[2] Webster, 89a.
[3] Id. 173a.
[4] Hazlitt's Dodsley, V 129: See also Marlowe, I 156, II 211; Peele, I 125, Tourneur, II 6 (the address to the skull), 37 (the address to the sword), cf. 58, 72, 120, 144; Jonson I 58b, II 221b, 348b; Chapman 202b, 258a (the game of cards), etc.

others. But it is only with metaphor in its various manifestations that we arrive at the highest dramatic form among tropes. Dramatic poetry, and especially Elizabethan tragedy, has been preëminently the field for the expression of human passion, and no form of language is so adapted to the expression of idealized passion as metaphor. "The metaphor," as Dr. Wood[1] says, "has in serious poetry usually a distinct element of feeling;" while simile and the more deliberate figures make their appeal more dispassionately to the imagination — the image-creating faculty — and to the understanding. Mere vividness of visual impression, mere definiteness of outline and clearness of conception, are not essential qualities of all trope, and especially of dramatic trope, where usually emotional association and the representative realization of human pathos and passion are far more important functions of figure. The great merit of metaphor, as has been said by Aristotle,[2] and many others after him, is that it is a perception of hidden resemblances, and such resemblances by their nature are partial and generally are inexact and vague. As Burke[3] has said, — "In reality poetry and rhetoric do not succeed in exact description so well as painting does; their business is to affect rather by sympathy than imitation; to display rather the effect of things on the mind of the speaker, or of others, than to present a clear idea of the things themselves." Or, as Coleridge[4] phrased the same idea : "The grandest efforts of poetry are where the imagination is called forth not to produce, a distinct form, but a strong working of the mind, . . . viz., the substitution of a sublime feeling of the unimaginable for a mere image."

Metaphor, its Various Forms as a Dramatic Figure

Exactness not an essential Merit in Trope

[1] "T. L. Beddoes, a Survival in Style," American Journal of Philology, IV 445-455.

[2] Rhetoric, Bk. III, ch. xi.

[3] On the Sublime and Beautiful, Pt. V (Works I 257). Burke has developed the whole subject very thoroughly : See Works I, pp. 88, 133, 136, 251, 255, etc.

[4] Lectures on Shakspere and Milton (Bohn ed.) p. 91. Further on the distinction between vague and vivid imagery cf. Hennequin, La Critique Scientifique, 40-43 (Paris, 1890).

The mere perception of analogy is not as such a poetical faculty. The mind of Sir Francis Bacon, so powerful and subtle in the perception of intellectual analogies, is standing evidence to the contrary. The sense of beauty, or the sense of passion, or both, in a high degree, are also necessary to the creative artist.

Two Poetic Types
In poetic art there always have been two types of mind: in the first place there is the mind supreme in the creation of mental images deeply informed with the sense of beauty, in the pictorial power attaching itself to human emotion; of which type Homer, in ancient poetry, is an example, and Spenser, very strikingly, in English poetry; simile, and usually prolonged and elaborate simile, is the form of expression natural to this type of mind; in the second place there is the type which usually fuses the outlines of the image in the heat of its passion, making the ideas always subservient to the emotion, instead of making the emotion, for the moment, subservient to the idea, to the picture, as is so often the case with Homer and the epic poets; Æschylus, among the ancients, and Shakspere, among the moderns, are the great exemplars of this school; and it is preëminently the dramatic school and the school of intense metaphor. It is probable that modern taste and instinct inclines more to the method of the dramatic school, but still it is too much, it seems to me, to assert, as Professor Sherman[1] apparently does, that the essential tendency of literary evolution is away from the expansive type and the school of simile, and is only toward the concentrative type and the school of

Strong Figures and Metaphor
metaphor. "It is very plain," writes Dr. Wood,[2] however, "that strong figures are the cornerstone of style,[3] but especially of English style." The bold use of trope is one of the first characteristics of the Romantic School in poetry, at each of the recurrent periods of its recrudescence. In a certain sense this is largely true of the romantic art of the Elizabethan drama. But conjoined with the merely

---

[1] Analytics of Literature, pp. 78 f.
[2] Op. cit.
[3] "... pure Poetry, the essence of which consists in bold figures and a lively imagery" (Bp. Hurd, Works, Vol. I, p. 99). Cf. also Dryden, Works ed. Scott and Saintsbury, V, 111 f.

bold and concentrative use of trope in this drama, there is the deliberate and frequent use of simile, not of the prolonged simile, it is true, but of the short and emphatic simile. Shakspere, especially in his earlier work, is full of it, and it is almost the chief characteristic of the style of Webster, the most intense of the Elizabethans after Shakspere. At the same time, moreover, the other tendency towards the expansive in style and towards deliberate and weaker figures, is continually reasserting itself in all periods of literary history,[1] although probably the final result on the whole is a blending of various styles such as we see in Milton and Tennyson; and the sympathetic or pregnant metaphor, as Biese[2] says, in its various forms and phases, has doubtless been a product of slow growth.

<small>Weaker Figures and Simile</small>

At any rate the dramatic metaphor, in infinite complexity of form and expression and in varying degrees of intensity, is abundantly illustrated in the Elizabethan drama. Passion and emotion rather than utilitarian economy[3] seem to me to be its function. Brevity and directness are doubtless the usual concomitants of passion and emotion, but they are hardly the primary motive of dramatic and other æsthetic metaphor. If we disregard the external marks of difference between metaphor, simile, and other tropes of a high degree of imaginative intensity, they all perhaps may be divided into two classes acccording to their subjective effect — a division which also corresponds roughly to the primary division among tropes according to the source from which the subject-matter of each is derived. The first class includes such tropes as primarily illustrate Aristotle's explanation[4] of the psychological effect of metaphor and simile as affording a gratification of intellectual curiosity in

<small>Dramatic Metaphor; its Function</small>

<small>Two Essential Classes in Trope: the Vivid Image versus the Sympathetic Metaphor</small>

---

[1] Homer is succeeded by the Latin epic poets; then Ariosto, Tasso, etc.; then Spenser, Milton, Wordsworth; and in our day typical minor poets like William Morris and other dreamers of dreams.

[2] Das Metaphorische in der dichterischen Phantasie, pp. 29-30.

[3] Cf. Spencer's Phil. of Style.

[4] Rhetoric, Bk. III c. x.; also Bk. I c. xi.

the perception of hidden analogies, of likeness in difference. Such are many nature similes and those which generally excel in vividness of image. The second and larger class, while sometimes also answering to the test of conveying instruction, primarily make their appeal remotely or directly to the human will, to "the will to live," in the phraseology of the Schopenhauerian philosophy. Such are the sympathetic metaphor and in fact most metaphors and similes involving human affairs and interests in one term or the other of the comparison. Nature similes involving "the pathetic fallacy," all personifications, full or concealed, and almost all forms of sententious figures are of this sort. By far the greater proportion of the figures used in dramatic poetry, where the comparison almost always involves the human in at least one of its terms, are of this class. The brief and intensive metaphor is so far distinguished from other forms of trope of this class in its greater directness, subtlety, and force of appeal to the emotional sympathies of "the will to live." Thus Macbeth's passionate cry, "Out, out, brief candle;" forces home upon the mind not so much a comparison conveying useful instruction, as an intense and sympathetic realization, through the humblest symbolism, of the brevity and uncertainty of life and a score of other emotions arising from the situation and the context, but far too complex and searching to be expressed by any circumlocution of literal language.

This form of figure, the sympathetic or intensive metaphor, brought to its perfection by Shakspere, is exemplified with varying degrees of power and success throughout the works of his contemporaries. Few, however, show it in great degree, although almost all show traces at least of a style of expression and feeling which was in the air of the Renaissance period. Marlowe's passion is too tumultuous, rhythmical, and grandiose to exhibit many examples of the concentrative metaphor and the brief and intensive simile. Marlowe like a true poet is fond of the nature picture with but slight emotional connotation:

The Intensive Metaphor in the Drama

In Marlowe

> "The horse that guide the golden eye of Heaven,
> And blow the morning from their nosterils,
> Making their fiery gait above the clouds."

> "their ensigns spread
> Look like the parti-colored clouds of heaven."

Intenser is:
> "Oh, thou art fairer than the evening air,
> Clad in the beauty of a thousand stars."

Or Faustus' passionate cry:
> "See where Christ's blood streams in the firmament."

Full of symbolism, too, is the concluding chorus of *Faustus:*
> "Cut is the branch that might have grown full straight,
> And burned is Apollo's laurel bough,
> That sometime grew within this learned man."

The diction of *Edward II* is somewhat more dramatic than elsewhere in Marlowe:
> "Brother, revenge it, and let these their heads
> *Preach* upon poles."

> "methinks you hang the heads,
> But we'll *advance* them, traitors!"

> "My heart is *as an anvil unto sorrow*,
> Which beats upon it like the Cyclops' hammers."

> "weep not for Mortimer,"
> That scorns the world, and, *as a traveller*,
> Goes to discover countries yet unknown."

And see Edward's language to his jailors.

Greene, Peele, and Lyly have little figure of this sort that is significant. Kyd's great reputation in his own time, we may conjecture, was partly due to his daring experiments in the art of violent and intensive imagery.

In Kyd

Tropes like the examples that follow must have had a striking and novel effect after the arid literature of the preceding two hundred years upon a public eager for sensation, but with tastes yet crude and unformed.[1]

---

[1] Perhaps, if we may conjecture from Henslow's diary, the best of these are from Jonson's hand; or else, according to Lamb (Spec. of Eng. Dram. Poets, p. 11), from Webster's; or, according to Coleridge (Table Talk, Bohn ed., p. 203), from Shakspere's.

> "A melancholy, discontented courtier
> Whose famished jaws look *like the chap of death.*"
>
> "Methinks since I *grew inward with revenge*,
> I cannot look with scorn enough on death."

See also the fanciful description of the classical inferno at the beginning of *The Spanish Tragedy*,[1] or Hieronimo's semi-lunatic allegory in his speech to the "Portingals."[2]

> "There is a path upon your left-hand side
> That leadeth from a guilty conscience
> Unto a forest of distrust and fear," etc.

Chapman's tragedies are replete with metaphor, but his manner is expatiatory, tortuous, and magniloquent, rather than concise and intense. Occasionally, however, he breaks out into the characteristic Elizabethan metaphor. For example:

In Chapman

> "my heart *shrugs* at it."[3]

> "I stroke again at him, and then *he slept.*"[4]

> "He died *splinted* with his chamber grooms."[5]

> "D'Ambois' sword . . . . .
> *Shot like a pointed comet* at the face
> Of manly Barrisor."[6]

Even Jonson in the midst of his resolute realism presents a few instances of similar phraseology.[7] But it is from the tragic and intense genius of Webster and of Tourneur that we must look for the greatest number of concentrative tropes. Tourneur is full of flash-light images:

In Tourneur

> "Your gravity becomes your perished soul
> As hoary mouldiness does rotten fruit."[8]

> "O, that marrowless age
> *Should stuff the hollow bones* with damn'd desires."[9]

Hippolito in *The Revenger's Tragedy* urges Antonio's friends to avenge the latter's wrongs at the hands of the Duchess' son; and,

---

[1] Hazlitt's Dodsley, V pp. 8-10. [6] Id. p. 147b.
[2] Id. p. 106. [7] See the examples quoted supra, pp. 134-135.
[3] Chapman, p. 337. [8] Tourneur, I 34.
[4] Id. p. 366. [9] Id. II 5.
[5] Id. p. 175.

in default of legal justice which is bribed, drawing his own sword, cries,

> "Nay, then, step forth *thou bribeless officer!*
> I bind you all *in steel* to bind you surely.
> Here let your oaths meet to be kept *and paid.*
> Which else will stick like rust and shame the blade.
> Strengthen my vow, that if, at the next sitting,
> *Judgment speak all in gold,* and spare the blood
> Of *such a serpent*—e'en before their seats
> To *let his soul out,* which *long time was found*
> *Guilty in heaven."*[1]

And Castiza, indignantly rejecting the evil suggestions of her mother, says to her,

> "I have endur'd you with an *ear of fire;*
> Your tongues have *struck hot irons on my face.*
> Mother, *come from that poisonous woman there."*[2]

See also:

> "Hast thou beguil'd her of salvation,
> And *rubbed hell o'er with honey?"*[3]

> "To have her train borne up, and her soul trail i' th' dirt."[4]

—and many others.

Similarly Webster:

In Webster   ". . . Sleep with the lion,
> And let this brood of secure foolish mice
> Play with your nostrils, till the time be ripe
> *For the bloody audit* and the fatal gripe."[5]

> "And so I leave thee,
> *With all the Furies hanging 'bout thy neck."*[6]

> "I have heard grief nam'd the eldest child of sin."[7]

> "These are two cupping-glasses that shall draw
> All my infected blood out." [*Showing the pistols.*][8]

> "Fate's a spaniel,
> We cannot beat it from us."[9]

[1] Tourneur, 37.
[2] Id. 51.
[3] Id. 54.
[4] Id. 123.
[5] Webster, 27b.
[6] Id. 35a.
[7] Id. 44b.
[8] Id. 47b.
[9] Id. 49a.

> "Her guilt *treads on
> Hot burning coulters*."[1]
>
> "Sir, your direction
> *Shall lead me by the hand*."[2]
>
> "I'll second you in all danger; and, howe'er,
> My life *keeps rank* with yours."[3]
>
> "You shall see me *wind my tongue about his heart*
> Like a skein of silk."[4]
>
> "Because I do not strike you,
> Or give you the lie, such foul preparatives
> Would show like *the stale injury of wine*,—
> I reserve my rage *to sit on my sword's point*."[5]
>
> "His memory to virtue and good men
> *Is still carousing Lethe*."[6]
>
> "Thy violent lust
> Shall, like the biting of the envenom'd aspic,
> *Steal thee to hell*."[7]

Webster's characteristic figure, however, is the deliberate comparison. But the emotional power of his similes, if somewhat dry, bitter, and conscious, is scarcely less than that of the deepest and most burning metaphors.

Out of the hurry and stress and profusion of metaphorical speech which gets to be characteristic of many of the Elizabethan dramatists result several tendencies which may be said to mark the drama of the time as a whole. First there is a great amount of cumulative and alternative trope. Figures are dealt out in overmeasure;[8] there is often a very riot of metaphors and similes; the poet delights to show his dexterity with language; few of the dramatists are free from the vice of punning and every sort of

Various Excesses in the Use of Tropes

---

[1] Webster, 74b.
[2] Id. 80a.
[3] Id. 92b.
[4] Id. 95b.
[5] Id. 117b.
[6] Id. 169a.
[7] Id. 172a.

[8] See the distinctions on the subject of accumulated and daring metaphor in The Treatise on The Sublime usually ascribed to Longinus XXXII 1, 2:

"Those outbursts of passion which drive onwards like a winter torrent draw with them as an indispensable accessory whole masses of metaphor . . .," etc. (Havel's translation, p. 58.)

fantastic playing with words; hyperbole is a familiar figure with them, and such is the superabundance of dramatic passion pressing forward for expression that the grossest exaggerations seldom shock them; conceits everywhere abound, witty, dainty, fantastic, feeble, eloquent,—of every sort. We feel the approach of the "metaphysical" school in poetry. Extremes meet in the same writer. Chapman is turgid, grandiose, extravagant in his tragedies; such sound and fury of metaphor, obscurely signifying weighty and impassioned things, can hardly be paralleled elsewhere in literature. At the same time his comedies are often witty, easy, and full of natural life. Involved metaphor is counterbalanced in him by a habit of logical and emphatic simile. So Webster, the deepest poet of passion of the age after Shakspere, prefers to use the dry and clear-cut simile to accentuate the emotion of pity and terror. Yet Webster, too, at times heaps metaphor upon metaphor. Bosola in *The Duchess of Malfi*[1] reproaches the duchess for her despair:

Cumulative Effects

"Leave this vain sorrow.
Things being at the worst begin to mend: the bee
When he hath shot his sting into your hand,
May then play with your eyelid.
Duchess: Good comfortable fellow,
Persuade a wretch that's broke upon the wheel
To have all his bones new set; entreat him live
To be executed again. Who must despatch me?
I account this world a tedious theatre,
For I do play a part in't 'gainst my will.
Bosola: Come, be of comfort, I will save your life.
Duchess: Indeed, I have not leisure to tend
So small a business.
Bosola: Now, by my life I pity you.
Duchess: Thou art a fool, then,
To waste thy pity on a thing so wretched
As cannot pity itself. *I am full of daggers.
Puff, let me blow these vipers from me.*"

Dramatic innuendo everywhere abounds in Webster. Excited imaginations naturally have resource to suggestion by metaphor

[1] Act IV sc. i (Works p. 85b); see also Works 21a.

and are loth to drop the game. A little snatch of dialogue between Bosola and Antonio in *The Duchess of Malfi* (Webster 70b) is typical :

> *Bosola :* You are a false steward.
> *Antonio :* Saucy slave, I'll pull thee up by the roots.
> *Bos. :* May be the ruin will crush you to pieces.
> *Ant. :* You are an impudent snake indeed, sir :
> Are you scarce warm, and do you show your sting ?
> You libel well, sir.
> *Bos. :* No, sir ; copy it out
> And I will set my hand to 't.

Chapman is particularly fond of massing metaphors. See, for example in *Byron's Conspiracy* King Henry's speech to Byron concerning La Fin :[1]

> "Why suffer you that ill-aboding vermin
> To breed so near your bosom ? be assured
> His haunts are ominous ; not the throats of ravens,
> Spent on infected houses, howls of dogs,
> When no sound stirs, at midnight ; apparitions
> And strokes of spirits clad in black men's shapes,
> Or ugly women's; the adverse decrees
> Of constellations, nor security
> In vicious peace, are surer fatal ushers
> Of femall mischiefs and mortalities
> Than this prodigious fiend is, where he fawns."

Sententious Tropes

This same tendency, connected as it is with the tendency to conceits and over-elaboration of figures, results also in a great profusion of tropes which for want of a better name may be called Sententious Figures,[2] including Allegory, Perfect and Imperfect, Fable, Parable, Proverb, and also metaphors and similes of a gnomic cast, such as are very frequent throughout the drama. A sort of implied

---

[1] Act III sc. i (pp. 230b-231a). See also the superb cumulative effects in Byron's dying speech, quoted above, pp. 134-135; and see Marlowe's *Tamburlaine* passim. The great examples of this sort of effect, however, are to be found in Shakspere. See the Dover cliff speech, *King Lear* IV vi; the apostrophe to England—"This royal throne of kings," in *Richard II*, Act II sc. i; etc.

[2] See further on sententious figures, infra, pp. 204 f.; see also : Greene, 179a (Friar Bacon's prophecy of Elizabeth, "Diana's rose"), 200a, 200b, 219a (fable

simile or metaphorical phrase or passage is the favorite form.
Lyly especially abounds in them; for example, "There is no surfeit so dangerous as that of honey, nor any poison so deadly as that of love; in the one physic cannot prevail, nor in the other counsel."[1] This sort of proportional simile with the sign of comparison omitted passes very readily into the imperfect allegory, as does also the pursued or compound metaphor which is likewise so frequent in the early dramatists. Indeed the compound metaphor Gerber[2] apparently treats as allegory. The general indirection and ethical impressiveness of these figures commended them to the Elizabethan writers. Greene and Chapman especially abound in them; Jonson also has many, especially proverbs and others of a colloquial cast; Webster is more dramatically sententious. The taste for this sort of thing in the earlier dramatists is connected with the tendency of contemporary literature to allegory and emblem. Notice has already been taken of the echoes of Spenser's imagery in Peele and in Marlowe.[3] The emblematic devices of Young Mortimer and Lancaster for Edward's "stately triumph" in Act II scene ii of Marlowe's *Edward II* recall also the Spenser of *The Visions* and similar imitations of mediæval and contemporary motives out of Petrarch and the French poets.

> "A lofty cedar-tree, fair flourishing,
> On whose top-branches kingly eagles perch,
> And by the bark a canker creeps me up,
> And gets into the highest bough of all:
> The motto, *Æque tandem.*"[4]

The Euphuistic employment of a fabulous natural history, which invaded the drama at this period, is a part of the same tendency to fable and emblem.

of the lion, the hind, and the fox); Marlowe, II 154–5; Webster, 32b (fable of the crocodile and the wren), and passim for sententious couplets and similes; Chapman, 185b (fable of the traveler, the north wind, and the sun); etc.

[1] Works I 112. See also his various prologues, especially the "Prologue at the Black Friars" to *Alexander and Campaspe*.

[2] Die Sprache als Kunst, II 98.

[3] Supra, pp. 25, 39.

[4] Marlowe, II 154–5.

Catachresis and Mixed Metaphor

Catachresis and mixed metaphor we naturally expect to find largely exemplified in a diction such as that of the Elizabethan dramatists, and far-fetched comparisons and metaphors subtle and elliptical beyond measure doubtless do abound; but the typically crude and grotesque mixed metaphor is much less frequent than might be expected. Too much real passion and emotional excitement dictated the utterances of these men to permit many lapses into mere senility and vacuity of imagery. Rant, extravagance, and hyperbole there is in abundance in Kyd, Marlowe, Chapman and others, but little mere incompetence and impotence of picture and phrase.[1] Chapman, it is true, is too often involved, obscure, and excessive, but with him it is rather a matter of tortuous phraseology, and of overwrought hyperbole, than of any weakness of the image-conceiving power. Seldom does he descend to mere absurdities like the following from La Fin's speech to Henry in Act I scene i of *Byron's Conspiracy*:[2]

> "Nor shall frowns and taunts, . . .
> Keep *my free throat from knocking at the sky.*"

Or later (Act IV scene i):[3]

> "tell our brother . . .
> . . . in what prayers we raise our hearts to heaven,
> That in more terror to his foes, and wonder,
> He may *drink earthquakes, and devour the thunder.*"

The love of hyperbole, indeed, was the great provocative of catachresis among the Elizabethans. But the heightening of figure throughout the greater years of the drama is emotional rather than visual or logical. Elliptical figures which border on the non-logical prevail, at least in tragedy—"good wits will apply" was the motto of the age. For those who care to apply the test there are few of these that cannot be resolved syllogistically after the manner of Lord Kames[4] or of Dr. Abbott,[5] but the process is not the real process psychologically underlying their composi-

---

[1] See examples of mixed metaphor in Marlowe, supra, pp. 36-37.
[2] Chapman, p. 217a.
[3] Id., p. 235b; see also 164b.
[4] Elements of Criticisms, II 282 f.
[5] Shaksperian Grammar, §§ 517 f.

tion. Later, and in comedy even as early as Lyly, intellectual fancy and mere conceits get the upper hand of nature and passion.

Of the rapid transition from image to image which borders on catachresis, but which is always characteristic of the highly metaphorical and impassioned style, Webster himself, exact and clear cut as his mental processes habitually are, offers several examples:

"Let the young man *play still upon the bit*,
Till we have brought and *train'd him to our lure*."[1]

"His smooth *crest hath cast a palped film*
Over Rome's eyes."[2]

Other passages in which simile treads upon the heel of simile exist in great number and have already been referred to.[3]

Conceits Conceits and verbal and intellectual jugglery of every type are a marked characteristic in greater or less degree of almost the entire body of Elizabethan literature. Under each dramatist reference already has been made to numerous examples of conceits and plays upon words. In tragedy they generally appear under the form of hyperbole. In romantic and popular comedy they assume every form, from Lyly's Euphuism and Shakspere's infinitely varied archness, artifice, and drollery, to Jonson's colloquialism, and the fantastical and metaphysical subleties of the later school.

In comedy and occasionally in more serious drama it must be borne in mind that these and similar aberrations from classical taste are very frequently in keeping and have a justification in the ethos of a drama which holds the mirror up to a life and a society so romantic, fantastic, and extravagant as that of the Elizabethan age in many respects was. The chief defect of frigid and "metaphysical" conceits is precisely the lack of such a justification in dramatic truth or other adequate æsthetic motive.

[1] Webster, p. 160b; cf. also 161b ("under his smooth calmness *cloaks a tempest*").
[2] Id. p. 162a.
[3] Supra, pp. xii, 177 f.

That extravagant forcing of the analogical faculty which is the basis of conceits, takes various forms in the Elizabethan dramatists.[1] Conceits that strangely intensify dramatic effect are not uncommon. Webster's similes, which often border on conceits in the remoteness and unexpectedness of their analogies, almost never fail to emphasize and enforce the exact tone of dramatic feeling desirable and desired in any given situation. Thus in *The White Devil* the taunting irony of Monticelso's speech to Francisco de Medici is accentuated by the seemingly careless strangeness of his phrase:

Dramatic Conceits

> "Come, come, my lord, *untie your folded thoughts,*
> *And let them dangle loose as a bride's hair:* —
> *Your sister's poison'd.*"[2]

Tourneur is even more impressive in such effects:

> "Hast thou beguil'd her of salvation
> And *rubb'd hell o'er with honey?*"[3]

> "Slaves are but nails to drive out one another."[4]

Or in that most dramatic interview between the two brothers Vindici and Hippolito and their mother in Act IV, scene iv, of *The Revenger's Tragedy*,[5] how sudden and intense is the emotional transition indicated by Vindici's ironical metaphor at sight of his mother's repentance:

> "Nay, an you draw tears once, go to bed....
> Brother, *it rains; 'twill spoil your dagger; house it.*"

Airy and fantastic conceits, the very false gallop of wits, are first exemplified in Lyly's comedies. The entire Euphuistic natural history is a string of conceits. But Lyly excels also in sprightly and witty dialogue elaborated through mazes of fantastic conceit. He delights to pursue airy poetical fancies through all the possible variations of metaphor. Here is a fragment of dialogue between Cupid and a Nymph of Diana:[6]

Airy and Fantastic Conceits

---

[1] On verbal conceits and plays on words in the drama, cf. A. W. Schlegel, Dramatic Art and Literature, trans. Black, p. 366.
[2] Webster, p. 27a. [4] Tourneur, II 103.
[3] Tourneur, II 54. [5] Id. 122.
[6] Lyly, I 223 (*Gallathea* I ii); see I 53 ("my palace is paved with grass,

Nymph: Love, good sir, what mean you by it? or what do you call it?

Cupid: A heat full of coldness, a sweet full of bitterness, a pain full of pleasantness; which maketh thoughts have eyes, and hearts ears; bred by desire, nursed by delight, weaned by jealousy, killed by dissembling, buried by ingratitude; and this is love, fair lady,—will you any?"

The conceits of love, following the motives of contemporary poetry, are frequently introduced by other dramatists. Chapman in *All Fools*, Act IV, scene i, draws a humorous picture of the extravagant lover:[1]

> "I had quite been drown'd in seas of tears
> Had not I taken hold in happy time
> Of this sweet hand; my heart had been consumed
> To a heap of ashes with the flames of love,
> Had it not sweetly been assuaged and cool'd
> With the moist kisses of these sugar'd lips."

And similarly Jonson:[2]

> "No more of Love's ungrateful tyranny,
> His wheels of torture, and his pits of birdlime,
> His nets of nooses, whirlpools of vexation,
> His mills to grind his servants into powder"—etc.

Chapman's comedies contain many light and charming conceits; thus:... "Indeed thou told'st me how gloriously he apprehended the favor of a great lady i' th' presence, *whose heart, he said, stood a tiptoe*[3] *in her eye to look at him*,"[4] or, "Up to the heart in love;"[5] or, "She hath exiled her eyes from sleep;"[6] or this: "Her blood went and came *of errands betwixt her face and her*

and *tiled* with stars;" cf. the French proverb—"dormir à la belle étoile;" cf. Webster, 152b: "This three months did we never house our heads But *in yon great star-chamber;* cf. Tourneur, I 139: "In yon star-chamber thou shalt answer it"); or see II 114 (Halfpenny's dream of prunes, currants, and raisins); or II 232 (Silvestris' wooing of Niobe); etc.

[1] Chapman, 68b.
[2] Jonson, II 377a (*The New Inn*, IV iii).
[3] Cf. Kyd, Hazlitt's Dodsley, IV 391 ("my blood 's a tiptoe").
[4] Chapman, 133b (*Mons. D'Olive* IV i).
[5] Chapman, 51a.
[6] Id. 328b.

heart, and these changes I can tell you are shrewd tell-tales."¹
Compare Webster, 132b;

> "I cannot set myself so many fathom
> Beneath the height of my true heart as fear."

Or see the gallant Captain Quintiliano's comparison of the service of a feast with the honorable service of the field, in *May-Day*, Act IV, scene iv.²

Jonson is full of comic conceits, at times grotesque and extravagant; satire and burlesque, however, is usually their motive. Thus, in *The Staple of News*,³ Act IV, scene i:

> "O, how my princess draws me with her looks,
> And hales me in, as eddies draw in boats,
> Or strong Charybdis ships that sail too near
> The shelves of love! The tides of your two eyes,
> Wind of your breath, are such as suck in all
> That do approach you."

Abstract and Metaphysical Conceits

Closely akin to the fantastic conceits so characteristic of the romantic comedy vein of this period are the abstract and "metaphysical" conceits which, occasionally developed in tragedy and comedy for dramatic purposes, point the way to the colder and more vicious style of the poetry of the fantastic school. Many of the subtler and finer effects of the peculiar Elizabethan dramatic phraseology depend upon figures of this sort, which are often tropological paradoxes. Thus in Chapman's *All Fools*, Act I, scene i, Valerio, whose father is thwarting his aspirations to gentility and trying to force him into "husbandry," exclaims:

> "My father? why, my father, does he think
> *To rob me of myself?*"⁴

Similarly in *Monsieur D'Olive*, Act IV, scene i:

> "You know the use of honor, that will ever
> *Retire into itself.*"⁵

Similarly Tourneur⁶ (though scarcely metaphorical):

> "Joy's a subtle elf.
> I think man's happiest *when he forgets himself.*"

---

¹ Chapman, p. 317a.
² Id. p. 300.
³ Jonson, II 317b.
⁴ Chapman, p. 49a.
⁵ Chapman, 130b.
⁶ Tourneur, II 124; cf. Webster, 49b, 83a.

And also: "What, brother? Am I far enough from myself?"[1]
Or: "Mother, come from that poisonous woman there."[2]
And Jonson,[3] translating Persius' "Ne te quæsiveris extra":

> "as if I lived
> To any other scale than what's my own,
> Or *sought myself without myself*, from home."[4]

Similar subtleties abound:

> "O, at that word
> I'm lost again; *you cannot find me yet;*
> I'm in a throng of happy apprehensions."[5]

> "'twas spoke by one
> That is most *inward with* the duke's son's lust."[6]

"Here was the .... fittest hour, to have *made my revenge familiar* with him."[7]

So Kyd:[8] "since I grew *inward* with revenge."

Kyd again:[9] "He had not *seen the back* of nineteen years."

Chapman:[10] "O, the infinite regions betwixt a woman's tongue and her heart! Similarly Jonson:[11]

> "If this were true now! but the space, the space,
> Between the breast and lips--Tiberius' heart
> Lies a thought farther than another man's."

Webster:[12]   "O, the secret of my prince,
>   Which I will wear on the inside of my heart."

So Shakspere:[13]   "I will wear him
>   In my heart's core."

Jonson:[14] "They say lines parallel do never meet,
>   He has met his parallel in wit and school-craft."

---

[1] Tourneur, II 24.   [2] Id. II 51.

[3] Jonson, II 350b (*The New Inn*, II i).

[4] Cf. Ford, II 287 (*Fancies Chaste and Noble* IV i): "Come home again .... to thine own simplicity."

[5] Tourneur, II 81.   [8] Hazlitt's Dodsley, V 168.

[6] Tourneur, II 59.   [9] Id. 105.

[7] Id. II 130.   [10] Chapman, 158b.

[11] Jonson, I 295b. Similarly see Shirley, *The Witty Fair One*, I iii (Mermaid ed., p. 13) and *Hyde Park*, III ii (p. 221); also Beaumont and Fletcher, *Philaster*, I i, (Mermaid ed. I, p. 111).

[12] Webster, 80a.   [14] Jonson, II 353b.

[13] *Hamlet*, III ii 70.

Ford:[1] "My soul
Runs circular in sorrow for revenge."
Tourneur, II 137: "All sorrows
Must run their circles into joys."
Chapman:[2] "Hereafter? 'Tis a supposed infinite."
Tourneur:[3]
"Make .... A drunkard clasp his teeth and not undo 'em,
To suffer *wet damnation* to run through 'em."

Sententious ideas similarly are often cast into the form of quasi-conceits for a juster emphasis, as in Jonson:[4] "It is a competency to him that he can be virtuous." Or Webster:[5]

"I have long served virtue
And ne'er ta'en wages of her."

Or Tourneur[6]: "Patience is the honest man's revenge."

Hyperbolical Conceits

Colossal conceits, conceits that become hyperboles, as well as those that are simply crude and extravagant, exist in great number throughout the Elizabethan drama. In the best passages and in the best authors we are never safe from them. Flamineo's dying speech in *The White Devil*,[7] in the very resolution of the tragic knot, is spoiled by this bit of atrocity, unworthy of Donne or of Cowley:

"My life was a black charnel. I have caught
An everlasting cold; I have lost my voice
Most irrecoverably."

And similarly in The *Duchess of Malfi*, this is part of Ferdinand's dying speech:

"Give me some wet hay; I am broken winded.
I do account this world but a dog-kennel."[8]

In Jonson's *Sad Shepherd*[9] Amie's love-plaints are such as this:

"I weep, and boil away myself in tears;
And then my panting heart would dry those fears;
I burn, though all the forest lend a shade," etc.

[1] Ford, I 188.
[2] Chapman, 169b.
[3] Tourneur, II 83.
[4] Jonson, I 162.
[5] Webster, 65a.
[6] Tourneur, I 153.
[7] Webster, 50b.
[8] Id. 100b.
[9] Jonson, II 50rb.

The height of the bizarre however is reached in Chapman's comparison :[1]

> "Love is a razor, cleansing being well used,
> But fetcheth blood, still being the least abused."

Or in his similes of the shoeing horn: "Make both their absences shoeing-horns to draw on the presence of Æmilia.[2] Shakspere makes use of the same comparison in *Troilus and Cressida*, V i 53, describing Menelaus as "a thrifty shoeing-horn in a chain, hanging at his brother's leg."

Worse in effect because seriously meant is Bussy D' Ambois' dying injunction :[3]

> "Tell them all that D' Ambois now is hasting
> To the eternal dwellers; that *a thunder*
> *Of all their sighs* together for their frailties
> Beheld in me, may quit my worthless fall
> *With a fit volley for my funeral.*"

— recalling Tourneur :[4]

> "His gasping sighs are like the falling noise
> Of some great building, when the ground-work breaks."

Worse yet is D' Amville's imprecation in the *Atheist's Tragedy*.[5]

> "Dead be your tongues! Drop out
> Mine eye-balls and let envious Fortune play
> At tennis with 'em."

Hyperbole, bombast, and extravagance are absent from few of the Elizabethans. Kyd, Marlowe, Greene, and Chapman show the most, although passages of it are to be found here and there in almost every playwright of the time. In fact hyperbolical expression was a recognized form of dramatic emphasis. The way had been prepared for it by the Herods, the devils, and the huffing young gallants of the mystery and morality plays. The passion and the imagination of the period as reflected in its minor writers, whatever qualities of exaltation and of beauty it has, is also at times fundamentally crude and violent, especially

<small>*Hyperbole in the Elizabethan Drama*</small>

[1] Chapman, 165a.
[2] Chapman, 291a; similarly, 136b, 137b.
[3] Id. 175b.
[4] Tourneur, I 136.
[5] Id. I 54.

in the popular drama, which was so largely freed from all restraints of literary form and tradition. The introduction of the element of literary form and tradition by Marlowe and his associates affected the use of hyperbole in two ways. In the first place it reduced the harshness and formlessness of the earlier rant into some sort of measure; and in the second place it tended to substitute poetical and idealized forms of passion for the mere barbarism of the earlier extravagance. *Tamburlaine's* magnificence and hyperbole is immeasurable but it is idealized. The weak points of the new style, however, were very quickly seen and satire of Kyd and Greene and the other early emulators and imitators of Marlowe in this vein begins at once. In the second part of *The Return from Parnassus*, Act III, sc. iv and following, in the part of Furor Poeticus, there is some significant burlesque of the new style. Tamburlaine's habitual hyperbolical insolence towards the gods —

"The God of wars resigns his room to me,
Meaning to make me general of the world:
Jove viewing me in arms, looks pale and wan,
Fearing my power should pull him from his throne,"—[1]

seems to be the general model of the burlesque invocation of Furor Poeticus:[2]

"Awake, you paltry trulls of Helicon,
Or, by this light, I'll swagger with you straight.
You, grandsire Phœbus, with your lovely eye,
The firmament's eternal vagabond,
The heaven's prompter that doth peep and pry
Into the acts of mortal tennis-balls,
Inspire me straight with some rare delicies,
Or I'll dismount thee from thy radiant coach,
And make thee a poor Cutchy [coachee?] here on earth."[3]

The romantic and swelling hyperbole of Marlowe and Chapman, however, with its frequent classical phraseology, soon gives way to a less profuse and more dramatic manner. The hyperbole of Titanic insolence yields to the hyperbole of violence and

[1] *I Tamburlaine*, V ii (Works I p. 102; cf. similarly pp. 189, 198, etc.).
[2] *Parnassus*, ed. Macray, p. 123.
[3] See also the reference to "three-piled hyperbole" in Biron's speech in *Love's Labor's Lost* V ii 407.

tragic exaggeration. Webster, for example, uses little hyperbole, but that little abounds in dramatic intensity:

"Hell to my affliction
Is mere snow-water."[1]

"In the sea's bottom sooner thou shalt make
A bonfire."[2]

"Other sins only speak; murder shrieks out:
The element of water moistens the earth,
But blood flies upward and bedews the heavens."[3]

Personification in the Drama

Personification as a dramatic mode was made familiar to the sixteenth century English public by the morality plays. "In itself," as Mr. Pollard says,[4] "as tending to didacticism and unreality, personification is wholly undramatic." This, of course, is to be understood merely of full, or formal, abstract personification. Personal metaphors, on the other hand, and tropes involving intense and emotional anthropomorphism, in themselves are oftentimes the most dramatic of all figures. What phrase, for example, could express more vividly the idea of the reproach of associates for another's cowardice or degeneracy than to say:

Personal Metaphors

"the scorn of their discourse
Turns *smiling back* upon your backwardness."[5]

Figures of this class, more than any other, are the foundation of the true Elizabethan dramatic diction. Striking examples are:

Chapman, 337a: "'fore heaven *my heart shrugs* at it."

315a: "Drunkards, *spew'd out of* taverns."

97a: "never shall my counsels cease *to knock
At thy impatient ears.*"

256a: "I would your dagger's point *had kiss'd* my heart."

Jonson, I 299a: "His thoughts *look through* his words."

[1] Webster, 15a.
[2] Id. 31b.
[3] Id. 90a.
[4] Engl. Miracle Plays, Introd., p. xliii.
[5] Tourneur, 1 9

138: "the plague that *treads on the heels* o' your foppery."

Webster, 118b: "till the grave *gather* one of us."

131a: "such a guilt as would have lain
Howling forever at your wounded heart,
And rose with you to judgment."

80a: "Sir, your direction *Shall lead me by the hand.*"

Tourneur, I 28: "Her modest blush fell to a *pale dislike.*"

Marlowe, I 223: "the gloomy shadow of the earth . . .
Leaps from the antarctic world into the sky."

II 202 "O my stars,
Why do you *lour* unkindly on a king?"

Formal and abstract personification, however, is very common, especially in the earlier drama, where it usually takes poetical or classical forms. Personifications of Death, the Fates, the Furies, Fortune, Occasion, and the like, abound throughout Greene, Peele, and Marlowe. They are very prominent also in Chapman's high-tragedy style. Among the more dramatic poets like Webster and Tourneur formal personification becomes rarer and briefer, as in Webster's

Formal Personification

"Lust carries her sharp whip
At her own girdle."

Or — " O sacred innocence, that sweetly sleeps
On turtles' feathers, whilst a guilty conscience
Is a black register wherein is writ
All our good deeds and bad."[2]

Or Vindici's apostrophe in Tourneur:[3]

"Sword, I durst make a promise of him to thee;
Thou shalt dis-heir him; it shall be thine honor."

Such personifications are full of meaning and dramatic force. The degree of feeling involved in any personification is usually the measure of its merit, and in the utterance of feeling personification never is an outworn form. Poverty of significance and of poetic emotion is the general characteristic of mere capital-letter personification, and this precisely is what distinguishes the man-

[1] P. 12b.   [2] P. 91b.   [3] II, p. 33.

ner of the English "classical" period from that of the Elizabethan period.

In regard to the general range of observation and the sources in nature and human life from which the Elizabethan dramatists included in this study draw their metaphors and similes the most striking fact to be noted is the more narrowly poetical character of the earlier dramatic writing and its reliance upon the more conventional artifices of composition, resulting in a much larger proportion of nature similes, and of nature similes handled after a more or less conventional method, than in the following and more dramatic period. In the treatment of nature indeed, although only a small part of their task, the dramatists of the entire period seldom advance beyond the conventional and ornamental manner. There is a tinge of the Euphuistic natural history, an odor of the lamp about almost all their observations of things natural. Poetical touches are not rare, but there is little evidence of much keenness or delicacy of nature-observation.[1] A few examples, however, are worth recording: Chapman 47a:

General Range and Sources of Tropes in the Drama

Treatment of Nature

"like the lark
Mounting the sky in shrill and cheerful notes,
Chanting his joys aspired."

65b: "Like a jackdaw, that, when he lights upon
A dainty morsel, kaa's and makes his brags,
And then some kite doth scoop it from him straight."

164a: "Here's nought but whispering with us; like a calm
Before a tempest, when the silent air
Lays her soft ear close to the earth to hearken
For that she fears steals on to ravish her."

207b: "that resembles
The weighty and the goodly bodied eagle,
Who, being on earth, before her shady wings
Can raise her into air, a mighty way
Close by the ground she runs."

245b: "We must ascend to our intention's top
Like clouds that be not seen till they be up."[2]

[1] Cf. Symonds, Essays Speculative and Suggestive, 417.
[2] See also Chapman, p. 543a.

Jonson, II 490a : "turf as soft and smooth as the mole's skin."

I 371b : "When she came in like starlight."

Jonson, I 291b : "to present the shapes
Of dangers greater than they are, like late
Or early shadows."

Marlowe, I 201 : "Thus are the coward villains fled for fear
Like summer vapors vanished by the sun."

Spenser's method of nature treatment, graceful and charming, but highly conventional, and following so strictly the poetical traditions, is, generally speaking, the accepted method of the Elizabethan drama. Spenser,[1] following Chaucer closely, enumerates the trees contained in his Wood of Error:

"The sailing pine, the cedar proud and tall,
The vine-prop elm, the poplar never dry,"

and so on; the obvious comment on which, neglecting consideration of the possible allegorical justification of the description, is that all these trees were never known in nature to grow together in one forest. In the same way Mr. J. A. Symonds[2] notes a flower passage in one of Ben Jonson's masques[3] in which there is a similar confusion of nature's ways. The true answer to such criticisms perhaps is that, however much such descriptions may err scientifically, æsthetically they are justifiable, at least so long as the reader's sense of beauty is satisfied and is still untroubled by suggestions *ab extra* of discord and discrepancy.[4]

The Pathetic Fallacy   The pathetic fallacy naturally is frequent in the nature similes of the dramatists. A charming illustration is found in one or two lines of the opening speech of Ben Jonson's *Sad Shepherd*.[5]

[1] *Fairy Queen*, I i 8. Cf. also "Virgil's Gnat" (Spenser, Globe ed., p. 506), and the flower passage in "Muiopotmos" (p. 534).

[2] Shaks. Pred., 351.

[3] "Pan's Anniversary" (Works III 184).

[4] See Aristotle's Poetic ch. xxv: "The poet errs if what he fabricates is impossible according to the art itself; but it will be right if the end of poetry is obtained by it." (Buckley's translation.)

[5] II 489. A similarly charming passage occurs in Shirley, *The Witty Fair One*, I ii.

> "Here she was wont to go! and here! and here!
> Just where those daisies, pinks, and violets grow:
> *The world may find the spring by following her:*
> For other print her airy steps ne'er left.
> Her treading would not bend a blade of grass,
> Or shake the downy blow-ball from his stalk!
> But like the soft west wind she shot along
> *And where she went the flowers took thickest root,*
> As she had sowed them with her odorous foot."

"The flattering green" is an epithet from Lyly.[1]

> "As when the moon *hath comforted the night*
> And set the world in silver of her light"

is a couplet from Chapman.[2] "The golden fawnings of the sun" is another phrase of his.[3] His fine simile of the oak in Arden[4] has many similar touches:

> "Then, as in Arden, I have seen an oak
> Long shook with tempests, and his lofty top
> Bent to his root, which being at length made loose,
> *Even groaning with his weight,* he 'gan to nod
> This way and that, as loth his curled brows,
> Which he had oft wrapt in the sky with storms,
> Should stoop; and yet, his radical fibres burst,
> Storm-like he fell, and *hid the fear-cold earth.*"

Others furnish various noteworthy illustrations of the same figure: Marlowe, I 46: "Always moving as *the restless* spheres."

174:   "Making the meteors . . .
> Run *tilting* round about the firmament,
> And break their burning lances in the air,"

Jonson, I 248a:

> "the loving air,
> That closed her body in his silken arms."

I 92: Perfumes "To keep the air in awe of her sweet nostrils."
Tourneur, I 17:

> "The lovely face of heaven was masqu'd with sorrow,
> The sighing winds did move the breast of earth,
> The heavy clouds hung down their mourning heads,
> And wept sad showers the day that he went hence."

See also in Tourneur, I 40–41, the description of the weeping sea

---

[1] I 173.   [2] P. 227a.   [3] P. 251a.   [4] P. 148; see also p. 445b.

embracing the body of Charlemont. But the passionate and imaginative appeal to the anthropomorphic instinct is nowhere more vividly uttered than in this apostrophe from Webster (p. 40b):

> "O thou soft natural death, that art joint-twin
> To sweetest slumber ! No rough-bearded comet
> Stares on thy mild departure ; the dull owl
> Beats not against thy casement ; the hoarse wolf
> Scents not thy carrion : pity winds thy corse,
> Whilst horror waits on princes."

Most striking of all dramatic examples of the pathetic fallacy, if only it were more removed from sensationalism, is Vindici's exclamation in *The Revenger's Tragedy*, V iii, on hearing a peal of thunder just as he and his fellow-conspirators are wreaking their murderous revenge :

> "Mark, Thunder !
> *Dost know thy cue, thou big-voic'd crier?*"

In fact throughout the nature similes of the Elizabethan dramatists the second term of the simile, or the aspect of nature brought into comparison with any given human or dramatic motive or idea, is usually kept subordinate, so that a vivid picture is seldom formed. The simile of the oak in Arden, just cited from Chapman, is an exception, but such exceptions are rare and Chapman's tragic manner at best is epic rather than dramatic. It is the remote or the curious or novel in nature that interest these poets, rather than the familiar and the deeply significant things such as the modern poet by preference observes. The Euphuistic natural history attracted them because of its romantic associations and of the ease with which it may be applied for sententious illustrations. Still the sky, the sun, the stars, clouds, flowers, and the like, frequently freshen the poetry of Greene Peele, and Marlowe. Simple images in Peele, like

> "As when of Leicester's hall and bower
> Thou wert the rose and sweetest flower,"

or   "Pale, like mallow flowers,"

or   "Why should so fair a star stand in a vale,
> And not be seen to sparkle in the sky?"

are the source of half the slender grace of his lines. And there are a few similar touches in Greene ; for example:

> "Gracious as the morning star of heaven."
>
> "Thy father's hair, like to the silver blooms
> That beautify the shrubs of Africa."

Thunder, comets, and other hyperbolical images are characteristic of Marlowe, but he has a few fine nature-similes:

I 145 :   "Their ensigns spread
Look like the parti-colored clouds of heaven."

I 179 : "My chariot, swifter than the racking clouds."

I 179 : "The horse that guide the golden eye of heaven
And blow the morning from their nosterils,
Making their fiery gait above the clouds."

II 263: "I go as whirlwinds rage before a storm."

I 276: "Oh, thou art fairer than the evening air
Clad in the beauty of a thousand stars."

But the range is not wide, nor is there any subtlety of observation in the nature similes of the pre-Shaksperian drama. Later the poetical touches are rarer, but the range of mental association becomes more subtle and novel, while at the same time, as already remarked, the intensity of the dramatic connotation almost swallows up the nature image itself. Thus Webster, 17a :

> "Like mistletoe on sear elms spent by weather,
> Let him cleave to her, and both rot together."

Or 172b,

> "Thou lovest me, Appius, as the earth loves rain :
> Thou fain wouldst swallow me."

Chapman, 147b:

> "D'Ambois, that like a laurel put in fire
> Sparkled and spit."

Similarly Jonson, I 157 : . . . "not utter a phrase but what shalt come forth steeped in the very brine of conceit, and sparkle like salt in fire."

Jonson, I 72a :

> "Made my cold passion stand upon my face,
> Like drops of dew on a stiff cake of ice."

But this borders on the bizarre, as do many of Jonson's colloquial comparisons:

I 266b: "like so many screaming grasshoppers
Held by the wings, fill every ear with noise."

I 349b: "All her looks are sweet,
As the first grapes or cherries."

But, generally speaking, nature is important in the drama only in large and conventional metaphors or as linked with man and human sympathies. In the Elizabethan drama, certainly, man was the chief center of interest, but man imaginatively conceived. Unless imagination be understood as something alien from human passion, Buckle's generalization[1] that imagination is most active in man chiefly when he is directly subject to the stimulus of natural objects and forces is not borne out by the dramatic literature of the age of Elizabeth. The storm and stress of human passion, reflected in this literature, excited men's imaginations throughout this period perhaps as much as they have ever been excited by natural phenomena in any wise. Certain aspects of nature there were during the days of Elizabeth, such as the new discoveries in astronomy and geography, which stirred men's thoughts profoundly, but nature, in dramatic literature at least, is reflected at second hand, and the larger part of its nature imagery seems borrowed from books, and especially from classical literature.

Treatment of Human Life

In the realm of human life, on the contrary, variety and range of interest and keenness and subtlety of observation rapidly developed and extended. Novelty, appositeness, and force are the marks of the significant tropes drawn from the field of human life in the typical Elizabethan drama. Here at least most of the studies are made from

---

[1] Hist. of Civilization in Engl. (N. Y., 1872), Vol. I., pp. 85 f. e. g. "Under some aspects, nature is more prominent than man, under others, man than nature. In the former case the imagination is more stimulated than the understanding, and to this class all the earliest civilizations belong. The imagination is excited by earthquakes and volcanoes, and by danger generally."

the living model, and the work is rammed with life, crude and boisterous, tragic and passionate, or tender and noble. The early school, it is true, offers little evidence of close observation or dramatic rendering. It was the function of the university wits to soften and enrich the diction of the popular drama, and to give it certain elements of literary form. Yet in such plays as Peele's *David and Bethsabe* and Greene's *James IV* the beginnings of the close observation of human life and character are evident. David, in the former, is an original study in passion, and Dorthea and Ateukin, in the latter, are the rude prototypes of many of the tender and forsaken ladies and the insinuating villains of the later drama. But the imagery of these authors shows little observation of human life, and consists mostly of conventional nature similes. Lyly with his fantastic prose and his lively colloquialisms is much more significant. Marlowe, of course, was the great originator of new dramatic forms and ideas, and his influence in the development of the drama of passion was supreme. But he is not rich in trope and his imagery reveals little closeness of observation of the ways of men and of the various aspects of human life. In Marlowe, however, the dramatic conception of character and of human passion and pathos first gathers a large and full life. Chapman in turn carries to an extreme the grandiose and epical tradition of tragedy of Marlowe and his school, but his comedies are of another bent, and his metaphors and similes are as a whole wide ranging and varied and display considerable observation of life. Webster exhibits the finished product of the minor Elizabethan tragedy and in Webster and Tourneur we find a new depth and acuteness of psychological observation. It is difficult to cite elsewhere in English literature, outside of Shakspere, home-thrusts, flash-lights turned upon the human heart in some of its states, that exceed many of the analogies and illustrations employed by these writers.

Webster, 81a: "*Pescara.* The Lord Ferdinand laughs
  Delio. Like a deadly cannon
  That lightens ere it smokes."

83b: "*Bosola.* Your brothers mean you safety and pity.

> The Duchess.   Pity!
> With such a pity men preserve alive
> Pheasants and quails, when they are not fat enough
> To be eaten."

32a: "Best natures do commit the grossest faults,
When they're given o'er to jealousy, as best wine,
Dying, makes strongest vinegar."

86b: "I am acquainted with sad misery
As the tann'd galley-slave is with his oar."

25a: "We endure the strokes like anvils or hard steel,
Till pain itself make us no pain to feel."

91b: "Here is a sight
As direful to my soul as is the sword
Unto a wretch hath slain his father."

94a: "I do not think but sorrow makes her look
Like to an oft-dy'd garment."

91a: "I stand like one
That long hath ta'en a sweet and golden dream;
I am angry with myself, now that I wake."

Tourneur, II 69:
"Here's Envy with a poor thin cover on't,
Like scarlet hid in lawn, easily spied through."

II 127: "Are not you she
For whose infect persuasions I could scarce
Kneel out my prayers, and had much ado,
In three hours' reading, to untwist so much
Of the black serpent as you wound about me?"

With these writers, as with Chapman and Jonson, all sides of human life are illustrated. The conventional in metaphor and simile is discarded for the novel and the strange:

Webster, 73b: "This intemperate noise
Fitly resembles deaf men's shrill discourse,
Who talk aloud, thinking all other men
To have their imperfection."

75b: "Laboring men
Count the clock oftenest, Cariola;
Are glad when their task's ended."

Or this feigned parallel for long service unrewarded (p. 78a):

> " 'Tis even like him, that in a winter night
> Takes a long slumber o'er a dying fire,
> A-loth to part from't ; yet parts thence as cold
> As when he first sat down."

Chapman, 447b: "I die *Willingly as an infant.*"

In Jonson illustrations of this sort are endless. The wealth of the Elizabethan drama in wide-ranging and new-coined metaphors and similes is practically inexhaustible, and is one of the striking proofs of its preëminence as a literary form in the qualities of vitality, and of what may be called, if not imagination, at least dramatic fancy.

It is further characteristic of this drama that its diction throughout is formative and fluent. There are few set forms and frequently recurring similes such as afflict the minor poetry of the eighteenth century period. The earlier conventionalities of nature treatment and most of the tricks of expression of the sixteenth century poets are quickly replaced by a new and generic diction. It is true, however, that as the drama declines there is observable a tendency to crystallize many metaphorical idioms into definite forms. Some of these are now obsolescent ; many have passed into the familiar language of the day ; the most striking ones, however, and especially those of a violent or passionate cast, were peculiar to this drama and have had little vogue outside of it. Such metaphors as "*to stab home* their discontents,"[1] "*massacre* his heart,"[2] and the like,[3] while frequently repeated in the drama, have been little used since. Other idiomatic metaphors characteristic of the Elizabethan drama, as also to some extent of Elizabethan poetry in general, are; Spotted and unspotted ;[4] Climbing, mounting ;[5] Cloak (with the disuse of cloaks in male attire the metaphor has naturally fallen into partial desuetude);[6] Pierce ;[7] Paint ;[8]—note also the frequent meta-

Diction Fluent, not Conventional

---

[1] Tourneur, II 139.
[2] Marlowe, I 94.
[3] See infra, p. 209.
[4] Lyly, Chapman, Jonson, Ford, etc.
[5] Lyly, Peele, Greene, Marlowe, Webster, etc.
[6] Lyly, Chapman, etc.
[7] Lyly, Peele, Marlowe, Chapman, etc.
[8] Peele, Greene, Marlowe, Webster, Jonson, etc.

SUMMARY AND CONCLUSIONS. 201

phorical use of the adjective "painted," as in Peele's phrase, "the painted paths of pleasant Ida,"[1] or Marlowe's "the painted spring."[2]—similarly, "enamelled";[3] Print;[4] Melt;[5] Drown— especially in Chapman, where its incessant use becomes an idiosyncrasy;[6] Tie, tangle, etc.[7] A list of similarly recurrent and characteristic metaphors might be extended almost indefinitely.[8] The metaphorical vocabulary of the drama was not narrow, and such repetitions and set comparisons as there are seldom degenerate into mannerisms.[9] Occasionally an approved poetical motive from an earlier period shows a long persistency and is frequently repeated in various dramatic contexts. The greatest favorite is the conventional poetical description of woman's beauty, which runs through many of the dramatists.[10] Jonson, in the fantastic tournament of compliment and courtship in Act V scene ii of *Cynthia's Revels*, presents a semi-serious burlesque of the manner: "You have a tongue steeped in honey, and a breath like a panther; your breasts and forehead are whiter than

[1] Peele, I 17.
[2] Marlowe, II 156.
[3] Peele, Ford, etc.
[4] Greene, Chapman, Ford, etc.
[5] Marlowe, Lyly, Kyd, Webster, etc.
[6] See also Webster, Jonson, Ford, etc.
[7] Lyly, Peele, Marlowe, etc.

[8] See especially; Fold, enwrap; Engine, instrument, etc.; Edge, whet, etc.; Poison; Hinge; Lock; Mirror, glass, mould, model, etc.; To weigh, to put in a balance, etc. (as in Greene's "thinks King Henry's son that Margaret's love Hangs in th' uncertain balance of proud time?"); To hammer (of thoughts, cares, etc.); Engraven on brows, sits on forehead, etc.; Lamps (of stars, of eyes, etc.); Scourge, whip; To sound a depth; Dowry (of beauty, etc.); Anvil; Branch; Furrow; Golden; Map; Mine (to undermine, etc.); Mushroom; Quench; Reap; Rip, rip up; Seal; Serpent, viper, etc.; Shadow; Shrine; Sift; Smother; Snare, net, springe, etc.; Surfeit, Usher; Wound, etc.

[9] By distributing the more striking metaphors under general topical headings in the preceding lists (supra, pp. 15 to 156), some indication is given of the significance of the choice of various peculiar classes of metaphors in the drama. Thus the great prevalence of certain violent and hyperbolical metaphors (see infra, p. 209) is highly significant of the mental and moral atmosphere of the times; and similarly of various coarse, colloquial and repulsive metaphors, such as entrails, beget, to be great with, bawd, dunghill, etc.

[10] See Lyly passim, e. g., II 42; Greene, 154a; Webster, 8a; Chapman, 13a, 50b, 208b, 275b; Ford, I 124, 147, II 13, III 46, etc.

goat's milk or May blossoms; a cloud is not so soft as your skin"[1]—and so on. And Jonson has also written the great classic of charming conceits of this sort in his song,

> "Do but look on her eyes, they do light
> All that love's world compriseth!"

Characteristics of the Period Reflected in the Metaphors and Similes of the Drama. All prominent aspects of life are represented and reflected in this varied drama; to name them all would but involve a repetition of our topical lists. A few significant phases, however, may be singled out for mention here. The aspects of the sky, of clouds and stars and the elements, especially in their violent manifestations, as in tempests, comets, eclipses, conflagrations, and the like, are perhaps the chief source of metaphors and similes drawn from nature. The Wordsworthian calm and mystic contemplation is far enough removed from the excited imagination of the Englishmen of this time. Next in order of prominence perhaps are the numerous references to animal life, as in Webster and Jonson. Under the miscellaneous aspects of life connected with man and his interests the number of tropes drawn from learning, books, the universities, and the like is remarkable. References to the stage and the drama are abundant and significant, and emphasize the literary self-consciousness of the time. Music, especially in its popular aspects, is a prominent theme to supply illustrations. The Elizabethan playwrights seem to pride themselves also on the abundance and facility of their references to the various professions and occupations of men. Life is studied at all points. Technical law terms, popular medical terms and references to diseases and to various remedies, the language of the merchant and the artisan, of the soldier, the sailor and the courtier, all are drawn upon. Metaphors from dress, jewels, and all sorts of male and female finery, illustrate the social history of the time. Had we no other means of information, we could infer from the metaphors of the drama that sports and amusements of all sorts were active

---

[1] Jonson, I 192b; similarly 194b; cf. also 224b, 349a, and II 149b, 237-8, 317b, 373a, 489a, 498b.

and common in the life of the Elizabethan Englishman.[1] Hunting and angling, card-playing and tennis, are frequently mentioned. Archery is not yet obsolete, and falconry and hawking are still pursued. Note that falconry also is a favorite source of the similes of the poet Spenser. The frequent use of illustrations drawn from voyages, from sea life and from ships and the life of sailors, indicates the new interests of the nation in these matters. The national sense of humor and of sympathetic interest in all the idiosyncrasies of common life is reflected in the rich fund of colloquial and comic images invented by Jonson in his comedies, but appearing previously to some extent also in Lyly, as well as in some of Jonson's contemporaries, such as Chapman and others. Note what oddities Jonson has seen in his walks about the London streets, which are reported in his similes. Thus, the size of a crowd he indicates by the saying that it was greater "than come to the launching of some three ships." The signs of the streets attract his attention: "When he is mounted," we are told of a foolish gallant, "he looks like the sign of the George." Of another: "He treads nicely like the fellow that walks upon ropes." He recalls the London plague: "the bells, in time of pestilence, ne'er made Like noise." He has watched the bargemen on the Thames: "I shall see you quoited Over the bar, as bargemen do their billets." These, and many more of the like, are merely little touches of observation thrown in like marginal sketches on his full-sized comedy etchings of London life.

The ethical preoccupation of the mind of the Englishman of the day, so different from the jaunty carelessness of the Englishman of the Restoration comedies, is reflected in many ways. Colors, used in a moral sense, supply many metaphors. Heaven and hell are frequently recurrent emblems. Devils and conjuring, perspective-glasses and witchcraft, are the sources of many similes. The images of death and the grave, so abundant in Webster,

Moralizing Tendency

---

[1] In Webster's *White Devil* (p. 246) the young Giovanni asks his uncle:
"What do the dead do, uncle? *do they eat,
Hear music, go a-hunting and be merry,
As we that live?*"

are not infrequent also in others. Death is on one side of them, and riotous and abundant life on the other. They live the life of the body in its fullness. The senses are continually in play and their habitual metaphors reflect this activity. The æsthetic senses of the eye and ear are fully alive. They are keenly awake to the pleasures of sight and the charms of music. But the other senses, too, are freely recorded. Metaphors of food, eating, thirst, surfeits, odors, smells, abound. On the other hand the fundamental ethical questions connected with the life of the individual and the welfare of the human soul are perpetually touched upon and made prominent in the favorite comparisons and metaphors of the Elizabethan playwrights. I have spoken of the abundance of figures didactic and sententious by virtue of their very form, such as allegory, fable, and proverb. But many simple metaphors and similes in their subject-matter as in their application show the same tendency. Chapman is gnomic and moral to a fault. Webster is full of a gloomy and world-weary philosophy of life. Kyd in *The Spanish Tragedy* writes an inverted *Hamlet*. Marlowe's passionate eagerness about the fundamental questions of human sin and fate is evident to the most superficial reader of his *Faustus*. Peele in *David and Bethsabe* went beyond his powers in attempting a psychological study of temptation and sin. What can exceed in caustic bitterness and melancholy the criticisms of life conveyed in some of Tourneur's, or Chapman's, or Webster's comparisons: See for example Byron's dying speech[1] from Chapman's *Byron's Tragedy*, and many similar passages elsewhere in Chapman. Thus 174a:

Sombre Criticism of Life

> "Man is as a tree that hath no top in cares,
> No root in comforts; all his power to live
> Is given to no end, but to have power to grieve."

140b: "Man is a torch borne in the wind ; a dream
But of a shadow, summ'd with all his substance."

271a: "like a man
Long buried, is a man that long hath lived :
Touch him, he falls to ashes."

[1] Supra, pp. 106.

329a : "'This is the inn where all Deucalion's race,
　　　　Sooner or later, must take up their lodging.
　　　　No privilege can free us from this prison :
　　　　No tears nor prayers can redeem from hence
　　　　A captived soul."

And Tourneur, II 124 : "Joy's a subtle elf.
　　I think man's happiest when he forgets himself."

And Webster, who is full of dark and pathetic reflections on human life and destiny, as, for example, in the brief colloquy between Francesco de Medicis and his young nephew, in *Vittoria Corombona* (p. 24b):

Giovanni: What do the dead do, uncle ? do they eat,
Hear music, go a hunting, and be merry,
As we that live ?
Fran. de Med. No coz; they sleep.
Giov. Lord, Lord, that I were dead !
I have not slept these six nights.— When do they wake ?
Fran. de Med. When God shall please"¹

Compare with this the Duchess' farewell to her son, in *The Duchess of Malfi*, III v (p. 83a):
　　　　　　　　　　" Farewell, boy :
Thou art happy that thou hast not understanding
To know thy misery ; for all our wit
And reading brings us to a truer sense
Of sorrow."

See also 47a :

" Are you grown an atheist ? Will you turn your body,
Which is the goodly palace of the soul,
To the soul's slaughter-house ? O, the cursed devil,
Which doth present us with all other sins
Thrice-candied o'er,— *despair* with gall and stibium ;
Yet we carouse it off."

88a : "Didst thou ever see a lark in a cage ? Such is the soul in the body. This world is like her little turf of grass ; and the heaven o'er our heads, like her looking-glass, only gives us a miserable knowledge of the small compass of our prison."

¹ See a similar passage in Beaumont and Fletcher, *Bonduca*, IV ii, in the dialogue between Caratach and his young nephew Hengo.

99a : " We are merely the stars' tennis balls, struck and bandied
Which way please them."

99a-b :   "In all our quest of greatness,
Like wanton boys, whose pastime is their care,
We follow after bubbles blown in the air.
Pleasure of life, what is't? only the good hours
Of an ague; merely a preparative to rest."

But gnomic and moral reflections of every sort are a marked trait of the serious drama of the entire period from *Gorboduc* to the closing of the theatres. The temperamental melancholy which underlies most of these moralizations is almost a national characteristic, seemingly recurrent in extreme manifestations at irregular intervals from the Anglo-Saxon period to Webster, from Swift to Carlyle. The reader of the Elizabethan tragedy, with its gloomy insistence on the darker sides of life, can more easily understand the motives and influences which prompted just at this time (1621) the preparation of Burton's curious Anatomy of Melancholy.[1]

If the serious and melancholy cast of mind which is reflected in the imagery of the dramatists of this period is a national trait, there are others, similarly revealed, which are rather characteristic of the entire Renaissance movement, although none the less congenial to the national temperament when roused and quickened by stimulating influences from without and within. The new sense of wonder and interest in the brave new world of the time and in its people, under the new life of the Renaissance, is one feature evident in the imagery and ideas of the new poetry. Far-fetched comparisons, that travel over the whole realm of nature and of the life of man with restless penetration, resulting in sudden and surprising juxtapositions of thought, are eagerly sought out, and quite as eagerly relished and applauded. The utmost fire and fullness of life, the pomp and gorgeousness

Renaissance Traits Reflected in the Drama

[1] Note also that one Elizabethan drama, Ford's *The Lover's Melancholy* (1628), — is directly based upon this book. See the discourse on melancholy in Chapman's (?) *Revenge for Honor* (Works p. 418); cf. Jonson's *Every Man in his Humor*, III i (Works I 25). But the Elizabethan references on melancholy are innumerable. Cf. Symonds, Shaks. Pred. 55–57.

of the external world, are pictured in every aspect. The incessant hyperbole and passion of this imagery, its frequent felicity, and its occasional lack of proportion, are indicative of a new and excited taste and of an unwonted rush of thoughts and feelings seeking representation. The artist sees too much and feels too intensely to be content with the ordinary prose-utterance of unimaginative men. Hence he seeks for poetical and unusual forms, which he fills with the new inventions that come so readily to him. Everything is drawn upon for ornament and use,— classical and Italian forms, models, motives, and plots, the whole of ancient story and mythology, all the new discoveries of science, and all the new discoveries in geography.[1] The strong literary and classical coloring of the drama is as indicative of its Renaissance origin, as its vivid realism, its varied inventiveness, and its sombre passion are of its national meaning and sympathy. Much of the Renaissance quality, tempered with much of the poet's own moonlight beauty and charm, had been rendered and revealed during the first of these flowering years of the drama in Spenser's *Faerie Queene*. Here is the pomp and gorgeousness of the external world, here the classical mythology newly wedded to fairy magic, here the sense of the new wonders of space and thought, together with the underlying seriousness and moral sense of the typical Englishman. But it was a poem for idealists; it lacked passion and penetrative power. Shakspere alone speaks to us the full message of the Elizabethan age. Outside of Shakspere we must supplement Spenser with the minor dramatists in order to find a chorus of poetic voices equally representative.

The pride of life and the pleasure in costly phrases and in the enumeration of sensuous and gorgeous details so characteristic of the entire poetry of the period and so typical of the Renaissance is a prominent feature of the imagery of the dramatists. The earlier writers are especially fond of introducing such passages. Thus Greene, in the opening scene of his *Orlando*

Costly and Gorgeous Images

[1] E. g. Marlowe, 1 83:
"We mean to travel to the Antarctic pole,
Conquering the people underneath our feet."

Furioso, fills the speeches of the princely suitors with a profusion of pompous illustration after this manner:

> "The bordering islands, seated here in ken,
> Whose shores are sprinkled with rich orient pearl,
> More bright of hue than were the margarites
> That Cæsar found in wealthy Albion;
> The sands of Tagus, all of burnished gold,
> Made Thetis never prouder on the clifts
> That overpeer the bright and golden shore,
> Than do the rubbish of my country seas."

Read also the sumptuous array of delicacies which Friar Bacon, in *Friar Bacon and Friar Bungay*, promises to provide for the princes through his magic art:

> "And for thy cates, rich Alexandria drugs,
> Fetched by carvels from Ægypt's richest straits,
> Found in the wealthy strand of Africa,
> Shall royalize the table of my king.
> Wines richer than th' Ægyptian courtesan
> Quaff'd to Augustus' kingly countermatch—"

and so on, including sugar-cane from Candy, spices from Persia, Afric dates, mirabolans of Spain, "conserves and suckets from Tiberias," and cates from Judea. Tamburlaine's illimitable spirit of geographical conquest is in a higher vein, but Greene's manner is resumed with even fuller sensuousness in Jonson, who is very fond of such images. "If thou wilt eat the spirit of gold, and drink dissolved pearl in wine, 'tis for thee," says Deliro to Fastidious Brisk in *Every Man out of his Humor*. And Mosca to Voltore, in *Volpone:*

> "When you do come to swim in golden lard,
> Up to the arms in honey, that your chin
> Is borne up stiff with fatness of the flood,
> Think on your vassal."

Similarly Volpone himself:

> "Thy baths shall be the juice of July-flowers,
> Spirit of roses, and of violets,
> The milk of unicorns, and panther's breath
> Gathered in bags, and mixed with Cretan wines.
> Our drink shall be prepared gold and amber."

See also the part of Sir Epicure Mammon throughout *The Alchemist*.[1]

Violent Metaphors

But passion, and passion the expression of which too often degenerates into hyperbole and violence, is the most striking feature of the serious drama of the minor Elizabethans, and especially of the Tragedy of Blood, as Mr. J. A. Symonds has named the earlier Elizabethan tragedy.[2] The extravagance which characterizes the plots and the catastrophes of many of the plays of Kyd, Marlowe, Tourneur, and others, is reflected in their use of metaphor and simile. For, in addition to the large amount of literary and elaborate hyperbole which marks the drama of the period, there is a sort of familiar and idiomatic hyperbole, revealing itself in the customary employment of startling and violent metaphors and comparisons, almost as matters of course. Such metaphors as "kill," "stab," "massacre," "drown," "smother," "rip," "poison," "infect," "thunder," "tempest," "eclipse," are extremely common.[3] A tendency to similar exaggeration, more softened, however, by long usage, and never so seriously meant, has been noticed in certain familiar French idioms.[4] Such metaphors as "bouleversé," "assassine," "assomme," "meurtri," "navré," and the like, correspond in form at least very closely to the English examples just given. Metaphors connected with swords and other weapons the Elizabethans seem to use with peculiar frequency and emphasis. The language of warfare and combats is made to lack none of the violence imaginable in the proper situations. Thus Peele, I 112 : "make his flesh my murdering falchion's food." I 113 : "with your swords write in the

[1] Cf. similarly, Shirley, *The Lady of Pleasure*, V i (Mermaid ed., pp. 350-351); and Massinger, *The City Madam* III iii.

[2] Shaks. Pred., ch. xii.

[3] Examples: *Stab:* Jonson, I 116b, 215a ; Chapman, 165a ; Tourneur, II 139 ; *Kill:* Chapman, 7b ("slain with our beauties"), 41a (murder); Marlowe, I 94, II 247 (massacre), II 264 ("thou kill'st thy mother's heart"); *Drown:* Chapman, (see supra, p. 122); Webster, 34a, 142b ; Jonson, I 295a, II 105a, etc.; *Smother:* Webster, 99a ("smother thy pity"), 135a ; Marlowe, I 96 ; Chapman, 217a, etc.; *Rip, rip up:* Chapman, 109b ; Peele, I 24 ("unrip not so your shames"); Greene, 212a ; Webster, 136b, 153a, etc.

[4] By Falkenheiner; cited in Gerber, *Die Sprache als Kunst*, II 264 note.

Book of Time." 1 238: "Sith they begin to *bathe their swords in blood.*" Marlowe, II 143: "To *greet* his lordship with a poniard." II 260: "I will whip you to death with my poniard's point." 297:

>"*Whet* thy sword on Sixtus' bones,
>That it may keenly *slice* the Catholics."

Tourneur, II 8:

>"Thy wrongs and mine are *for one scabbard fit.*"

II 58: "Sword, thou wast never a back-biter yet.
>I'll pierce him to his face, he shall die looking upon me.
>Thy veins are swell'd with lust,—this shall unfill 'em."

Webster, 125b:

>"You would have lock'd your poniard in my heart."

Chapman, 259b:

>"My sword, that all the wars . . .
>Hath sheathed betwixt his hilt and horrid point."

Ford, II 307: "Your sword talks an answer" (cf. III 32).

The language of these dramatists is sometimes curious in ferocity, doing more than ample justice to a traditional conception of the Italianate manner: Thus Chapman, 168a:

>"I'll bind his arm in silk, and rub his flesh,
>To make the vein swell, that his soul may gush
>Into some kennel."

366b: "I stroke again at him, and then he slept,
>His life-blood boiling out at every wound,
>In streams as clear as any liquid ruby."

441b: "Would it were possible
>*To kill even thy eternity.*"

Webster, 36b:

>"And yet methinks that this revenge is poor,
>Because it steals upon him like a thief."

49b: "Naught grieves but that you are too few to feed
>The famine of our vengeance."

But violent metaphors are often used to signify commoner things. Thus Tourneur, II 78:

> "Here came a letter now
> *New-bleeding* from their pens."

Webster, 76b:

> "I *will plant my soul* in mine ears, to hear you."

Chapman, 315a:

> "*Stuff'd his soul*
> With damn'd opinions and unhallow'd thoughts."

The same passionate way of feeling and speaking gives them sharper senses and livelier imaginations than men in quieter times possess. Volpone[1] in the midst of his villanies hears a noise and cries out:

> "Hark! who's there?
> I hear some footing; officers, the saffi,
> Come to apprehend us! *I do feel the brand
> Hissing already at my forehead: now
> Mine ears are boring.*"

Chapman is fond of the classical metaphor, "to eat one's heart."[2] The metaphor of heaping up evil on another's breast is another favorite of this same general stamp:

Tourneur, II 105:

> "Hoping at last
> To pile up all my wishes on his breast."

Chapman, 109a:

> "All the pains
> Two faithful lovers feel, that thus are parted, . . .
> . . . on thy heart
> Be heap'd and press'd down, till thy soul depart."[3]

Jonson, I 17a:

> "Heap worse on ill, make up a pile of hatred."

Other and various illustrations of the same method of utterance are:

---

[1] Jonson, I 373-4. On this form of imagination in general see Longinus On the Sublime, XV 1 2. Further examples may be seen in Massinger, *A New Way to Pay Old Debts*, IV ii 17 22, and Beaumont and Fletcher, *Thierry and Theodoret*, I i (Mermaid ed. I p. 297).

[2] Chapman, 161b, 176b, 217a.

[3] See also Chapman, 157b, 175b.

Marlowe, II 217: "*Unbowel* straight this breast."
Webster, 12b: "Spit thy poison."
44b: "I am falling to pieces."
Chapman, 176a: "Her wounds Manlessly *digg'd* in her."
Tourneur, II 22: "O, one incestuous kiss *picks open Hell*."
II 59: "O, there's a wicked whisper; *hell is in his ear*."
II 74: "Make him curse and swear, *and so die black*."

We have thus reviewed in some of their more striking manifestations the leading forms of metaphor and simile characteristic of the minor Elizabethan playwrights, emphasizing some of the more dramatic types and peculiarities of imaginative diction. We have noted the general range of observation and the main sources in nature and in human life commanded by these writers. A few of the chief characteristics of the period, illustrating, in Charles Lamb's phrase,[1] "what may be called the moral sense of our ancestors," as reflected in their choice of illustration and trope, consciously or unconsciously made, have received brief special mention. The didactic and moralizing tendency of the early dramatists, their love of literary and classical ornament, their attitude towards Nature, their treatment of common life, the prominence with them of the senses and of coarse and colloquial images, their abundance in the rich coloring and their profuse employment of the pomp and fire and fullness of life of the Renaissance, their conception of the passions and their methods of rendering them

Final Recapitulation

all these things as entering into the imagery of the minor Elizabethan drama have been touched upon. This drama was the most vital and the most popular form of literature existing in its day. Its significance and its greatness lie above everything else in its showing of strenuous character in strenuous action. In music and rhythm of verse it is not supreme. There is nothing in it to correspond to the choral odes of the Greek drama. In structure of plot and in narrative felicity it is often deficient.

[1] Specimens, Preface, p. iv.

In dignity and power of imaginative language it is uneven and careless, however vivid and fresh and forcible is its diction. Its interest is centered too narrowly in the life of the individual and in the reaction of personal forces and passions. But in this special sphere it presents an imaginative transcript of life, for uncompromising fidelity, for tragic and romantic feeling, for strenuous reality, hardly rivaled in the world's literature. These qualities are adequately reflected in the metaphor and simile employed in this drama.

BIBLIOGRAPHICAL INDEX.

TEXTS OF THE DRAMATISTS.

George Chapman, Plays, ed. R. H. Shepherd, London 1874, pp. 1-340, 351-380.
Robert Greene, Dramatic and Poetical Works of Greene and Peele, ed. Dyce, London, 1861. (Greene pp. 1-320.)
GORBODUC, or FERREX AND PORREX: in The Works of Thos. Sackville, ed. R. W. Sackville-West, London 1859 (pp. 1-92).
Ben Jonson, Works, ed. Gifford and Cunningham, London [1876], 3 vols. Vol. I pp. 463; vol. II pp. 1-515.
Thomas Kyd: *Jeronimo*, in vol. IV pp. 345-396, and *The Spanish Tragedy*, in vol. V pp. 1-173 of Dodsley's Collection of Old English Plays, ed. W. C. Hazlitt, London 1874.
John Lyly, Dramatic Works, ed. F. W. Fairholt, 2 vols. London 1858; pp. 298, and 284.
Christopher Marlowe, Works, ed. A. H. Bullen, 3 vols. Boston 1885; vols. I 1-283, II 1-298.
George Peele, Works, ed. A. H. Bullen, 2 vols. Boston 1888; vols. I pp. 1-347, II 1-86.
Cyril Tourneur, Plays and Poems, ed. J. C. Collins, 2 vols. London 1878; vols. I pp. 1-155, II 1-150.
John Webster, Works, ed. Dyce, London 1859; pp. 1-180.

GENERAL REFERENCES.

E. A. Abbott, Shakespearian Grammar, London 1879.
Aristotle, Rhetoric, translated J. E. C. Welldon, London 1886.
— Rhetoric and Poetic, translated T. Buckley, (Bohn) London 1890.
Beaumont and Fletcher, Works, ed. Dyce, New York 1890, 2 vols.
— Best Plays, ed. Strachey (Mermaid Series), London 1893. 2 vols.
A. Biese, Das Metaphorische in der dichterischen Phantasie, Berlin 1889 (pp. 35).
F. Brinkmann, Die Metaphern, Bonn 1878.
S. Brooke, Primer of English Literature, New York 1879.
E. B. Browning, Poetical Works, New York 1885, 5 vols.
F. Brunetière, Nouvelles Questions de Critique, Paris 1890.
H. T. Buckle, History of Civilization in England, 2 vols. New York 1872.
E. Burke, Works, Boston 1881; vol I 67-262, On the Sublime and Beautiful.
T. Campbell, Specimens of the British Poets, London 1845.
Chalmers and Johnson, eds., The Works of the English Poets, London 1810, 21 vols.
Chaucer, Complete Works, ed. Skeat, Oxford 1894, 6 vols.
S. T. Coleridge, Miscellanies, Æsthetic and Literary, London (Bohn) 1885.

J. P. Collier, History of English Dramatic Poetry to the Time of Shakespeare, 3 vols. London 1879.
Dryden, Works, ed. Scott and Saintsbury, Edinburgh 1883 (vols. V and VI).
F. G. Fleay, Biographical Chronicle of the English Drama, 1559–1642, 2 vols. London 1891.
John Ford, Works, ed. Gifford and Dyce, 3 vols. London 1869.
G. Gerber, Die Sprache als Kunst, 2 vols., 2d. ed., Berlin 1885.
E. Gosse, The Jacobean Poets, New York 1894.
    Seventeenth Century Studies, 2d. ed., London 1885.
H. E Greene, A Grouping of Figures of Speech (reprinted from the Publications of the Modern Language Association of America, N. S. vol. I No. 4), Baltimore 1893.
F. B. Gummere, The Anglo-Saxon Metaphor, Halle 1881.
    Old English Ballads, Boston 1894.
H. Hallam, Introduction to the Literature of Europe in the Fifteenth, Sixteenth, and Seventeenth Centuries, 4 vols. in 2, New York 1886.
Wm. Hazlitt, Miscellaneous Works, 3 vols. Boston N. D.
E. Hennequin, La Critique Scientifique, 2d. ed., Paris 1890.
Henry Home, Lord Kames, Elements of Criticism, 2 vols., Edinburgh 1807.
Leigh Hunt, Imagination and Fancy, London 1883.
R. Hurd, Works, London 1811, 8 vols.
R. C. Jebb, Attic Orators, London 1893, 2 vols.
    – Introduction to Homer, Boston 1893.
F. Klaeber, Das Bild bei Chaucer, Berlin 1893.
Charles Lamb, Specimens of the English Dramatic Poets who lived about the Time of Shakespeare, London (Bohn) 1854.
Landmann, Euphues, Heilbronn 1887.
Longinus, On the Sublime, trans. Havell, London 1890.
J. R. Lowell, The Old English Dramatists, Boston 1892.
    Works, Riverside edition, 10 vols., Boston 1892.
Massinger, Plays, ed. Gifford and Cunningham, London [1872].
A. Mézières, Predecesseurs et Contemporains de Shakespeare 3d. ed., Paris 1881.
    – Contemporains et Successeurs de Shakespeare, 3d ed., Paris 1881.
Wm. Minto, Manual of English Prose Literature, Boston 1891.
    Characteristics of English Poets from Chaucer to Shirley, Boston, 1889.
Max Müller, The Science of Thought, New York 1887.
The Pilgrimage to Parnassus, with the Two Parts of the Return from Parnassus, ed. W. D. Macray, Oxford 1886.
A. W. Pollard, English Miracle Plays, Moralities, and Interludes, Oxford 1890.
Quintilian, De Institutione Oratoria; in Nisard's Collection des Auteurs Latins, Paris 1875.
Retrospective Review, 16 vols., 3 series, 1820–6, 1828, 1853-4.
A. W. Schlegel, Dramatic Art and Literature, trans. Black, London (Bohn) 1889.

Shakspere, Works, ed. W. A. Wright (The Cambridge Shakspere) London and New York 1891 3, 9 vols.
L. A. Sherman, Analytics of Literature, Boston 1893.
J. Shirley, Best Plays, ed. E. Gosse (Mermaid Series), London 1888.
Sidney, Defense of Poesy, ed. A. S. Cook, Boston 1890.
- Poems, ed. Grosart ("Early English Poets"), London 1877, 3 vols.
Herbert Spencer, The Philosophy of Style (with notes), New York 1891 (pp. 55).
Edmund Spenser, Complete Works, ed. Morris and Hales (Globe ed.), London 1890.
A. C. Swinburne, Essays and Studies, London 1888.
— A Study of Ben Jonson, London 1889.
. George Chapman, a Critical Essay, London 1875; also in the Poems and Minor Translations of Chapman, London 1875.
J. A. Symonds, Shakspere's Predecessors in the English Drama, London 1884.
— Ben Jonson ("English Worthies" Series), New York 1886.
— Introduction to Webster and Tourneur, in Mermaid ed., London 1888.
— Essays Speculative and Suggestive, New York 1894.
— In the Key of Blue and other Prose Essays, London and New York 1893.
H. A. Taine, History of English Literature, translated H. Van Laun, 2 vols. New York 1872.
A. Tennyson, Works, New York and London 1893.
A. H. Tolman, The Style of Anglo-Saxon Poetry (reprinted from the Transactions of the Modern Language Association, vol. III, 1887).
H. Ulrici, Shakspeare's Dramatic Art, translated L. Dora Schmitz, 2 vols., London (Bohn) 1892.
T. H. Ward, ed., The English Poets, 4 vols., London and New York 1880.
A. W. Ward, History of English Dramatic Literature, 2 vols., London 1875.
Thos. Warton, History of English Poetry, ed. W. C. Hazlitt, 4 vols., London 1871.
Webster and Tourneur, Best Plays, ed. J. A. Symonds (Mermaid Series), London 1888.
E. A. Whipple, Literature of the Age of Elizabeth, Boston 1891.
Thomas Wilson, The Arte of Rhetorique [London] 1553.
Henry Wood, T. L. Beddoes, a Survival in Style (in American Journal of Philology IV 445-455).

www.ingramcontent.com/pod-product-compliance
Lightning Source LLC
Chambersburg PA
CBHW021812230426
43669CB00008B/729